BLOOD ON THE STONE

ADVANCE PRAISE FOR *BLOOD ON THE STONE*

'A masterly account of the dark side of the diamond trade. Smillie's scalpel has cut very deep.'

—Matthew Hart, author of *Diamond:
the history of a cold-blooded love affair*

'Required reading for anyone who still believes the diamond trade is only about love, honor and trust... A devastating, important work... Read this before you buy another diamond.'

—Greg Campbell, co-author of *Flawless:
Inside the World's Largest Diamond Heist*

'Smillie's compelling narrative of the journey from teacher to prosecutor is touching and breathtaking.'

—Peta Thornycroft, award-winning
Zimbabwean journalist

'Very high-octane...by far the most interesting and illuminating account of the blood diamond campaign.'

—Lansana Gberie, author of
A Dirty War in West Africa

'Ian Smillie was among the first international and most eloquent investigators who understood and publicly denounced the use of "blood diamonds"... In *Blood on the Stone*, he links his own experiences and deep knowledge of the diamond trade to the history of... how these gemstones with no intrinsic value drive conflict, corruption and mayhem. It is an important story, and one that needs to be understood if the world is to help end the misery of conflicts driven by commodities and greed.'

—Douglas Farah, co-author of *Merchant of Death: Money,
Guns, Planes and the Man Who Makes War Possible*

'Global Witness, after first alerting the world to the horror of blood diamonds in 1998, has worked closely with Partnership Africa Canada on the campaign to stop diamonds funding war. Smillie's book is a fascinating read about the world of diamonds, war and greed.'

—Charmian Gooch, co-founder, Global Witness

BLOOD ON THE STONE

GREED, CORRUPTION AND WAR
IN THE GLOBAL DIAMOND TRADE

IAN SMILLIE

ANTHEM PRESS
LONDON · NEW YORK · DELHI

International Development Research Centre
Ottawa • Cairo • Dakar • Montevideo • Nairobi • New Delhi • Singapore

Anthem Press
An imprint of Wimbledon Publishing Company
www.anthempress.com

This edition first published in UK and USA 2010
by ANTHEM PRESS
75-76 Blackfriars Road, London SE1 8HA, UK
or PO Box 9779, London SW19 7ZG, UK
and
244 Madison Ave. #116, New York, NY 10016, USA

A copublication with the
International Development Research Centre
PO Box 8500, Ottawa, ON K1G 3H9, Canada
www.idrc.ca / info@idrc.ca
ISBN 978-1-55250-498-7 (e-book)

British Library Cataloguing in Publication Data
A catalogue record for this book is available from the British Library.

Library of Congress Cataloging in Publication Data
A catalog record for this book has been requested.

ISBN-13: 978 0 85728 979 7 (Hbk)
ISBN-10: 0 85728 979 9 (Hbk)

ISBN-13: 978 0 85728 963 6 (Pbk)
ISBN-10: 0 85728 963 2 (Pbk)

ISBN-13: 978 0 85728 987 2 (eBook)
ISBN-10: 0 85728 987 X (eBook)

For Sharon

'What do you know about diamonds, Bruce?'
'They're forever.'
'Corny.'
'They're a girl's best friend.'
'Which decade are you from?'
'They're not cheap.'
'Yeah.'
'Hoods call them "ice".'
'They're wrong.'
'And they're probably trouble.'
'That's for certain.'

– *The Big Killing*, Robert Wilson

CONTENTS

GLOSSARY

AFRC	Armed Forces Ruling Council (Sierra Leone)
AMAL	*Afwaj al Muqawama al Lubnaniya*, ('Lebanese Resistance Detachments')
ANC	African National Congress (South Africa)
ASCorp	Angolan Selling Corporation
CAR	Central African Republic
CAST	Consolidated African Selection Trust
CENADEP	*Centre National d'Appui au Développement et à la Participation Populaire* (DRC)
CSO	Central Selling Organization (De Beers)
DIAMANG	*Companhia de Diamantes de Angola*
DRC	Democratic Republic of the Congo
DTC	Diamond Trading Company (De Beers)
ECOMOG	Economic Community (of West African States) Monitoring Group
ECOWAS	Economic Community of West African States
ENDIAMA	*Empresa Nacional de Diamantes de Angola*
HRD	*Hoge Raad voor Diamant* ('Diamond High Council')
IDI	International Diamond Industries
IDMA	International Diamond Manufacturers' Association
IDSO	International Diamond Security Organisation
IMF	International Monetary Fund
KP	Kimberley Process
KPCS	Kimberley Process Certification Scheme
LURD	Liberians United for Reconciliation and Democracy
MIBA	*Société Minière de Bakwanga*
MLC	*Mouvement de libération du Congo*
MONUA	United Nations Observer Mission in Angola
MPLA	*Movimento Popular de Libertação de Angola*

NGO	Non governmental organization
NMJD	Network Movement for Justice and Development (Sierra Leone)
NPFL	National Patriotic Front of Liberia
NPRC	National Provisional Ruling Council (Sierra Leone)
OCHA	(UN) Office for the Coordination of Humanitarian Assistance
OECD	Organization for Economic Cooperation and Development
PAC	Partnership Africa Canada
PLO	Palestine Liberation Organization
RCD	*Rassemblement congolais pour la démocratie*
RUF	Revolutionary United Front
SLST	Sierra Leone Selection Trust
SWAPO	Southwest Africa People's Organization
UNAMSIL	United Nations Mission in Sierra Leone
UNAVEM	United Nations Angola Verification Mission
UNITA	*União para la Independência Total de Angola*
WDC	World Diamond Council
WFDB	World Federation of Diamond Bourses

PREFACE

Many people helped bring this book to fruition. Sharon Capeling-Alakija gave me invaluable editorial advice as the book began, along with encouragement that has endured. In 1999, Ralph Hazleton, Lansana Gberie and I started to work on the issue of conflict diamonds, eventually travelling the globe – if not always physically together, together at least in spirit. This book benefited enormously from their efforts and their company. My old friend Cloudy Beltz caught many errors in the first draft, including a grammatical mistake in the first line of the prologue. Many other people have wittingly or unwittingly helped me in understanding diamonds. They include Andrew Bone, Chaim Even-Zohar, Stéphane Fischler, Simon Gilbert, Martin Rapaport, Matt Runci and Richard Wake-Walker. For ideas and encouragement at various points on the trail, thanks are due to Charaf Ahmimed, Shawn Blore, Abu Brima, Deborah De Young, Christian Dietrich, Annie Dunnebacke, Susanne Emond, Dorothée Gizenga, Charmian Gooch, Corinna Gilfillan, Andrew Grant, Karen Hurston, Susan Isaac, Adrian Labor, Josée Létourneau, Flora MacDonald, Bernard Taylor and Alex Yearsley. Some of them commented on early chapters of the book, as did Joan Baxter, Barbara Brown, Jim Freedman, Matthew Hart, Don Hubert, Terry Jones, Nick Koumjian and Don Law-West. To all I am very grateful.

I am grateful as well to my old *alma mater* Partnership Africa Canada (PAC) and the many individuals and organizations that have supported the campaign on conflict diamonds. These include the Canadian Department of Foreign Affairs and International Trade, the Canadian International Development Agency, the British Department for International Development, Irish Aid, the John D. and Catherine T. MacArthur Foundation, Oxfam, World Vision, the Canadian Autoworkers Social Justice Fund, Inter Pares, the Canadian Catholic Organizations for Development and Peace, Cordaid and many others. I am especially grateful to the International Development Research Centre for its long-time support to the cause, and for its help in allowing me to finish the book. Needless to say, the opinions and any errors or omissions are mine alone.

A brief note on names: throughout the book, the Ivory Coast is referred to by its official name, Côte d'Ivoire. The Democratic Republic of the Congo – often shortened to 'DRC' – was known as Zaire between 1971 and 1998. I have avoided 'Zaire' wherever possible, in order to avoid confusion. When I use the term 'Congolese' I am referring to this country. The DRC was once a Belgian colony. There is another country – a former French colony – known as the Republic of Congo. Its capital, Brazzaville, lies directly across the River Congo from Kinshasa, the capital of the DRC. Whenever I refer to the Republic of Congo, I will use the term Congo-Brazzaville. The distinction is important, not least because of the hundreds of millions of dollars worth of illicit diamonds that have crossed the river between the two countries.

Ian Smillie
Ottawa, June 2010

PROLOGUE

This book is about how diamonds fuelled some of the most brutal wars in Africa. More than three million people died as a result of these wars in the 1990s and the early 2000s; many more millions of lives have been damaged, and the existence of entire nations has been called into question. The book is also about a campaign that began in 1998 to stop these 'conflict' or 'blood diamonds'. It is a campaign in which I have been deeply involved, but in this book I have mostly kept myself out of the story because it is one that involves hundreds of individuals, organizations and governments, each contributing in their own way.

How the campaign began for me, however, is a tale worth telling, not least because of the places it has taken me over a period of ten years: from the killing fields of Sierra Leone to the diamond bourses of Antwerp; from the back streets of Jaffa in Israel to the august Security Council in New York; from Moscow to the barren lands of Canada's Northwest Territories, to refugee camps in Guinea, the Clinton White House and the witness stand of a war crimes trial in The Hague.

In 1997, a small group of individuals began meeting at the Ottawa offices of a non governmental organization (NGO) called Partnership Africa Canada (PAC) to talk about the war then raging in the small West African nation of Sierra Leone. It was an eclectic group of people who were concerned that this increasingly horrific war had received so little attention – from the humanitarian aid community, the media and the United Nations. Tens of thousands of people had been killed, and fully half the population of the country had been displaced by marauding rebels, who marked their passing by chopping the hands off innocent civilians. Our little gathering, which we called the 'Sierra Leone Working Group' comprised two or three Sierra Leonean-Canadians, a couple of people like myself who had once worked in Sierra Leone, and others who had come to know the country in other ways.

1

Years before, and fresh out of university, I went to Sierra Leone to teach secondary school. I was posted to Koidu Town in Kono District in 1967, the heart of the country's lucrative diamond mining industry. It was, in almost every respect except for location and climate, a replica of the Klondike gold rush – a wild west kind of town with thousands of illicit diamond diggers, a vibrant Lebanese diamond mafia, and a company exporting two million carats a year worth of the best diamonds in the world to the cutting and polishing factories of Antwerp and beyond. In those days, people like me saw development in terms of roads, schools and hospitals. And all of these things were being built. In Koidu, some of my students walked five miles to school every day, and most could expect trouble at home if they didn't do well in class. Koidu Secondary School, the only high school in the country's fourth largest town, was two years old when I arrived, but parents, town elders and especially the students, wanted it to grow and thrive. None of them, and none of the teachers, could possibly imagine what was to come. Twenty five years of bad government, mismanagement and corruption put Sierra Leone on the slippery slope to a war without precedent for its senselessness and its savagery. And the diamonds – which we teachers and students more or less ignored in those long ago days – would be at the epicentre of the tragedy.

I'm not sure if those of us in the Sierra Leone Working Group had a clear idea of where we were going in our 1997 and 1998 meetings. We raised a bit of money, and as the war worsened we talked with not a little irony about 'peace-building'. Finally, towards the end of 1998, one member of the group interrupted a discussion and said, 'Look, this war is all about diamonds, and until something is done about that, it will never end.' It was a eureka moment. Adrian Labor, a young Sierra Leonean who had recently immigrated to Canada, worked as a computer programmer at the International Development Research Centre. He had hit the nail on the head. Reports about diamond theft by the Revolutionary United Front (RUF) were common, but none of the solutions proposed by those studying the war had addressed this issue. In fact, having lived in the diamond area, I saw Labor's point so clearly that I wondered why I had not thought of it myself. Within a couple of months we had put together a modest funding proposal to study the issue. Working as a free-lance consultant and writer, I had the time that would be required if we could get some travel money, and if we could find others to work on it. We asked 12 Canadian NGOs to give us $2000 each, and all but one said yes. We then asked for a matching grant from the Peacebuilding Fund of the Canadian Department of Foreign Affairs, and officials there too said yes.

I had known Ralph Hazleton as a casual acquaintance for several years. He had a Ph.D. in economics and a mixed career in academia and international development. He had run CARE relief operations in Liberia and then in Goma during the Rwanda crisis, and we had met, coincidentally, in Freetown, the capital of Sierra Leone, in 1996. Following a quadruple-heart bypass, Ralph had gone into semi-retirement, but now he was itching for an interesting assignment. When I suggested our project to him – all work and almost no pay – he said yes without hesitation. Lansana Gberie was a journalist in Freetown for six years, reporting through the early days of the escalating war. He received a US government fellowship, and for a time worked on the Kansas City *Star*, alma mater of Ernest Hemingway, before going to Wilfrid Laurier University for a master's degree. He called me out of the blue from Toronto, where he had entered a Ph.D. program, and in short order, we had the team.

We worked on the issue through 1999, and as we delved into it, we discovered that diamonds in Sierra Leone were like a strand of wool dangling from a sweater. If you pull on it, the entire sweater begins to unravel, and if you pull on it long enough, you might find that it is connected to a lot of other things as well. That was the case with Sierra Leone diamonds. They were intimately connected to the war that had been fought in neighbouring Liberia until 1997, and they were now a mainstay in the expansionist ideas of Liberian warlord-turned-president, Charles Taylor. Conflict diamonds – as they came to be known – were what had kept a war in Angola going for almost two decades. The diamonds were laundered in half a dozen ways before they arrived in jewellery shops, but because nobody had ever asked questions before, most of those involved in the cover-up had taken no great pains to hide their trail. Antwerp, the centre of the world's diamond trade, had for years been importing hundreds of millions of dollars worth of diamonds from countries where none were mined. No questions were asked.

We discovered that we were not alone. A year before, a small British NGO, Global Witness, had published a hard-hitting report on blood diamonds in Angola. The people at Global Witness became allies as our work progressed. And we were helped indirectly by the United Nations. The UN Security Council had mandated its Sanctions Committee on Angola to set up an Expert Panel to study how and why the rebel group, UNITA, was able to sell hundreds of millions of dollars worth of stolen diamonds into the legitimate trade every year, with complete impunity. In January 2000 we released our report, *The Heart of the Matter: Sierra Leone, Diamonds and Human Security*. The report accused Liberian President Charles Taylor of masterminding one of the worst wars on the African continent, paying for it with diamonds. We accused the diamond industry of complicity, and we said that Antwerp and the government of Belgium bore special responsibility for the traffic in illicit gems. And while we described the giant diamond conglomerate, De Beers, as part of the problem, we said that as the largest and most powerful player in the diamond world, it had a special responsibility to become part of the solution. The report helped take the war away, intellectually speaking, from the realm of what is often portrayed as mindless African savagery, placing it squarely into a more realistic construct: power and money.

The Heart of the Matter created a media sensation, at least it seemed that way to us. It resulted in front page stories in newspapers in Canada, Sierra Leone, Belgium and South Africa, and wide coverage elsewhere. The Belgian media accused us of being part of a Canadian plot to destroy the Belgian diamond industry. Canadian Foreign Minister Lloyd Axworthy had more than one discussion with Belgium's Foreign Minister, Louis Michel, trying to persuade him that there was no conspiracy.

By the time the report came out, a peace accord had been reached in Sierra Leone, and a UN peacekeeping force had at last been sent to supervise the agreement. But in May 2000, the RUF kidnapped 500 UN peacekeepers as they moved towards the diamond fields, and the war began anew. Sierra Leone's 'CNN moment' had at last arrived, and some of the world's best journalists flocked to Freetown. But now, instead of interpreting the war in terms of 'the coming anarchy' and a 'clash of civilizations', reporters could see more clearly what was at the root of it.

It is important to say that diamonds did not *cause* the war in Sierra Leone. Nor did they cause the wars in Angola and the Democratic Republic of the Congo. They did, however, pay for the rebel effort in these wars, making them significantly more horrific and long-lived than could ever have been the case without diamonds. It is also important that these wars not be described only in terms of greed. An academic debate grew up as the conflict diamond issue gathered steam, as to whether wars funded by diamonds, oil and tropical hardwood were about greed, or about grievance. The real answer is *both*. Where grievance is concerned, it is worth noting that most power-hungry despots and warlords have grievances. Even a teenager who robs a corner store may have a grievance. UNITA had a grievance and a clear political agenda: power. In Sierra Leone, the RUF had a clear political agenda: power – even though it had no ethnic or political backing from anybody. What they failed to understand is that public support tends to dissipate when you terrorize the people you say you want to liberate. In the Congo, it was about power. But in all of the cases described in this book, there was a heavy overlay of greed as well. Whatever legitimate grievances the RUF may have had when it began, by the mid 1990s these had all been discredited by their terror tactics and their determined focus on diamonds. Going after the diamonds was their way of winning the war. Going after the diamonds was our way of trying to stop the war.

In the summer of 2000, I received a call from the United Nations Department of Political Affairs: would I allow my name to stand for inclusion on a UN Security Council Expert Panel that was being assembled to examine the connection between diamonds, weapons and the war in Sierra Leone? Not expecting for a moment to be appointed, I said 'sure'. Not long afterwards, however, I received a second call saying that I had been appointed by the Secretary General of the United Nations as a member of 'the five-member Panel of Experts on Sierra Leone, to collect information on possible violations of the arms embargo and to report to the Council with observations and recommendations.' Other members of the team included a senior Indian police officer seconded from Interpol, a Belgian arms-tracking expert, a Senegalese air traffic control expert, and a Cameroonian diplomat who acted as our chairman.

Much of our work took place in Sierra Leone, but the unravelling sweater took us much father afield. In South Africa we investigated individuals suspected of diamond trafficking and gunrunning. In Israel, three of us visited the flat of a mercenary who was wanted in Colombia for training the paramilitary force of a Medellin drug cartel, and who had a chequered career in both Sierra Leone and Liberia. He served us tea and cookies and kept a pistol on the sideboard during our discussion. Some of my colleagues went to Ukraine and the United Arab Emirates in search of gunrunners, and I spent a lot of time in Antwerp and Tel Aviv talking to people in the diamond industry. I came to realize that while there is a great deal of corruption and denial in the world of diamonds, there are also many decent people who were appalled to discover what their industry was contributing to. And though we met thieves, smugglers, killers and some of the world's most repulsive scum, we also met some very brave people who told us things that would have cost them their lives had they been discovered. One of the most harrowing interviews for me was an hour-long session with the President of Liberia, Charles Taylor.

Taylor had been billed as one of the star villains in the PAC report, *The Heart of the Matter*, and I had been told by a senior Liberian exile that I was regarded in his country as an enemy of the state. Under no circumstances should I go to Liberia. But I assumed I would be safe enough under the banner of the UN Security Council. And as it turned out, Taylor, assuming we were inclined to recommend sanctions against his government, wanted to put his best foot forward. As a result, we were able to interview almost everyone we asked to see, even though, from most, we received the company line: Liberia was in no way involved in the Sierra Leone conflict, and wanted only peace in the region. We asked a lot of questions to which we already had answers – in the form of international flight plans of weapons-carrying aircraft, radio intercepts, photos, and information from half a dozen different police and security agencies. In Liberia we were mostly told lies. Then, on our last day we were taken to the Presidential Mansion for an interview with the big man. The event had a surreal quality to it, because until that morning, I had begun to assume that they might not have connected me with *The Heart of the Matter*. The *Monrovia Guardian* that morning, however, quoted directly from the PAC report, using my name and saying that the UN Panel had come to Liberia to 'concoct facts' that would condemn the country to hardship sanctions. As we waited in an anteroom of the Mansion – which is more like a dilapidated five story hotel than a Presidential palace – a television in the corner gave us the latest news from CNN's Elsa Klensch 'Fashion File'. I stared at the screen. *What in the name of God am I doing here*, I wondered.

We had been warned against anything more than pleasantries if Taylor was in a bad mood, and 'bad mood' would reveal itself to us soon enough. But he was in a good mood. His windowless office was draped in brocade, with seriously scuffed imitation Louis XVI furniture, and large colourful pictures of Jesus, Mary and diverse saints hung high enough around the room to avoid reaching fingers. Taylor was charming and disarming and he told us lie after lie. He said that he had not provided training, sanctuary or weapons for the RUF. He denied knowledge of foreign gunrunners to whom he had given huge amounts of money and diplomatic Liberian passports. He said he had nothing to do with stolen diamonds. He said he was only interested in peace, and had enough problems of his own without meddling in those of other countries. He denied breaking the UN embargo on weapons, but said he did need weapons to fight his own dissidents. He asked, rather oddly, that we recommend a lifting of the UN arms embargo on Liberia, because he needed guns.

Instead, we recommended that it be tightened. We had found much more evidence than I had thought possible on weapons trafficking, diamond smuggling, and even management of the RUF war from behind the Liberian border. We recommended a ban on all 'Liberian' diamonds and we recommended a travel ban for Charles Taylor, his family, his cabinet ministers and other senior officials. We also recommended a ban on timber exports from Liberia, because Taylor's deforestation project was another source of hard currency for hard weapons. That part of the recommendation never made it into the Security Council resolution that eventually passed. China and France said that they were unwilling to harm the pathetically weak Liberian economy any more than necessary without clear evidence that timber sales were being used to buy weapons. Although the International Monetary Fund had complained that the proceeds from timber sales were going into 'off-budget' accounts – that is, to accounts controlled directly by Taylor – France and China nevertheless held the day on timber, coincident with the fact, perhaps, that they were the two largest importers of Liberian hardwood. It would take a lot more war and many more deaths before the Security Council would return to the issue of Liberian timber, eventually agreeing to an embargo in May, 2003.

When the resolution against Liberia was being debated in the Security Council, my fellow panel members and I were present in the chamber. We heard praise for the quality and depth of our report from several countries, and criticism from Russia, whose delegate said that some of the recommendations on diamonds were 'too radical'. We heard a long rant from a Gambian delegate who seemed to have missed the entire point of our exposé of diamond trafficking through his country. The Liberian Foreign Minister, Monie Captan, had come to New York to listen to the debate and to make Liberia's case one last time. A lawyer by training, Captan was smooth, even persuasive, especially for journalists who had not followed the story in any detail. He attacked me personally in his speech, something not often done in the Security Council. Later I was asked by a journalist how that made me feel. 'Proud,' I said, 'The truth hurts – at last.'

At the beginning of 2001 I returned to PAC where we were beginning a larger program of study on diamonds in Southern Africa, in the Democratic Republic of the Congo, Canada, India and elsewhere. We teamed up with a courageous Sierra Leonean organization, the Network Movement for

Justice and Development, and a Belgian organization, the International Peace Information Service, which had done outstanding work on the illicit weapons trade. PAC became a member of the Kimberley Process, a conclave of governments, industry representatives and NGOs that met a dozen times between May 2000 and November 2002, trying to create an international certification system for rough diamonds.

There were more adventures ahead for all of us. The UN reports on Angola and Sierra Leone had named Burkina Faso as a supplier of illicit weapons to Charles Taylor and as a conduit for diamonds moving out of the region. Lansana Gberie volunteered to go there to investigate the story in greater detail. Such was the paranoia in Burkina Faso that Lansana was immediately arrested on arrival at Ouagadougou airport. Our telephone calls and e-mail traffic, it turned out, had been intercepted by the authorities. It was only after a few tense hours of interrogation that he was put on a plane back to Abidjan. Other odd things happened. Some of the many people who assisted us were not what they seemed. John Pape, Director of the International Labour Resource and Information Group in Johannesburg, provided Ralph Hazleton with useful information and advice for a paper about the economic impact of diamonds in Southern Africa. Pape was well regarded in South Africa as a gentle and committed researcher. He was also something else. His real name was James Kilgore, and he was the last fugitive member of the Symbionese Liberation Army which in 1974 had kidnapped media heiress Patty Hearst, robbed banks and left a trail of murder and mayhem across Southern California. In November 2002, the FBI finally caught up with him and he was extradited to the United States where he was eventually tried and sentenced to six years in prison. In May, 2009 he was the final member of the SLA to be released from prison.

Among the hundreds of diamond meetings I have attended, a few stand out. In January 2001, the White House organized a meeting on conflict diamonds. If the visit with Charles Taylor was surreal, this meeting had similar overtones, not least because the Clinton administration had only ten days remaining, and had left the conflict diamond issue too late to make any difference. At a coffee break, I spoke to Alex Yearsley of Global Witness. As we stuffed paper napkins with the White House crest into our pockets, I asked him where he thought we could possibly go from here. What neither of us imagined was that three American politicians would nominate Global Witness and Partnership Africa Canada for the 2003 Nobel Peace Prize. Tony Hall, a Democratic Congressman from Ohio, and Frank Wolf, a Republican from

Virginia, had been indefatigable champions of the conflict diamond issue in the United States. Along with Vermont Senator Patrick Leahy they wrote a three-page nomination letter to the Nobel Committee of the Norwegian Parliament. Considering how much Hall and Wolf had done themselves, and considering how many organizations and individuals had contributed to the effort, this was an unusually generous act, one that helped strengthen our resolve when the battle for a genuine, credible system of diamond controls sometimes seemed too distant.

But there were other incentives. During a visit to Sierra Leone in 2002, I ran into one of my former students from Koidu Secondary School. Esther was 14 in those days, a shy Form 2 student from a wealthy Kono family. Now 49, she sat in the guest house where I was staying and told me her story. She had finished school and married, and she and her husband had developed a profitable little diamond business in Koidu. As the war closed in on them, they made plans to escape 'out the back way' with their two teenage daughters if the rebels ever came. Inevitably they did come. They came from the front, and they also came 'the back way'. Their first order of business was to behead Esther's husband in front of the family, splattering them all with his blood. The next was to start demanding. She gave them everything – the keys to the car, the house, whatever money she could lay her hands on, and for some reason they let her and the girls go. Esther's only thought was for the girls as they walked for weeks through the bush, eating grass and berries and drinking bad water. Esther's arms are permanently scarred from insect bites and the cuts inflicted by elephant grass. Finally they reached a refugee camp in Guinea, and after many months were able to make their way to Freetown.

In Freetown they stayed with an uncle, and Esther managed to get the girls into school. They created whatever might pass under such circumstances for a normal life. When I saw her, the war was over, and Esther was about to go back to Koidu to see what had happened. She knew that the town had been destroyed, but the family still had land, and there were still the diamonds. If she could get a little money together, she would be able to rent a pump and do some digging again. 'Esther,' I said, after some thought, 'Don't you think the diamonds are a curse?' 'Yes,' she said. 'A curse. But what else is there?'

CHAPTER 1

OF JUDGEMENT AND CUNNING WORK: DIRTY DIAMONDS

And thou shalt make the breastplate of judgment with cunning work...and the second row shall be an emerald, a sapphire and a diamond.

– Exodus 28:13, 18

Sir Percy Sillitoe, newly retired head of MI5, Britain's chief spymaster, was casting about for something to do in life when he was approached by Sir Ernest Oppenheimer, Chairman of the giant diamond cartel, De Beers.[1] As Sillitoe tells it, Oppenheimer wanted him to investigate illegal African diamond smuggling, a perennial problem that was turning into a massive drain on the company and a threat to De Beers' domination of the industry. It was 1953, and Sillitoe would spend the next three years travelling across Africa investigating the problem and establishing a covert diamond police force known as the International Diamond Security Organization (IDSO). One of the IDSO's operatives in West Africa was Fred Kamil, a Lebanese whose parents had settled in Liberia. Working in the family retail business, Kamil inadvertently found himself involved with men engaged in a massive diamond smuggling operation into Liberia from Sierra Leone. In the course of events, his business was ruined and he vowed to seek revenge on 'the callousness of the cursed trade which had wrecked my business at Robertsport, and the careers of so many'.[2] Kamil made his way to Sierra Leone where he says he was recruited by the IDSO.

The Madingo tribe is one of the most prominent and most dispersed ethnolinguistic groups in Africa, stretching from the River Niger in the west to the mouth of the Gambia River in the east, and north as far as the deserts of Mauretania. Their trading networks across West Africa are legend: once slaves; now agricultural products, cloth, gold and diamonds. The diamonds were Kamil's fixation. He soon infiltrated illicit Madingo diamond gangs and led armed raids on smuggling routes, catching dozens of what he called 'little and medium-sized fish'. He always missed the big ones, however, because of what he viewed as odd and unfathomable policies within the company and the IDSO. Gone from Sierra Leone by the end of the 1950s, he hints in his memoirs at dark deeds and massive corruption in the highest places of the diamond industry.

Enter Ian Fleming. Fleming had been a journalist for ten years before serving in British naval intelligence during the Second World War. Following the war he returned to journalism, but women, travel, expensive tastes and a Jamaican villa called *Goldeneye* demanded a more remunerative occupation. Over a seven week period in 1952, he dashed off a spy thriller, calling it *Casino Royale*. The book and a television production were successful, and in the next couple of years he wrote two more James Bond novels, *Live and Let Die*, and *Moonraker*. Fleming's interest in diamonds began in 1954 when he met Percy Sillitoe and heard about his new job with De Beers. Fleming's fourth novel, *Diamonds are Forever*, and arguably the worst of the 14 he eventually wrote, appeared in 1956, and it was obviously influenced by what Sillitoe had told him. It is the only Bond novel in which Fleming referred to an actual person:

'Things are getting too hot. At the mines. I don't like it at all. There's been a big intelligence man down from London. You've read about him. This man Sillitoe. They say he's been hired by the Diamond Corporation. There've been a lot of new regulations and all the punishments have been doubled...'[3]

The following year, Fleming wrote a series of articles for the *Sunday Times* dealing with Sillitoe's work, and later compiled the stories into a non-fiction book called *The Diamond Smugglers*. Sillitoe's legend grew, courtesy of an IDSO deputy named John Blaize, who provided most of the details that Fleming used in *The Diamond Smugglers*. Meeting secretly in Tangier, they discussed Sillitoe and the IDSO operation while strolling through the Kasbah, sipping mint tea in the gardens of the Minzah, and over Cuba Libres in suitably darkened bars and nightclubs.

In *The Diamond Smugglers*, Fleming explains that while De Beers may well have worried about the threat smuggling posed to its control over the diamond industry, the company's ultimate motive behind the hiring of Sillitoe and the creation of IDSO was bigger, and infinitely more important. Stopping the 'biggest smuggling operation in the world' – partly in Southern Africa, but mainly out of Sierra Leone via Liberia – was De Beers' 'patriotic duty'. Fleming explained it this way: the boom in gem diamonds was a hedge against inflation everywhere. 'As for industrial diamonds', he has Blaize explain, 'these are used for machine tools, and they're being stockpiled in the armaments race.'[4] Fleming laced the book with Soviet intrigue, saying that 'industrial diamonds are one of the sinews of peace', lifting a phrase from Churchill. He included a world map in the book which showed 'light', 'medium' and 'heavy' diamond smuggling traffic. The heaviest traffic on the supply side was from Monrovia, and on the end-user side, the heaviest lines depicting smuggled diamonds were drawn from Antwerp, via Berlin and Zurich, to Moscow. Fleming asks Blaize about reports of huge new diamond finds in Russia, but Blaize replies that 'No one's ever seen anything to back that story up.' He then asks rhetorically, 'If the Russians have got all that supply on tap, why would they be paying above world prices in Liberia and Belgium, as we know they're doing?'

Sillitoe's police work was successful, but the real solution to the diamond smuggling from Sierra Leone was commercial. One company, the Sierra Leone Selection Trust (SLST), had a diamond monopoly throughout the country. This was reduced to 450 square miles in 1955, and for the first time ordinary Sierra Leoneans were allowed to mine legally. The colonial government invited De Beers to set up buying stations in areas surrendered by SLST, partly to create a legal and taxable outlet, partly to stop smuggling. De Beers sent a small battalion of young school leavers and retired army types to sit in tin sheds with piles of cash to buy diamonds that once went across the border to Liberia. This novel solution – paying Sierra Leoneans for diamonds that they dug out of land which SLST had treated as its own – worked. 'And so, in a brief blaze of glory,' as Blaize explained it to Fleming, 'IDSO wound up its activities and prepared to disband.'

'Once the Diamond Corporation had set itself up in Sierra Leone and was ousting the IDB [illicit diamond buying] by straight commercial methods, there was nothing more for us to do that couldn't be done by the mine security staffs and by the local police forces in Africa.'[5]

Apart from a few loose ends and a skeleton organization with a watching brief, there was little more to be done. The Soviets had been foiled, the smugglers had been stopped, and all was well with the diamond world. Sir Percy went back to Britain where he helped establish a private security firm. Fred Kamil developed a neurotic grudge against De Beers and Harry Oppenheimer which culminated when he hijacked an aircraft in 1972, expecting to find Oppenheimer's former son-in-law on board. This was supposed to result in high-level negotiations between Kamil and Oppenheimer, but instead led to 21 unpleasant months in a Malawi prison. Ian Fleming became rich and famous, and John Blaize disappeared forever. Mainly because he never existed.

In fact most of the Percy Sillitoe story and Ian Fleming's intrigues were exaggerations or wildly incorrect. Sir Percy had never been 'approached by Ernest Oppenheimer'. When he retired from MI5, he opened a candy shop in Eastbourne. After two days of selling sweets to kiddies, he closed the shop, and following months of depression and failed attempts at writing his memoirs, he applied to a blind advertisement that had been placed in *The Times* by De Beers. Flying to Cape Town, he finally did meet with Oppenheimer, who told him that a vast, communist-directed diamond smuggling ring was at work throughout Africa.[6] One of the field operators chosen for Sillitoe was J. H. du Plessis, a former member of the South African police, who in due course wrote his memoirs (everyone at this time, it seems, was writing memoirs, filled with both pseudonyms and pseudo facts). Du Plessis wrote that 'certain of my superiors had made it clear to me that without the incredibly huge flow of illicit industrial diamonds from Central Africa to behind the Iron Curtain, the development of the Russian H-bomb would have been delayed by many years. Diamonds, thousands upon thousands of industrial diamonds, helped to make the precision tools and instruments which made the Russian H-bomb...'[7] Not only that, diamonds, he wrote, were financing anti-west uprisings in Greece, Lebanon, Syria, Algeria, the Far East, and 'a dozen other places'.

Coming from a long career as a police officer and eight years as head of Britain's counter-espionage organization, the Cold Warrior in Sillitoe must have bristled at what he was hearing. In fact, however, it made little sense. Industrial diamonds are not rare or expensive, and with the exception of a brief moment during World War II, they never were. And industrial diamonds are not used to make H-bombs or any other kind of bomb. They are used in machine tools for cutting and grinding, and they would have been readily available to the Russians – if they needed to import them – from many commercial sources. In any case, by the time Sillitoe was on the job, and certainly by the time Ian Fleming wrote *The Diamond Smugglers*, the Russians were well into the mining of their own kimberlite pipes in Yakutia, a fact that could not possibly have been lost on De Beers, which – only months later – was negotiating with the Russians to buy *their* goods.

The huge smuggling racket out of Sierra Leone certainly existed, but the Sillitoe gambit was in actual fact about a foreign exchange problem. And it was about Sierra Leone's gem diamonds, which were never sent covertly over, under or anywhere near the Iron Curtain. Easily laundered in Antwerp, they went straight into the legitimate trade, and from there into the jewellery shops of London, Paris and New York. 'John Blaize', in reality a former MI5 employee named John Collard, probably fed Ian Fleming his stories more for the Cuba Libres than anything else. In fact in the three short years that IDSO existed, there were only half a dozen people charged with diamond smuggling, and no evidence was ever found – despite all of Ian Fleming's dark innuendo and outright nonsense – that any smuggled African diamonds were going to the Soviet Union.

So what was IDSO all about? Certainly it had to do with smuggling and the very real threat that widespread leakage posed to the De Beers cartel. De Beers wanted to choke off the Liberian channel. By setting up sting operations and sending thugs like Fred Kamil to crash about in the rainforest, they may well have gone some way towards this goal. By establishing their own buying agents in Sierra Leone, however, and by persuading the British colonial government to waive tight, post-war foreign exchange rules, they went much further. This gave them the hard currency they needed in order to compete in Sierra Leone with Liberia – where the currency was the US dollar. In order to get the currency restrictions lifted, they needed someone of Sillitoe's stature, and they needed a Cold War excuse. In the end, De Beers got its cake and ate it too.

But not for long, as more recent events will show. Before leaving the 1950s, however, there are two footnotes to the IDSO story. One is the incredible arrogance that runs through the tales these men tell. If they were in any way typical of the late colonial mind, it is no wonder that the British Empire fell apart so quickly in the following decade. There is no conception anywhere in their writing that Africans had any role to play in the diamond business, except as hewers of kimberlite and drawers of gravel. A photograph in

The Diamond Smugglers shows three grown men handling a massive jackhammer; the caption reads 'Native *boys* at the face of the Williamson mine'. And Ian Fleming quotes 'John Blaize' on the subject of using X-rays to check miners: 'You see, you can't go on X-raying men, even if they're black, again and again. They get loaded with gamma rays.' Later he says that Blaize was scathing about Liberia, 'with good cause'. 'He despised many of the comic opera Negroes in official positions, but he thought even less of the white men who backed them and often incited them in their venality.' Fleming puts these words into the mouth of 'Blaize', but the arrogance, racism, thinly veiled anti-Semitism and stupidity that run through *The Diamond Smugglers* shed a whole new light on the creator of James Bond, gazing knowledgeably out from the dust jacket of his book in a jejune Cecil Beaton pose, cigarette and cigarette holder held *just so* for the camera.

Worse is the legacy of Fred Kamil, who would not be remembered at all had he not committed his exaggerations to paper. Born Fouad Bu Kamil in a small Druse village in Lebanon, he did indeed move to Liberia and he did become involved with IDSO, although many of his tales are fabricated, as one might expect of a man so unbalanced as to hijack an aircraft in order to meet Harry Oppenheimer. He too looks out from the dust jacket of his book, cigarette in hand; glowering; ready to take on the world. In his book he recalls a touching love affair with 'Ann', the wife of an American missionary in Liberia. Kamil writes of Ann's husband, 'John', 'a small man with reddish hair, standing with his bible in his left hand to leave his right hand free to point his finger towards Salvation'. Is 'Ann' the mother of a woman who was still searching for Fred Kamil almost half a century after his adventures in West Africa? Writing in 2002, there was little doubt in her chilling tale. A man she calls 'Amin' in a short memoir was a reformed alcoholic who had been befriended by her missionary parents in Monrovia in the early 1950s. Her father had baptized him when he renounced Islam, and they were close for several years. One night in 1956, when 'John' was away, 'Amin' attacked her mother, brutally and repeatedly, and returned on two subsequent nights to do it again. Eventually the missionaries confronted 'Amin', who by now was drinking heavily again and was involved with diamond smugglers. They forgave him because Jesus taught forgiveness, and eventually they moved on to other times and other countries. But they did not forget. Half a century later, John's daughter, who was three years old at the time, still remembered, as did her parents. 'There is no vengeance in any of our hearts,' she writes.

'If there is any emotion, it is sorrow that he chose the road he did... I want him to know that he is forgiven.'[8]

◆

During the 1990s, perhaps 25 per cent of the world's trade in rough diamonds was infected by smuggling, tax evasion, money laundering, sanction-busting, war and state collapse. This represented almost $2 billion worth of illicit behaviour in a rough diamond trade that was worth about $7.8 billion in 2002. The extent of the problem started to become clear in the late 1990s, when two NGOs, Global Witness in Britain and Partnership Africa Canada, exposed the relationship between diamonds and the wars in Angola and Sierra Leone. Here the issue was *conflict* diamonds, a sub set of the larger problem, but infinitely worse in its effect.[9] Conflict diamonds, or 'blood diamonds', are diamonds used by rebel movements to buy weapons and fuel war.

In its search for conflict diamonds from Sierra Leone, a UN Expert Panel noted the much greater volume of *illicit* diamonds. Part of the difficulty in understanding diamond statistics is that once rough diamonds arrive in Europe, India and elsewhere, they are sorted, traded across borders, re-sorted and re-traded – possibly many times – before they actually get to a cutting and polishing factory. The UN report said that

> This obscuring of origins makes the diamond industry vulnerable to a wide variety of illicit behaviour. It is no secret that diamonds are stolen from virtually every mining area in the world. Diamonds have long been used as an unofficial hard currency for international transactions. As with other precious commodities, they lend themselves to money laundering operations. Because they are small and easily concealed, they are readily moved from one country to another for the purpose of tax evasion, money laundering or to circumvent trade agreements. Virtually all of these diamonds eventually find their way into the legitimate trade. And all of these illicit transactions are made easier by the industry's long history of secrecy. Secrecy in the diamond industry is understandable for security reasons, but secrecy also obscures illicit behaviour.[10]

Conflict diamonds entered the system in the same way that illicit diamonds entered the system, just as they had for a century. Someone carried them to a trading centre – Antwerp, Bombay or New York, for example – smuggling them past customs or simply making a false declaration. Regardless, there was no difficulty in finding a buyer. Or a dealer would travel to Africa and purchase them from rebels or their agent, or a third party. From there he would take them to Belgium or another country, smuggling them past customs or making a false declaration.

Diamonds have always lent themselves to theft and smuggling, and they have served a wide variety of interests as a ready alternative to both soft and hard currency. They are small; they have a high value to weight ratio; they may not be a great investment, but they keep their value. And historically, they have been completely unregulated. Most governments gave up long ago trying to tax diamond exports and imports in any meaningful way because diamonds have been virtually impossible to trace and to police.

In the past, customs departments in most countries could call on technical expertise to examine and assess diamonds. With the exception of Belgium and Israel, however, non-mining countries had no in-house diamond expertise in their customs departments, and even in Belgium and Israel the main purpose was valuation, not identification. Diamonds passed unhindered and mostly unchecked across US, Swiss, British and other EU borders, the value and origin recorded by customs departments as presented by the importer. Licensing and other regulations have been stringent in some producing countries – South Africa, Botswana, Namibia, Russia – but elsewhere, especially in major consuming countries such as the US, there were none. Anyone could buy and sell diamonds; values were rarely checked; there was no reconciliation between what a dealer bought and what he sold.

One of the most blatant examples of diamond laundering in the 1990s was carried out in the free trade zones of the Geneva and Zurich airports. These facilities, known as *freilager*, were discovered by a UN Expert Panel almost accidentally when it toured the Geneva airport in 2000. Under the watchful eye of Swiss customs agents, parcels of diamonds arrived in the *freilager*. Some might be imported into Switzerland directly, but this was a tiny proportion of the whole, as there is no significant cutting and polishing industry in Switzerland, nor are there any bourses for rough diamonds. Most of the diamonds were taken to small rented rooms in the airport, specially fitted with diamond scales and bright lights. There, the parcels were opened, sorted, repackaged and re-exported. In some cases, the original parcel was simply re-labelled and re-invoiced. Members of the UN Panel were astounded to see one such transaction take place before their very eyes, as they were discussing the system with a senior Swiss customs official. The Panel members may have been surprised, but the customs official was not, because nothing illegal was actually occurring.

A very simple but effective laundering operation, however, was taking place. Customs officials throughout the world are usually interested in where goods have been shipped from, rather than where they have actually been produced. A Ford produced in Germany might contain an engine made in Italy, body panels made in France and electronics from Japan, but when it is shipped to Sweden, it is recorded as a German vehicle. Where diamonds are concerned, customs agents are similarly interested in the 'country of provenance' rather than the 'country of origin'. 'Country of origin' refers to the place where the diamonds were mined. 'Country of provenance' refers to the place they were last shipped from. The 'provenance' designation had become so common that it had lost its actual meaning, and statistics in many countries used the term 'origin' and 'provenance' interchangeably.

The confusion was significant. By arranging a pit stop in Switzerland, and by changing labels and invoices in the *freilager*, dealers were able to obscure, with the stroke of a pen, the actual origin of huge volumes of diamonds. Thus Britain recorded the import of £107 million worth of rough unsorted diamonds in 1999, of which £44.2 million was said to have been Swiss in 'origin'.[11] These could obviously have been Swiss in provenance only, not origin, but the story is not simply one of semantics. Switzerland that year had recorded the import of only Sfr 1.5 million in rough diamonds (less than US$1 million), so it could not possibly have exported the amount declared to British customs. The reason for the discrepancy – the apparent disappearance of more than $70 million in diamonds – had to do with what Swiss customs agents recorded and did not record. If diamonds were simply passing through the *freilager* and did not actually enter the country, no records were kept. The reason was simple enough: huge volumes of goods to which no value is added and which only stop in transit for a few hours could skew national trade statistics if they were included. So they were not.

But that was only the beginning of the obfuscation. Once the diamonds were sorted in Britain, many of them made their way back to Switzerland. Britain was stated as the 'origin' of 96.7 per cent of all Swiss imports of sorted and/ or partially treated diamonds in 1999. Having become Swiss on their way to Britain, they now became British on their way back to Switzerland. Then, that same year, 96.4 per cent of sorted or partially treated Swiss diamond exports went to Israel where they were recorded as being 'Swiss'.[12] Thus, diamonds that began their journey somewhere in Africa became Swiss, British and then Swiss again on their way to Israel. There may have been nothing nefarious in the bulk of these transactions. Many of the diamonds passing through Switzerland were De Beers diamonds on their way from Africa to London for sorting. De Beers used the Swiss transit stop for security reasons and to minimize British taxes. The loophole was technically legal and was not used to obscure the origin of the diamonds. Opacity was, however, a by-product of the process. For others, it was a heaven sent opportunity to launder illicit goods.

Switzerland was not alone; the same facilities existed in a dozen places, making the laundering of illicit goods child's play. Stung by international criticism, Switzerland began to record statistics on transit diamonds in 2001, and provisions in the new diamond certification system, described in Chapter 12, have now made this sort of laundering more difficult. But there is a lot more to it, as the unfolding story will show.

The diamond trade is secretive; perhaps more secretive than any other. Multi-million dollar deals were, until recently, often made on a handshake; tens of millions of dollars worth of diamonds have been sent across borders and across continents on approval, with little or no paper work. Some of this was traditional – a way of doing business in a trade that is heavily populated by small (and a few very large) family-run businesses, and by people who have known each other for generations. Some of it had to do with security and the transportation of high value goods from one place to another. And some of it had to do with theft, tax evasion and money laundering. In 2002, police arrested 22 jewellers on New York's 47th Street for buying 'fenced' goods. The next year, eleven more were busted for money laundering and a further 30 diamond wholesalers were forced to submit four years worth of corporate records, tax returns and financial statements to a grand jury.

There are other reasons for secrets. In order to keep its control over the market, De Beers bought all the diamonds it could for generations, no questions asked. In doing so, it had to deal in the 1950s and onward with a wide array of strange and incompatible bedfellows. Apartheid South Africa, the home of De Beers, was an inappropriate partner for newly independent diamond producing nations elsewhere in Africa – Congo, Tanzania, Sierra Leone, Guinea. And it was an even more inappropriate partner for the Soviet Union after its discovery of diamonds in the 1950s. In addition, having dealt with the Portuguese colonists of Angola until the mid 1970s, and the apartheid regime of Southwest Africa until the late 1980s, De Beers had some fancy and very confidential footwork to do in making friends with the new management. This was successfully expedited, in part through the distribution of large blocks of equity to the new regimes and by an assiduous avoidance of public attention.

By value, almost 60 percent of all gem diamonds are mined in Africa, and until recent discoveries in Canada, the percentage was higher. As some African diamond producing countries slipped into corruption and chaos during the 1960s and 1970s, diamond buyers remained on the scene but they began to conduct their business in new ways. Formal diamond production in Sierra Leone, for example, fell from two million carats in 1970 to only 48,000 carats in 1988. Declining resources were partially responsible, but there was an added factor: one of the most corrupt regimes on the continent's west coast. The same was true in the Democratic Republic of the Congo (DRC), known from 1971 to 1997 as Zaire. There was no drop, however, in the overall supply of Zairian diamonds reaching the world's trading centres, of which Antwerp had become the most important. All that was required was a degree of secrecy, and few questions would be asked when the diamonds were declared on arrival at Belgian customs.

Between the 1950s and the mid 1980s, the diamond scene in Africa changed. A significant proportion of the production of countries like the Congo, Sierra Leone, Angola and others was being hidden under a veil of secrecy that cloaked a vast network of corruption, theft and smuggling. Diamonds were also being used for money laundering – as a means of moving cash in cashless societies, or in economies where currency no longer had value. Lebanese traders in Sierra Leone, for example, have for decades smuggled diamonds out of the country as a way of repatriating profits, or of obtaining the hard currency needed to buy imports for other commercial activities: vehicles, petroleum products, rice and other foodstuffs.

Most governments learned long ago that taxes on diamonds – even very low taxes – lead inevitably to smuggling because diamonds can be so easily concealed, and because the nature of the trade is so opaque. Export duties are typically set at about three per cent in producing countries, and import duties are frequently zero in trading, cutting and polishing countries. Other attempts at restricting trade have been strenuously and effectively avoided as well. A dramatic example can be found in the DRC. An Israeli firm, International

Diamond Industries (IDI), obtained an 18 month monopoly on diamond exports from the DRC in September 2000. The DRC Minister of Mines defended the monopoly at the time, saying, 'This is the optimum way for the Congo diamond production to be marketed in a transparent manner that will inspire trust and confidence in the country's certificate of origin, which will accompany each and every parcel to be exported by IDI'.[13] It did nothing of the kind, in part because it was little more than a thinly disguised attempt by President Laurent Kabila to direct more of the industry's profits his way. He cancelled the licenses of all the other dealers – bought earlier for $100,000 each – and is said to have received a multimillion dollar payment for the favour.[14]

Exports from the DRC, however, immediately fell, while across the river in Brazzaville, the capital of a country with almost no diamonds at all, there was a sudden and dramatic change. Belgian diamond imports from Brazzaville – which stood at zero in August that year – jumped by October to $37 million.[15]

Congo Brazzaville played this role for years, in part because of the massive corruption and predatory behaviour of the DRC's long-time dictator, Mobutu Sese Seko. Under his helmsmanship, formal diamond production in the Congo apparently fell from 18 million carats in 1961, to 12 million in 1970 and only 8 million in 1980, finally levelling off at about 6.5 million carats in the 1990s. Production 'apparently' fell to these levels, because these are the figures that were recorded. But Mobutu 'informalized' much of the diamond industry, bringing it and its profits under his own control and that of his cronies. Miners, middlemen and diamantaires devised a simple way to avoid his rapacious appetite and a heavy system of informal taxation (otherwise known as 'bribery'). They simply smuggled their product across the river to Brazzaville. The ups and downs of Belgian diamond imports from Brazzaville are, in fact, a relatively good barometer of war and corruption in the DRC. In 1997, when the DRC was undergoing the chaotic transfer of power from Mobutu to Kabila, Belgium imported $454.6 million worth of diamonds from Brazzaville. By 1999, however, things had settled down and it looked as though Kabila might actually be a new wind sweeping away the corruption and cronyism of the past. That year Belgium imported only $14.4 million worth of diamonds from Brazzaville, and there was growth in imports from the DRC. By 2000, however, the blush was off the Kabila rose, and the volume from Brazzaville soared to $116.6 million, almost doubling again in 2001 to $223.8 million.[16]

Many of the statistics in this book relate to the diamond trade between various countries and Belgium. This is partly because more than 80 per cent of the world's rough diamonds pass through Antwerp every year. But the main reason is that Belgium kept and published statistics on its diamond trade. Most other countries did not. Diamonds statistics have either been kept under lock and key – as in Russia where diamonds were treated until 2005 as a 'strategic mineral' – or they were simply not published out of neglect or lack of interest. Where statistics were available, however, they often bore no relation to reciprocal statistics in other countries. The transit issue was one area of confusion. Another had to do with definitions. For example Canadian diamonds exported to Belgium under one customs code were recorded as arriving in Belgium under another, making it difficult and sometimes impossible to reconcile trade figures. On top of that, there was not much reliable information on what a particular mining country was capable of producing in a year, so anomalies between actual production and exports were difficult to track. This was not so difficult in the case of Liberia, a country with few diamond resources, but the country recorded in Belgium as the origin of an astonishing $2.2 billion in rough diamonds arriving in Antwerp between 1994 and 1999. Until this 'anomaly' was pointed out by the NGO, Partnership Africa Canada, however, nobody did anything about it. (The UN Security Council finally banned all 'Liberian' diamonds 18 months later, in May 2001.)

The statistical fog was part of a further subterfuge in the diamond trade, not unlike the Swiss manoeuvre, but not always involving the actual movement of anything more than paper. During the 1990s, diamonds were imported into Belgium as Sierra Leonean, Ivorian, Guinean, Gambian and Liberian, in volumes far exceeding what these countries produced. The difference between official rough diamond exports from these five West African countries and imports into Belgium during the period 1994–9 averaged about $660 million per annum. In other words, there was an unexplained $660 million worth of diamonds showing up every year in Belgium. Some of the diamonds declared as Gambian may well have passed through Gambia, and many of the 'Liberian' diamonds were smuggled from Sierra Leone. But a large part of the billions of dollars worth labelled as Liberian never went anywhere near Liberia, one of the most unsettled and dangerous countries on earth during the years in question. It may be assumed, therefore, that most of these diamonds were one of two things: they were diamonds produced in the countries recorded by Belgian import authorities and not recorded as exports (i.e. they were smuggled out); or they were diamonds produced elsewhere and imported into Belgium under false declarations. Liberian diamond production has never been significant in either volume or quality, and Gambia has no diamonds whatsoever. The excess in import over export, therefore, represented illicit diamonds, and the value was staggering: almost ten per cent of annual world production.

During the 1990s, additional estimates of illicit goods could be added to these. For example, the head of the Angolan Selling Corporation (ASCorp) said that between $350 and $420 million in smuggled diamonds left Angola in 2000, representing about five per cent of world supply.[17] Most Belgian diamond imports from the Republic of Congo (Brazzaville) could be counted as illicit. Congo Brazzaville is a country with few diamonds of its own, yet it exported $2.2 billion worth of gems between 1994 and 1999, or $377 million annually on average, and a further $116 million in 2000 and $224 million in 2001. The 1994–9 annual average represented five per cent of world supply, a very large proportion for a country with no serious diamond mining of its own. South Africa exported $200–250 million worth of diamonds of 'questionable origin' in a year. These included mine thefts along with smuggled goods from Angola, the DRC and elsewhere.[18] Mine thefts in other countries could be added to the total. These vary, but have been estimated at as much as 30 per cent from Namibia's Namdeb in 1999, and 2–3 per cent of Botswana's $2 billion annual production.[19] There has been laundering and theft in other diamond producing countries, as well as through major trading, cutting and polishing countries: Israel, India, Switzerland, Britain, the United States. And the same was true in smaller centres. Exports of rough diamonds from the United Arab Emirates (Dubai) to Belgium increased exponentially in the late 1990s: from $2.5 million in 1997 to $149.5 million in 2001. Large increases were recorded in shipments from the UAE to Israel as well. Hong Kong rough diamond exports to Belgium increased by 370 per cent between 1997 and 2001.

In addition, there was a Russian phenomenon known in the diamond trade as 'submarining'. As much as one third of Russia's $1.6 billion worth of diamonds was sold within Russia to Russian cutters and polishers. Many of these diamonds could not be processed economically in Russia, and the surplus was 'exported', escaping official statistics and agreements. Another term for this phenomenon is 'leakage'. Because these diamonds were laundered under other labels, the leakage did not show up in import figures elsewhere as diamonds of Russian origin.[20] Another word that might be used is 'illicit'. Or maybe 'crooked'.

There is double counting in some of these figures, made inevitable by the secrecy that has historically surrounded diamond statistics. Some of the smuggled Angolan goods may have been counted in the figures of Brazzaville or countries in West Africa, for example. But these figures, and the potential in countries for which there are no figures, suggest that an estimate of 25 per cent of world trade as illicit was more than possible, and that it may actually be conservative. This means that on average up to the beginning of 2003, when a new certification scheme came into play, one rough diamond in every five was stolen, used for money laundering or had evaded taxes.

Why was the level so high? The reasons are simple enough: the value, portability and accessibility of diamonds; the inherent secrecy of the trade, lack of government controls, an absence of data for checking even the most rudimentary movement of diamonds within and between countries; little detection and few penalties. These 'reasons' represent the *opportunity*. The historic *motivation* was predominantly tax evasion and money laundering. Where money laundering is concerned, diamonds offered an attractive alternative to hard currency, often in short supply in Africa. More recently, however, there have also been links to drug money, organized crime and international terrorism, as will be seen in subsequent chapters. At the far end of the spectrum are conflict diamonds. These are illicit diamonds taken one step further – to pay for weapons in rebel wars. Here, the effect has been devastating. Over the past two decades, millions of people have died in wars that have been fuelled by, or fought for diamonds. More millions have been displaced and entire countries have been ruined. But the diamonds never stopped flowing; no scarcity arose; few diamantaires were arrested charged or even chastised for dealing in illicit or conflict diamonds; and no fiancée was ever denied an engagement ring because of shortages or dramatic price increases.

CHAPTER 2

THE RIVER OF BIG RETURNS: GEOLOGY AND HISTORY

This ornament is but the guilèd shore
To a most Dangerous Sea
— Shakespeare, *The Merchant of Venice*

Diamonds, the purest form of carbon, are formed in a marriage of great heat and immense pressure occurring in two types of rock – eclogite and peridotite – 75 to 125 miles below the earth's surface. The crystallization resulting from the process may have taken place very quickly, or may have occurred over millions of years, but it happened when the world was much younger than it is today. Most diamonds were formed not millions of years ago, but a billion or more. Most have come to the surface, or almost to the surface, through gassy eruptions pushing their way through ancient 'diamond stability zones' or cratons, and rising through the earth's crust to its surface, taking diamonds with them. These small volcanoes last occurred 50 million years ago, producing carrot-shaped 'pipes' of gray-green rock called 'kimberlite'. Many kimberlite pipes never made it to the surface, and of the thousands that did – and known today – only a few dozen passed through diamond stability zones. And of the 5000 that actually contain diamonds, fewer than 100 have proven economically viable. The diamond-bearing pipes vary in size at the surface. The biggest, at Fort à la Corne in Saskatchewan, is a kilometre across, while the smallest ones are only meters from one side to the other. The nature of the kimberlite eruption – the heat, pressure and the speed with which the rock and diamonds were brought to the surface – determines the size, quality and volume of the stones it contains. The ratio of diamonds to kimberlite may

27

be as low as one part in 20 million, but a very good mine will produce three to five carats a ton. In non metric terms, this represents about 150 tons of rock and gravel for every ounce of diamonds.

De Beers' first big mine, in Kimberley, South Africa, opened in 1871, and over the next 43 years before it was closed, it yielded 14.5 million carats worth of diamonds. Today, only the 'Big Hole' remains, almost half a mile deep and a quarter of a mile across. The most recent finds in Canada's Arctic are producing pits that are half a mile wide. Millions of tons of kimberlite and waste rock will be mined from them in order to produce upwards of a million dollars worth of diamonds a day.

But the earliest diamond finds, and the diamonds that contribute most to conflict and instability have a different history. They are almost exclusively 'alluvial' diamonds. Alluvial diamonds were produced in the same way as those found in kimberlite pipes, but over time the top of the pipe was worn away by erosion. The soft kimberlite, exposed to a million winters, summers and rainy seasons, or perhaps 50 million, has crumbled and washed away down countless streams and rivers, whose course has changed time and again over the aeons. Glaciers may have pushed the gravel a hundred miles or a thousand miles away from its source, sometimes into oceans, or what became oceans. Diamonds found in one country today may have their source in another. Or the precise source may not actually be known. These alluvial diamonds are often found within a few feet of the earth's surface and may be scattered in varying degrees of concentration over hundreds of square miles. Unlike the kimberlite mines, which require heavy equipment and which can be readily policed, alluvial diamonds are more accessible to labour-intensive digging methods. And the vast areas over which they are scattered are much more difficult to control.

Diamonds, known since ancient times, were first mined in India. The earliest references are in Sanskrit manuscripts dating from 300 B.C. It was undoubtedly Indian diamonds that adorned the breastplate of the high priest described in Exodus 28:18: 'And thou shalt make the breastplate of judgement with cunning work... And thou shalt set in it settings of stones, even four rows of stones: the first row shall be a sardius, a topaz, and a carbuncle... And the second row shall be an emerald, a sapphire and a diamond.' There are other references, in Ezekiel and Jeremiah – and in Zechariah, where the hearts of people are set against the words of the prophets: 'hearts as an *adamant* stone'. *Adamant*, today an English word meaning unyielding or inflexible, is derived from the Greek *adamas*, meaning unconquerable. This word gave the diamond – *le diamant* – its modern name. Pliny the Elder, writing in the first century A.D. recounted the legend of the Valley of Diamonds, found somewhere in the East. 'The most valuable thing on earth is diamond,' he wrote, 'known only to kings and engendered in the finest gold. Six kinds are known and, of these, the Indian and Arabian are of such unspeakable hardness that when laid on the anvil they give the blow back with such force to shatter hammer and anvil to pieces.'[1]

Any 'Arabian' diamonds had made their way to that land in the baggage of traders, almost certainly from India, where the first diamonds had been discovered six or eight centuries earlier. In those times, diamonds were valued because of their hardness, and because they were said to possess supernatural powers, ensuring victory in battle, warding off the evil eye, serving as an antidote to poison. Uncut, they had little of the beauty associated with them today, but their rarity, hardness and magical properties placed them in great demand. Marc Antony is said to have worn a gold-embroidered robe decorated with diamond buttons at the coronation of Cleopatra in 33 B.C.[2]

It was several centuries more before the real secret of the diamond would be released, first by simple polishing, then by more scientific cutting and polishing which would reveal the diamond's refraction, its reflection, and its dispersion of light. These give the diamond its special brilliance and 'fire'. Charlemagne, King of the Franks and in 800 founder of the Holy Roman Empire, wore two partially polished diamonds. And uncut diamonds can be seen in the portraits of European kings and princes of the 13th and 14th centuries. A thriving cutting industry was established in Venice in the early 14th Century, and smaller centres sprang up by the end of the century in Paris, Bruges, Antwerp and Lisbon. By the middle of the 17th century, diamonds adorned the crowns and sceptres of Europe's richest and most powerful monarchs. Cardinal Mazarin, chief minister to Louis XIV, bought the diamonds of England's beheaded monarch, Charles I, from Oliver Cromwell, adding to the Sun King's growing collection. Louis also bought a great blue Indian stone which would eventually produce the 44 carat Hope Diamond. Known originally as the 'Tavernier Blue', it had made its way to France in a pouch carried by Jean-Baptiste Tavernier, an inveterate diamond dealer who visited India six times during the 17th century. Tavernier sold many diamonds to the King, becoming wealthy in the process, but none was more valuable than the blue diamond he had carried from the Golconda mines in central India. For this one, Louis paid 220,000 *livres*, almost $2 million in modern terms.

But India's days as a diamond producer were ending. After 1750, the country that produced the Hope Diamond, the 108-carat Koh-i-Noor, the 280-carat Great Mogul and the 140-carat Regent – perhaps as much as 30 million carats altogether over time – was eclipsed as a producer by Brazil. As in India, it was gold miners who discovered diamonds in the Portuguese colony. The first finds in 1725, in rivers in the eastern province of Minas Gerais, led to others in Mato Grasso and elsewhere. During the last half of the 18th century, diamond production varied between 25,000 and 50,000 carats annually, rising to almost 200,000 carats a year by the 1850s. But Brazil's mining days were also numbered, and the by the end of the 19th century the country had become a relatively minor diamond producer.

Just as Brazil eclipsed India, a new source of diamonds would soon surpass dwindling supplies from South America. The modern diamond era begins, or so legend has it, with a 15 year-old South African boy named Erasmus Jacobs, out one day in 1867 looking for sticks. Instead, he found a 21 carat diamond which became known, appropriately, as the 'Eureka Diamond'. Erasmus Jacobs' mother gave it to a neighbour for nothing, and eventually it found its way to Britain where it was cut into a 10.73 carat diamond. It changed hands many times before being bought in 1967 by De Beers for repatriation to South Africa as a museum piece. Not long after the Jacobs discovery, the rush was on. One of the best early South African sites was on a farm near Kimberley, owned by two brothers named De Beer. They had bought the farm for £50 and must have thought they were turning a handsome profit when they sold it to a consortium of diggers for six thousand guineas, disappearing themselves into history but leaving their name behind with one of the most fabled companies of all time. By 1872 there were 50,000 diggers in the area, and eventually the De Beers farm yielded £600 million worth of diamonds.

Until the late 1870s, little was understood about the geology of diamonds. Indian diamonds were alluvial, and to this day their source remains unknown. The Brazilian diamonds were also alluvial, and in South Africa at first, there was no reason to assume that they originated in anything other than the shallow, yellow, oxidized kimberlite in which they were first discovered. As diggers burrowed into darker blue ground which they thought contained no diamonds, they began to look for entrepreneurs or fools who might buy out their claims. One of the former was a young man fresh from England, Barney Barnato. Twenty four years old in 1876, he began buying up leases, and he dug deeper into the blue rock that would soon take its name from the town nearby. Starting with an investment of £3000, he turned it into £90,000 before the year was out. The story will return shortly to Barney Barnato, sitting at the edge of what would soon become the Big Hole under the covetous gaze of another young man in a hurry, Cecil Rhodes.

But there were diamonds to be found elsewhere in Africa. The search began in the so-called Congo Free State in 1906 – 'so-called' because the colony had been, in fact, the personal property of Belgium's King Leopold II since the 1880s, and was anything but free. The Congo became a setting for enormous atrocities after Leopold planted his blood-stained flag and began systematic looting of ivory, timber, cotton, palm oil, rubber, gold, copper and tin. Forced labour, burned villages, starved hostages, massacres and the outright extermination of any resistance were the order of the day. Famine and epidemics raged, but the work and the exports continued. Authoritative modern calculations suggest that the population of the Congo dropped by a staggering ten million people between 1880 and 1920[3] – a crime of genocidal proportions. The first Congolese diamonds were discovered in 1907, a year before international public outrage finally forced Leopold to transfer authority for his colony to the Belgian government. The diamonds were alluvial, found in the Tshikapa River, not far from the Angolan border, and they provided a trail which led eventually to the discovery of diamonds in that Portuguese colony in 1912.

The next major find was in the German Protectorate of Southwest Africa, now Namibia. In 1908 a former De Beers employee shovelling sand off a railway line found something he recognized. It was the first of what would be tens of millions of diamonds. These were also alluvial stones, found along a desolate, under-populated coastal strip of land extending some 350 km north of the Orange River. Within a year most of the known diamond fields were being mined by small German syndicates or partnerships, usually on 50-year concessions in territory the German government had declared off limits to anyone without a permit. This was the *Sperrgebiet* or 'Forbidden Territory' where to this day trespassers face prison sentences or stiff fines – and worse if they are found with diamonds.

Soon there were important finds further north in West Africa. Diamonds were discovered in the Gold Coast, now Ghana, in 1919, and by 1930 there was a respectable diamond mining industry in the Eastern Province. Sierra Leonean diamonds were discovered in Kono District in 1930, when a small geological survey team found a crystal by the Gboraba stream. The team had been examining stream-bed gravels for heavy minerals; instead the crystal turned out to be a diamond. The next day, they found another diamond at the same site. The Sierra Leone colony, Britain's first in West Africa, had been suffering from economic stagnation and depression for nearly a century because of its dire lack of resources. But the discovery, which was duly reported to colonial authorities, elicited little interest until it came to the attention of the Consolidated African Selection Trust (CAST) which was mining the Gold Coast diamonds. A prospecting party from CAST arrived in March 1931 and not long afterwards it became apparent that Sierra Leone would be an important source of high-value alluvial gem diamonds.

Minor deposits were also discovered during these years in Guinea, Liberia and Côte d'Ivoire, and in the 1940s, a Canadian geologist, John Williamson, stumbled on one of the world's largest kimberlite pipes in the British Protectorate of Tanganyika, now Tanzania. The surface of the Williamson kimberlite is 361 acres. Although its gem content was low, the Williamson Mine became an important source of industrial diamonds during the Second World War.

Alluvial diamonds were found in Russia in the nineteenth century, but it was not until the 1950s that the major Yakutia diamond deposits were uncovered, half of them north of the Arctic Circle. Legend has it that a Russian geologist discovered the first kimberlite pipe by following a fox with a blue-stained belly to its lair. By 1959, 120 pipes had been discovered and there were more to come. And in Africa, the search for new sources of diamonds continued. Prospecting began in British Bechuanaland, now Botswana, in 1956, and here it was ants rather than foxes that helped geologists in their search. In constructing their giant anthills, some brought useful indicator materials to the surface – or so the story goes. The first kimberlite pipe was found in 1967 and the first mine, Orapa, went into production in 1971. Botswana's diamond statistics are today, truly breathtaking. In 2008 the country's only diamond mining company, Debswana, produced more than 32 million carats worth of diamonds, generating revenues of $3.3 billion.[4] That year, diamonds contributed one third of Botswana's annual GDP, made up three quarters of the value of the country's exports, and produced about half of all the direct revenues flowing to the treasury. This single industry, with only four operating diamond mines, produced an astonishing 25.7 per cent of the world's rough diamonds by value.

Australia has long been a source of minor alluvial diamond deposits but there were few of commercial value until a major discovery was made in

Western Australia in 1979. Within five years the Argyle mine was producing 30 million carats a year, and by the end of the 1980s, Australia had become the source of almost one third of all the world's diamonds by weight. Only five per cent of Australian diamonds are gem quality, but the finds made significant changes in world production.

Canadian discoveries in 1991 – 300 kilometres northeast of Yellowknife – took the industry by surprise again. Some of the world's biggest mining companies, including De Beers, had been prospecting in Canada for years but had come up with little or nothing. Like John Williamson in Tanganyika, the geological prospecting team in Sierra Leone and others who made important but unexpected diamond discoveries, the Canadian find was made by a dogged, badly funded team of two: a prospector and a geologist, tracking geological clues from the backwoods of Arkansas, along glacial moraines and across mountains into the frozen lands of the Northwest Territories. From the outset, their discovery promised to be important. But as late as 1998, Canadian diamonds were still not on the production radar: by weight, 32 per cent of world production came out of Australia, 20 per cent more or less from the Democratic Republic of the Congo, 16 per cent each from Botswana and Russia, nine per cent from Angola, and five per cent from all the other countries combined. Canada represented only 0.23 per cent of world production by weight. By value, however, the story was changing. Botswana came out on top in 2008 with more than 25 per cent of the estimated $12.7 billion world total. Russia was next at 19.7 per cent; South Africa came in at 9.7 per cent and Angola at 9.5 per cent. Canada, in production for less than a decade, had surpassed all but Botswana and Russia, with 17.7 per cent of world production by value, and estimates suggest that this will continue to rise.[5]

CHAPTER 3

DE BEERS: THE DELICATE EQUIPOISE

The whole of my stones I sold to De Beers, for if I had placed them on the open market I should have upset the delicate equipoise of diamond values. When I came finally to cast up my accounts, I found that I had secured a fortune of a trifle over a quarter of a million pounds. The wealth did not dazzle me so much as solemnize me... It had been bought with men's blood.

– John Buchan, *Prester John*, 1910

In the1870s, almost a decade after the diamond rush began in South Africa, there were still great fortunes to be made, and there were great fortune hunters aiming to make them. One of these was a pale young Englishman who had arrived in South Africa at the age of seventeen, intending to become a cotton farmer. Instead, he wound up in Kimberley where he bought a diamond claim and rented out steam-powered water pumps to other miners when their diggings flooded. On April Fool's Day, 1880, with assets of £200,000, Cecil John Rhodes, then 28, formed the De Beers Mining Company, merging his own interests with two other syndicates and taking over a major part of the mine on land that had once been the farm of the De Beers brothers. From its inception, however, the De Beers Company and Cecil Rhodes were interested in more than diamonds. The company's charter – with not a little arrogance – allowed it, among other things, to 'take steps for good government of any territory, raise and maintain a standing army, and undertake warlike operations'. *Warlike operations.*

But diamonds came first. As Rhodes was gaining control of one part of South Africa's diamonds, Barney Barnato, a former London music hall

35

entertainer, was buying up the rest. His Central Diamond Mining Company controlled the 'Big Hole' which would, before it was finished, produce three and a half tons of diamonds. Barnato had made an arrangement with a French company, *La Compagnie Française des Diamants du Cap* – known appropriately as 'The French Company' – to form part of Kimberley Central. But diamonds were flooding the market and prices fluctuated wildly. It was Rhodes who devised the idea of stabilizing the price through an amalgamation of all the companies. And by 'all', he meant *all*. By 1887, there was only one independent company left – Barnato's 'Central'. After tackling him head-on and failing, Rhodes approached Barnato, whom he had once called a 'little prancer', with a friendly offer that might suit them both where price-fixing was concerned. He would buy the French interests in the French Company outright and give them to Barnato in return for £300,000 cash and 70,000 shares of Kimberley Central. This gave Barnato cash as well as all of the French Company – at a more reasonable price than would have been possible in a bidding war.

A former business partner once said of Rhodes that 'as an opponent, he would do far less harm than he does as a sort of half-and-half friend.'[1] Barnato, having sold Rhodes one fifth of his company as a half-and-half friend, now found himself with a formidable opponent. In the end, it cost Rhodes £2 million more to get the rest of Kimberley Central's shares, driving them up in the process by a factor of more than three. He succeeded, but there was still one hurdle. A group of Kimberley Central's smaller shareholders went to court to have the merger blocked. Rhodes made one last deal with Barnato, dissolving Kimberley Central and paying off all the shareholders with what would be the biggest cheque ever written up to that time. On 18 July 1889, De Beers Consolidated Mines Ltd. wrote the cheque – for £5,338,650 – completing the takeover, and cementing with the stroke of a pen the future of the cartel, and the price of diamonds, for the foreseeable future.

Over the next few months, Rhodes bought up the few remaining independent mines in South Africa, and by 1890 he controlled over 95 per cent of the world's diamond production. He then established some of the principles that would stay with the company long after he was gone. He began to withhold diamonds in order to drive prices up, cutting Kimberley production by one third. He decided that there should be a single channel for the distribution of diamonds, and he worked with London merchants to create a syndicate that would take everything his mines produced, controlling the price as the diamonds moved further along the pipeline toward the consumer. He began to think about market generation, calculating the number of weddings that would take place in what had already become his biggest market, the United States.

And he had ideas about the need for class legislation. 'I prefer land to niggers,' he once said. Now he believed that 'there must be Pass Laws and Peace Preservation acts... we have got to treat the natives, where they are in a state of barbarism,' he said, 'in a different way to ourselves. We are to be the lords over them.'[2] He then looked as though he might take over the world, beginning with the premiership of the Cape Colony, a 'Cape to Cairo' railway and the colonization of half of central Africa. 'I would annex the planets if I could,' he once said. 'I often think of that.' At 48, however, Rhodes' ambition, greed and heart gave out. He died in 1902, single and alone, leaving his money and his name to a prestigious scholarship fund at Oxford University. He was buried on a hilltop in Southern Rhodesia, one of the two British colonies that bore his name – until such time as the people he had colonized could gain independence and erase his name from the map.

The syndicate that Rhodes helped to establish in London comprised the city's ten leading Jewish diamond merchants. For a thousand years, the diamond industry had been dominated by Jews, a by-product of money-lending when gems were used as collateral. Mediaeval European guilds prohibited Jews from a wide variety of crafts, but diamond cutting and polishing was not one of them, and so the craft followed the trade. The trade and the cutting industry developed first in Lisbon and then Antwerp, under Spanish control until 1714. But when the Spanish Inquisition began in 1478, Jews were forced to flee. Taking diamonds and their skills with them, they set up a new centre in Amsterdam. During the 18th century, with growing British domination of India and control over the trade routes from Brazil, the locus for diamond commerce began shifting to London, and so did the Jewish diamond entrepreneurs of Amsterdam. While the trade moved to London, the cutting and polishing gradually shifted to Antwerp, setting the stage for a diamond pipeline which continues to this day.

The flood of South African diamonds appeared fortuitously, just as supplies from India and Brazil began to dwindle. That was the good news for London traders. The bad news was that the flood created chaos in the marketplace, and the top ten London merchants, some of whom had helped finance Cecil Rhodes in his takeover of Kimberley Central, now saw great wisdom in his plan to control the supply of diamonds. By controlling the supply, demand – and therefore price – could be assured. Anton Dunkelsbuhler, one of the London ten, had worked with Rhodes and maintained a small buying office in South Africa. In 1902, after the death of Rhodes, he sent one of his young diamond sorters, a naturalized British citizen who had emigrated from Germany six years earlier, to run the South African operation. Ernest Oppenheimer, who would eventually play king of diamonds to Cecil Rhodes' knave, soon became a fixture in South Africa's gold and diamond industries, but not as a sorter or buyer. Money and deal-making would be his forte – for Dunkelsbuhler, for the syndicate, and for himself.

In 1914, at the outset of World War I, there were significant German interests in South African gold. And the hard-won De Beers monopoly had been broken by the discovery of diamonds in German Southwest Africa. Oppenheimer turned both of these problems to his own advantage. In 1917 he created a company that would buy up a considerable amount of a troubled mining firm, Consolidated Mines Selection Ltd., principally the part owned by German interests. Distancing himself from South Africa's traditional financial sources in London, he used political connections, friends, family, charm and guile to attract American money into the venture. He called the new company the Anglo American Corporation. It sounded important, and the name was politically adroit. And in Southwest Africa he used Rhodes' Kimberley Central takeover technique on the German diamond operations. He offered German investors, fearful of imminent expropriation, cash or shares in Anglo American in return for their diamond operations, most of which has been abandoned at the start of World War I. He called the new company, of which he was Chairman and Managing Director, Consolidated Diamond Mines.

Then he began to think about De Beers. By 1925, Oppenheimer had major interests in diamond operations in Angola and the Congo as well as Southwest Africa. With the support of London and New York bankers, he created his own syndicate, joining forces with a nephew of Barney Barnato, Solly Joel. Joel had retained some of Barnato's interests in diamonds and, as a major shareholder in De Beers, he also held a seat on the De Beers board. At the same time, Oppenheimer bought up as much De Beers stock as he and his family could afford. De Beers held out against Oppenheimer as long as its directors and financiers could, but by the end of 1929, inside or outside, Ernest Oppenheimer had become the most important player in the company. Five days before Christmas, age 49 and now *Sir* Ernest Oppenheimer – the

German diamond sorter from Friedberg – was unanimously elected Chairman of the Board.

Oppenheimer incorporated Consolidated Diamond Mines into De Beers, and when the exchanges and refinancing were complete, Anglo American surfaced as De Beers' controlling shareholder. Timing was an important factor in what came next. Oppenheimer had written to his brother that he intended to make De Beers 'the absolute controlling factor in the diamond world.'[3] This was not an idle fancy. With the depression, the bottom had fallen out of the diamond market. The only recently reconstituted syndicate of London buyers had stockpiled stones it could not sell, but by 1932, the price of diamonds had dropped by half, even though Oppenheimer had virtually halted South African production. Something had to give, and unless action was taken, the entire diamond price structure devised by Cecil Rhodes fifty years earlier would collapse.

Oppenheimer solved the problem by restructuring the Syndicate in London into a more sustainable marketing mechanism that he called the Diamond Trading Company (DTC). This created a platform that would enable him to impose long term stability on the entire diamond trade. From then on, only the De Beers-owned DTC would allocate diamonds to manufacturers and wholesalers. There would be no uncontrolled selling. De Beers would mine diamonds, and it would manage the new and more stable marketing distribution mechanism. It was a cartel that would benefit even non-De Beers mining firms, one that would be able to resist unforeseen economic setbacks and unpredicted world events. The new operation would buy up as many loose diamonds as it could on the 'open market' – diamonds mined in obscure places; diamonds stolen from De Beers' own mines and smuggled to other places; *all* diamonds.

At its height, and for half a century between the 1930s and the 1980s, De Beers wielded absolute control over all aspects of the rough diamond industry, handling directly more than 80 per cent of all the diamonds produced in the world. Sir Ernest Oppenheimer died in 1957, and was succeeded by the company's managing director, his son Harry. The same age his father had been when he ascended the throne, Harry would steer the company through the shoals of apartheid, the storms of the Cold War, and the discovery of vast quantities of diamonds in other parts of the world. But some of the biggest challenges for De Beers lay ahead for Harry's son, Nicky. When Harry retired in the 1980s, he created an inner cabinet of senior managers to look after the business. Nicky, the heir apparent, worked his way through the corporate labyrinth, and finally became Chairman of the De Beers Group in 1998. In 2009, *Forbes* put his net worth at $5 billion.

The De Beers system for controlling the industry was a sophisticated advance on the basic tenets established by Cecil Rhodes. On the one hand, De Beers bought up as many diamonds as it could lay its hands on, funnelling them all through its London operation, known alternatively as the Diamond Trading Company, the Central Selling Organization (CSO), and more recently, again, as the Diamond Trading Corporation. Its own diamonds, taken from its own mines, went through the system that way, and De Beers made arrangements with governments and mining companies throughout the world to do the same for them. And it set up buying offices throughout the world to mop up loose supplies and other goods on the 'outside market'. The idea was to manage as much of the world's production as possible, in order to maintain control, and thus stability, throughout the industry. Although independent diamond mining firms would often criticize De Beers, they rarely did it publicly, for the benefits of working with De Beers far outweighed the limitations of independence. The entire industry benefited from De Beers management of both supply and demand, and most of all, from the resulting high prices for a commodity that was becoming less and less rare with each year that passed.

On the demand side, De Beers sold, and continues to sell diamonds to a very select set of customers. Much has changed for De Beers in the new millennium, and the company no longer sells, as it one did, in volumes limited enough to maintain price levels. But the company still sells only to pre-approved traders, cutters and polishers. These select few are known as 'sightholders'. Until 2003, when the number was slashed by one third, there were about 125 of them.

Several times a year in London and Southern Africa, sightholders gather at an event called a 'sight', where each is given a smart yellow and black briefcase and sent into a room with lights, scales and other equipment for examining gems. In the case are diamonds, wrapped in pieces of folded paper. The diamonds are assigned to a sightholder based on what has been requested in terms of volume, colour, caratage and price. But De Beers will add other diamonds as well, in order to get rid of stones that it cannot otherwise apportion. Sightholders may sit and examine the allocation to their hearts' content, but with the exception of very special stones, there is little picking and choosing. The brilliance of the system is that De Beers is able to unload everything it wants to move, using the sightholders to pass on unwanted goods to customers further down the pipeline.

De Beers also advertises. Sir Ernest understood, like Rhodes, the importance of cultivating the market, and as more and more diamonds became available, it became necessary to find new customers. 'A diamond is forever' is thought by many to be the greatest advertising slogan of the 20th century, and perhaps it will remain so in the 21st. According to legend, an exhausted, overworked copywriter in the New York ad firm of N.W. Ayer was working late one night in 1948 on a presentation that had to be made the next day. 'Dog tired,' Frances Gerety said, 'I put my head down and said, "Please God, send me a line".' Then she sat up and wrote the famous slogan that would serve De Beers so well for more than half a century.[4] It was a good line, and it may have come from God, but New York author and playwright Anita Loos also had something to do with it, and never got much credit. In 1925 she wrote a book called *Gentlemen Prefer Blondes*, which later became a Broadway play. In 1953 it was made into a movie that produced another famous slogan – 'diamonds are a girl's best friend'. In the original book, however, Loos had her gold-digging heroine, Lorelei Lee, speaking clearly of diamonds and forever: 'Kissing your hand makes you feel very very good but a diamond and safire (*sic*) bracelet lasts forever.'[5]

New markets for diamonds were cultivated in North America before World War II, and in the 1960s, attention turned to Japan. When the advertising campaign began there in 1968, only one Japanese woman in 20 received a diamond engagement ring. Within 20 years, the number had risen to 15 in every 20, and then rose further. De Beers has spent upwards of $200 million a year on advertising, and yet paradoxically, it was not possible until the end of 2002 to buy a polished De Beers diamond anywhere. There was, in effect, no such thing, because De Beers' business was restricted to unpolished rough diamonds alone.[6]

In the 1950s and 1960s, India opened up entirely new possibilities for the diamond industry by expanding its cutting and polishing industry. Small and inexpensive stones, once confined to the industrial marketplace, could now benefit from India's cheap labour, and could be sold in the much more profitable gem market. The focus was on volume rather than quality, and the diamonds were often 'single cuts' – stones so small they are given just a few basic facets. But these stones created gems that were much more affordable for a new market of less affluent buyers. By 1998 there were 660,000 people working India's cutting and polishing industry. This kind of growth in a new type of product vastly expanded the global market for diamonds.

◆

A 'cartel', sometimes called a 'trust', is a collusive association of independent enterprises, formed to monopolize the production and distribution of a product, and to control prices. Cartels, trusts and monopolistic behaviour are variously regulated in industrialized countries, but nowhere as explicitly as in the United States. The 1890 Sherman Antitrust Act was promulgated at a time when government, labour and the public at large feared that combinations of big business threatened the very essence of free enterprise and the rights of the small entrepreneur. Arguments for antitrust laws favour both the consumer, by preventing collusion on prices, and business at large, by encouraging innovation and opportunities for individual enterprise. The antitrust laws, according to a 1972 US Supreme Court decision, 'are the Magna Carta of free enterprise. They are as important to the preservation of economic freedom and our free enterprise system as the Bill of Rights is to the protection of our fundamental freedoms.'[7]

Given this almost evangelical American conviction, it was predetermined that De Beers would sooner or later run afoul of the US Justice Department. For years the company was largely immune from US antitrust laws because it did no business in the United States, conducting sales to American sightholders outside of the country. But in 1973 the Justice Department discovered that De Beers owned half of Christensen Diamond Products, a US company that received industrial diamonds from the mother house. It was a clear case of a US De Beers presence, if not collusion. The case had been difficult to make because De Beers records were buried in a maze of some 300 interlocking corporations, many of them hidden behind Dutch and Luxembourg registrations. US government lawyers nevertheless concluded that De Beers had engaged in a 'conspiracy... to suppress competition' and that 'much was done with full knowledge that there was grave risk of violating US antitrust laws.'[8] De Beers, however, scampered quickly away from the charge by divesting itself of the Christensen stock, knowing in any case that Christensen would have very few options in the future when it went shopping for diamonds.

Then, in 1992, both De Beers and General Electric raised the price of industrial diamonds, the first price hike in five years. The ever-vigilant Justice Department smelled another rat, and in 1994 filed a suit against the two companies for price fixing. General Electric was acquitted, but the De Beers indictment remained outstanding because De Beers never appeared in court to defend itself, remaining under a Justice Department cloud for another decade.

While De Beers consistently and successfully avoided direct confrontation with US authorities, it is unrepentant in its defence of the cartel. In a 1999 speech, Nicky Oppenheimer introduced himself by saying,

> I am chairman of De Beers, a company that likes to think of itself as the world's best know and longest running monopoly. We set out, as a matter of policy, to break the commandments of Mr. Sherman. We make no pretence that we are not seeking to manage the diamond market, to control supply, to manage prices and to act collusively with our partners in the business.[9]

But Oppenheimer defended what De Beers prefers to call 'single channel marketing' in two ways. First, by controlling the price De Beers protects the consumer, ensuring that the purchase retains its value. He said that any company dealing in a total luxury 'cannot behave as an evil monopoly exploiting the masses, because at the end of the day they do not have a compelling need to purchase.' And secondly, 'single channel marketing has exercised an extraordinary beneficial influence upon the whole of the diamond industry, and particularly many of the economies of Africa.' This, he argued, was a good reason for considering a review of American antitrust laws as part of a new engagement with Africa.

Both arguments hold water, but both leak as well. There is a two-tier market for diamonds, and while retail diamond prices do rise, the resale value for 'used' diamonds is very different. In his 1982 book, much despised in the diamond industry, Edward Jay Epstein wrote about the problem. In a chapter entitled 'Have you ever tried to sell a diamond?' the author devotes several pages to the trials and tribulations of those who *have* tried, mostly without getting their investment back. The benefits of the diamond industry to Africa is a larger question, addressed at length in Chapter 10. Suffice to say here that whatever they have contributed to Africa in a positive sense, diamonds have also contributed to great suffering.

◆

Perhaps the most sensitive part of De Beers' delicate equipoise during the second half of the 20th century was apartheid. In 1948, South Africa's

Nationalist Party, led by Hendrik Verwoerd, came to power on a platform that would strip the non-white population of its most basic human and political rights. The issue soon became international, especially in the late 1950s as Britain's African colonies began to achieve independence, and it boiled over in 1961 when South Africa was expelled from the Commonwealth. One by one, countries in which De Beers had important commercial interests – Ghana, Sierra Leone, Tanzania – broke relations with South Africa.

Harry Oppenheimer opposed apartheid openly. He financed the opposition United Party, ran for parliament, and was one of the few UP candidates to be elected. For nearly a decade he sat with a small group of opposition MPs, unable to exercise much influence over the growing institutionalization of racism by the government. He did not contest the 1958 election, however, and in 1959 the United Party split on the issue of the black vote. While a conservative wing wanted to give up on the debate, a more liberal group, including Oppenheimer, wanted to leave the door open. When the conservatives prevailed, Oppenheimer left the party, turning his attention and his financial support to a new initiative, the Progressive Party. For most of the next three decades, the Progressive Party's only Member of Parliament, Helen Suzman, stood out as the country's lone voice against apartheid in the legislature.

Harry Oppenheimer's liberal politics did not protect De Beers from the firestorm of opposition to apartheid that raged throughout Africa. The company, inherently secretive, became more so. By 1964, the trails leading from diamond mines in independent African countries to De Beers had all been heavily camouflaged. Harry Oppenheimer spoke of a 'considerable reorganization' of the group and said that the '[diamond] buying operations in the newly independent African states are now, in every case, undertaken by companies registered and managed outside the Republic of South Africa, and which are not subsidiaries of De Beers.'[10] In fact De Beers remained very much in control of dozens of innocuously named companies which were precisely that, subsidiaries of De Beers, registered in Switzerland, Luxembourg, Liechtenstein and elsewhere. Most African governments knew all about it, but the smokescreen provided adequate political cover for them and for De Beers.

India was also a fierce opponent of South African apartheid, and officially, all trade ties were extinguished by the early 1960s. But India's growing cutting and polishing industry needed rough diamonds, and Indian sightholders did not want to become secondary buyers beholden to Antwerp middlemen. The Indian government, therefore, became directly involved, setting up the

Hindustan Diamond Company (HDC) which could purchase diamonds wholesale and then sell them to Indian diamantaires. The HDC was initially a joint-venture operation between the Indian government and companies based in Bermuda, companies in which, not coincidentally, De Beers had a stake. Similar front operations were established in London and elsewhere to provide the Soviet Union with deniability. De Beers had been buying most of Russia's diamonds since their discovery a decade earlier, but in 1963, at Soviet insistence, De Beers' annual report stated that 'On account of Russian support for the boycotting of trade with South Africa, our contract to buy Russian diamonds has not been renewed.'[11]

The complete truth was somewhat different, and it underlined a clear understanding by African governments, India, the Soviet Union and others, that the De Beers approach to diamonds was the only thing that returned value. If De Beers were to fail – because of apartheid or any other reason – the golden egg that it produced so reliably from one year to the next would simply disappear.

By 2000, when Harry Oppenheimer died, full of years, the company had weathered the storm. Nelson Mandela said 'The preamble to our founding constitution speaks of honouring those who suffered for justice and freedom in our country, and respecting those who have worked to build and develop our country. Chief among the latter must stand Harry Oppenheimer and his family... His support for democratic and philanthropic causes was, in my experience, always without hesitation and reserve.'[12]

♦

De Beers is nothing, if not ruthless in the defence of its empire and its basic operating principles. The Israeli diamond cutting industry grew tremendously in the 1970s, in part because repeated devaluations and cheaper labour gave it a significant competitive edge over Antwerp and New York. By 1975 there were 20,000 Israeli jobs in the diamond industry, which represented almost 40 per cent of the country's non agricultural exports. Israeli buyers were purchasing rough diamonds at a premium in New York and Antwerp, and they were also buying directly from smugglers in Africa, most notably in Liberia. The purchases, 80 per cent financed by Israeli banks at rates below inflation, had generated a stockpile that by 1977 exceeded six million carats. Something had to be done if De Beers was to prevent a wholesale disruption of its 'delicate equipoise'. First, the company began to pull in some of its markers with Israeli banks. Harry Oppenheimer and one of his managing directors served on boards of Barclays International and the Union Bank of Israel, both of which had direct and indirect interests in the Israeli diamond industry. De Beers raised the price of diamonds just as – not coincidentally – the interest rates on diamond purchases in Israel rose by half. And the company dropped 40 Israeli sightholders. Caught between higher prices, a tightening supply and a severe diamond recession, Israeli firms were forced to off-load diamonds. Dozens of diamond firms went bankrupt, the Israeli stockpile disappeared and by the mid 1980s the situation had returned to the 'normal' preferred by De Beers.[13]

Not all of De Beers' manipulation was as kosher, however, and occasionally it backfired. During the 1950s, the company had an agreement with the giant independent mining firm, Selection Trust, to buy its diamonds – mined mainly in Sierra Leone and Ghana – using an agreed valuation formula. De Beers had a 20 per cent equity holding in the Ghanaian subsidiary, Consolidated African Selection Trust, and two seats on the Board, one occupied by Philip Oppenheimer, Harry's cousin. When Edward Wharton-Tigar became Managing Director of CAST in 1955, he discovered that the job came with several lucrative board memberships in companies of the De Beers group. He found it 'curious that the chief executive of a diamond-mining company, which was not even in the De Beers group, should receive more financial reward from companies which *bought* the product than from those which produced it.' In addition to the 'puzzling perks' for directors 'who did nothing to earn them', Wharton-Tigar began to smell a rat in the diamond prices being paid to CAST by De Beers. He discovered that the company would actually have been £1 million better off each year by selling on the open market, no mean sum in 1955. He then did a 13-year analysis of what De Beers had paid, and he physically doctored several shipments of diamonds going from CAST to De Beers. He found that regardless of what was in them, the average price paid by De Beers per carat was always the same – even when all the gem diamonds had been removed. Complaints were met at first by threats from De Beers, to which CAST responded with counter-threats. De Beers usually meets a challenge with an offer that cannot be refused, however, and in this case it was an admission of 'error' and a cheque to compensate.[14] De Beers bought as many of Wharton-Tigar's books as it could, and the issue was quickly and quietly buried.

It seldom works that well for the complainant, however. In the early 1980s, Zaire's President Mobutu Sese Seko thought he could get a better deal from independent diamond companies than he could from De Beers. He began negotiations with three that were willing to offer him higher prices, until the market was suddenly flooded by De Beers with Zaire-quality diamonds at much lower prices. The offer evaporated along with Mobutu's dreams of higher income. Adding insult to injury, De Beers positioned buyers in Bujumbura and in Brazzaville, across the river from Kinshasa, and Mobutu suddenly discovered that he had significantly fewer diamonds at his disposal, regardless of price. Harry Oppenheimer, suggesting that the episode had been a lesson *pour encourager les autres*, said, 'I think you will find that over the period ahead people... may come to the conclusion that the Zaire experiment should be looked upon as a warning rather than as an example.'[15]

De Beers has managed its love-hate relationship with governments and that part of the diamond industry that lies outside its own perimeter with incredible agility and success. But one set of De Beers stakeholders had, by the end of the 1990s, become seriously disenchanted with the company's performance: its shareholders. During the 1990s, De Beers was forced to hold back on sales in order to maintain price stability. The holdback had been made necessary by independent post-Cold War Russian and Angolan diamonds flooding onto the open market, and by the 1997 Asian economic crisis which resulted in a sudden shrinkage in demand. In a year, the Japanese diamond market dropped from 33 per cent to only 18 per cent of world demand. A year earlier, Australia's Argyle Diamond Mine went independent of De Beers, and the discovery of diamonds in Canada by firms over which De Beers had no control meant that in a few short years the company's grip on the supply of rough diamonds had dropped from 80 per cent to something nearer 60 per cent. Holding back sales, however, meant two things: lower profits and a growing stockpile of diamonds. At the end of 1998 the stockpile was valued at $4.8 billion, none of it earning a penny in interest. De Beers' share price, which stood at 178 rand in 1997, was trading at only 98 rand six months later. Among other things, this encouraged a wave of new investors in the company, investors for whom short-term gain was the primary objective. The De Beers emphasis, however, had always been on the long run, a willingness to wait out downturns and to forego profits until the inevitable upturn occurred. But as stock prices languished, impatient investors complained.

In 1998, the company went through a radical restructuring. The direct links between De Beers and Anglo American were severed, although each continued to own about one third of the other. The purpose of the separation, according to De Beers, was to 'assemble all the diamond skills and expertise which have long been De Beers' special strength in one independent, dedicated and integrated company, led by a highly focused management team, free to devote its full attention to its core role – the discovery, mining and marketing of diamonds.'[16] And in 2000, De Beers announced an even more radical move: its monopolistic approach would be transformed into what the company now called a 'supplier of choice' strategy. Instead of manipulating supply (and building up a useless tonnage of diamonds in its London vaults), De Beers would focus on the demand side, revamping its advertising to stress a new 'forevermark', pushing its sightholders to advertise more themselves – $200 million more by 2004 – and 'adding value' to its product. Part of the new added value was a guarantee that diamonds from De Beers would be free of the taint of conflict. Part of it was the 'forevermark', aimed at driving diamonds more clearly up-market. 'We want to see stores pushing the preciousness of diamonds rather than treating them as a commodity you can discount,' explained Gary Ralfe, De Beers Managing Director.[17] And part of the 'supplier of choice' strategy was a reshuffling of the sightholder list, rewarding those companies that had advertised most and 'pushed preciousness' most aggressively, dropping many others from the list. India did best out of the change, while in Antwerp, the managing director of the Diamond High Council said, like many diamantaires over the previous century, 'We are angry! We do not accept it!'[18] But they did. To make the change complete, De Beers started marketing its own cut diamonds in 2002 through a partnership with the luxury goods manufacturer, LVMH, going into direct competition, some feared, with its very own customers.[19]

In 1998, when De Beers detached itself from Anglo American, Nicky Oppenheimer talked about secrecy. 'The diamond industry has always been secretive. De Beers lived in that environment where you didn't want to be open. You wanted to do business without regard to the outside world... Funnily enough, when you do change and become more open, the sky doesn't fall in.'[20] Perhaps the sky didn't fall in, but after two years in the open, De Beers decided to look for shelter again, buying the company's shares from its cranky shareholders, delisting itself from the world's stock markets, and transforming itself into a completely private company. The deal, which cost a stunning $18.7 billion, was completed in June 2001, and bore a striking resemblance to Cecil Rhodes' buyout of Kimberley Central 110 years before. In 2001 the company posted total net earnings of $776 million on diamond sales and other income totalling $5.5 billion. The following year, the numbers were higher. De Beers SA was now controlled by a new Luxembourg company called DB Investments. Anglo American owned 45 per cent of the setup; the Oppenheimer family 40 per cent and the government of Botswana 15 per cent. Nicky remained Chairman of De Beers SA as well as its two subsidiaries, De Beers Centenary, and De Beers Consolidated Mines. He explained the change as a 'need to liberate De Beers from the inherent short-termism of the stock market, thus enabling it to take the long view and tailor its decisions more closely to the needs of the diamond industry.'

Nothing, it seems, is forever.

CHAPTER 4

STRANGE PLUMBING: THE DIAMOND PIPELINE

In the Big Rock Candy Mountain the jails are made of tin,
You can slip right out again, as soon as they put you in.
— *Big Rock Candy Mountain*, Harry McClintock, 1897

If you have never purchased a diamond and have time one afternoon, go to your local jeweller and do some comparison shopping. Buying a diamond is, according to an American industry survey, one of the most anxiety-ridden experiences an ordinary shopper can have. Good diamonds are hugely expensive, but the variations in price and quality are enormous. When you are buying something for love, you don't want to be a piker, but you don't want to be cheated. Should you go to Tiffany? Zales? E-bay? How do you even know the $5000 sparkler they are showing you is a diamond? A stone bought from Cartier will inevitably cost considerably more than an identical stone bought from a jeweller in a shopping mall, but this is more about class distinction and a reflection of the cost of retail space than anything to do with the real value of the diamond. A diamond is a diamond, whether it is sold on Fifth Avenue, 47th Street, or over the Internet. The issues are image and quality.

To the trained eye, there are four criteria in judging and pricing a diamond: cut, colour, clarity, and carats – what the industry calls 'the four Cs'. The weight of the diamond, measured in carats – five carats to a gram – is an obvious price factor, but there are many other variables. Among the styles available, the most common is the round 'brilliant' found in most engagement rings. But there are many others – the emerald cut, the princess cut, the radiant cut, the pear, oval, heart, marquise, all with many variations. The brilliant cut shows off the best features of a diamond, reflecting both its brilliance and the 'fire' which results from the dispersion of light through a diamond's facets. A brilliant has 57 or 58 facets, 33 in the crown, which is the top of the diamond, above what is called the girdle, and 24 or 25 in the pavilion, the part below the girdle. The flat top of the diamond is called the table. A diamond whose table is too large or too small will not reflect the light from the pavilion properly. If the depth of the pavilion is out of proportion to the diameter of the stone, the same will happen. The larger the table, however, the higher the crown, and therefore, the heavier the stone. What is traded for weight will be at the expense of other aspects. The ideal table is between 56 and 62 per cent of the diameter; more or less than this and the stone will not do its lighting work properly. The depth of the pavilion is important for the same reasons. Too shallow and the stone will seem lifeless, with what diamantaires call a 'fish eye'. Other features will also affect the value – an additional facet to cover a flaw, the width of the girdle, the quality of the polish, the overall symmetry of the diamond and its facets. The value of a diamond lies more in its proportions than the actual shape. A well cut diamond that maximizes the fire will be worth more than one where bad proportions have reduced the fire.

Diamonds range in colour from transparent and colourless, to various shades of yellow and brown. More unusual colours – blue, pink, red – also exist, and depending on the intensity of the colour and the diamond's other attributes, such stones can be very valuable. The fourth C, clarity, is equally important. Small internal flaws, known as inclusions, range from minute cracks to small crystals that might be visible only under a powerful magnifying glass, what diamantaires call a loupe.

Tiny differences, invisible to the naked eye and possibly still invisible to an uneducated buyer even under a loupe, can make a mighty difference, however. Two diamonds of almost the same size may fetch very different prices. Take two on offer at the same time on e-bay: Diamond A is a 1.5 carat round brilliant, selling for $4250. Diamond B, only slightly larger at 1.53 carats, is selling for $8195. Diamond A's table is too big; Diamond B's is just right, but both have an incorrectly proportioned pavilion. Diamond A has 'J' colouring, which means that it is 'very slightly tinted' through the crown, whereas Diamond B is two grades up – 'H', meaning it is colourless through the crown, and only 'very slightly tinted' through the pavilion. If it had been an 'exceptional white' – four more grades up the scale – it would have been worth considerably more. Where clarity is concerned, Diamond A is an 'SI1', meaning it has slight imperfections, while its $8195 cousin is a 'VS', one grade up and bearing only 'very slight inclusions. This is still a long way from the top 'flawless' grade. A 'D' flawless exceptional white, with all the right proportions, might sell for $13,000 or more, but this would be a rare diamond, and one for which the market is small. At the bottom end of the scale, a low-grade 1.5 carat round brilliant could sell for as little as $750, but it too would have a small market and would not be a very attractive stone.

An even bigger spread can be seen between industrial and gem-quality diamonds. Rough industrial stones are worth pennies at the mine and only five or ten dollars a carat in the industrial marketplace. The highest price ever paid for a polished gem diamond, on the other hand, was realized at a Christie's auction in 2009. A five carat Fancy Vivid pink sold for $10.8 million, or $2.1 million per carat. The Hong Kong sale was remarkable not just for the amount realized, but because it came on the heels of the worst global recession in a lifetime and achieved a price that was 40 per cent more than Christie's high-end estimate. A more remarkable sale took place in 2010. A 507-carat rough diamond – the Cullinan Heritage, mined in South Africa the year before – fetched $35.3 million at auction, double the previous record for an uncut diamond.

In order to get a 1.5 carat gem out of a rough diamond, a cutter must start with a stone of about four carats. This will yield the hypothetical 1.5 carat diamond, and probably a smaller one as well. Professional mining firms will have a good idea of the value of a top quality four carat rough diamond, and might be able to sell it in Antwerp for $7000 or $8000. But what about a digger in a water-filled pit in the remote wilds of the Central African Republic? Over the years, diggers have become fairly savvy about diamonds, distinguishing the most lucrative characteristics moderately well. A very good four carat stone might fetch as much as $1000 from an up-country dealer who really wants it. By the time it gets to the capital city and is assessed for export, it will probably carry a price tag of $3000 or $4000, and this may double by the time it gets to Antwerp. Between that point and the time it is set into a ring, it will rise again in price until it has yielded one stone worth upwards of $10,000, and another worth perhaps $3000. These figures may double again when the stones finally appear in the jewellery store.

Each year, Tacy Ltd., an Israeli firm specializing in diamond industry analysis, produces a chart describing the 'diamond pipeline'. It estimates the cost of global rough diamond production, and tracks the volume and price of diamonds as they go from trading centres to cutting centres and into the jewellery shops of Europe, Japan and North America. In 2008, the estimated direct mining cost of production was $7.2 billion worldwide. At the end of the pipeline, retail sales of diamond jewellery totalled $64.8 billion.[1] There is a big mark-up at the retail end of the chain, where the difference between the cost of jewellery production is almost exactly half of what it will sell for in the shops. But the biggest mark-up of all is at the beginning of the pipeline, between the cost of mining and what mining firms receive for their product. Here the difference is a stunning 97 per cent. The Jwaneng mine in Botswana is said to have a 94 per cent profit margin, while Ekati – the first Canadian mine – has a 'low' profitability of only 55 per cent. Most major diamond mines repay their capital investments, which can be as high as a billion dollars, in as little as two or three years. The initial costs may be high, but after the start-up, the sailing is usually as clear as it gets. The Marsfontein mine in South Africa is said to have recovered its capital costs in only five working days. This level of profitability explains why the government of Botswana insists on partnering 50-50 with De Beers, and why other governments, such as that of Mobutu Sese Seko in the Congo, have tried to get their hands on even bigger pieces of the action.

Before diamonds can enter the system, however, they have to be located. And while there may be good money at some stages of the pipeline, if you search and never find a diamond, there is no profit at all. Where alluvial diamonds are concerned, every digger is a prospector. At the other end of the scale are companies like Rio Tinto and BHP Billiton, which spend millions every year looking for diamonds, mostly without success. De Beers, which spent $111 million in 2003 on exploration, began prospecting in Canada in the late 1970s, but its first mine at Snap Lake did not come on stream until 2008. And the Snap Lake property was not discovered by De Beers, despite a payroll supporting some of the best diamond geologists in the world. De Beers obtained Snap Lake by buying out a junior mining firm named Winspear for more than $200 million. This was about ten times more than Winspear had spent over an 18 year period in searching for diamonds. 'Juniors' like Winspear are a dime a dozen, and so are their share prices, but they represent a key link in the pipeline, because like Winspear, one in a thousand *will* strike it rich; not so much through good fortune as through long, hard work, over long hard years.

Chuck Fipke, a very determined geologist, began looking for diamonds in Canada in 1982, and seven years later, with his partner Stewart Blusson, had been reduced to selling company shares to orthodontists at barbeques in Kelowna in order to raise the money needed to keep going. By the time he made a deal in 1990 with BHP, one of Australia's oldest and largest mining firms, his company, Dia Met, was as close to bankruptcy as it was to reaching its goal. BHP brought more than orthodontists to the deal; it brought $500 million in exploration and development money, and the following year the investment paid off. Although today Fipke owns only ten per cent of the Ekati mother lode he discovered, it produces four million carats of rough diamonds in a year, six per cent by value of the world's total. Ten per cent of the Ekati profits will buy all the steaks for all the barbeques in Kelowna for the rest of time.

Junior mining firms are not all staffed by people like Fipke and Blusson, however. Many are get-rich-quick outfits that do more mining of stock markets than anything else. Some, operating under desperate circumstances in Africa, have been corrupted by other opportunities, paying bribes and offering kickbacks to horn their way into operations abandoned by larger companies amidst escalating chaos and anarchy. Some have turned to other business opportunities, importing weapons and mercenaries in order to protect their meagre investments and to curry favour with despotic governments. Later chapters will introduce some that were created *only* for this purpose.

◆

Once it has been found, the quality of the actual diamond is everything. Most of the features in a good stone will be visible to the dealer who sells the rough diamond, before cutting and polishing. But there are many bends in the diamond pipeline, and many calculations are made along the way. If the diamond is taken from a kimberlite mine, as in the case of Botswana or Canada, the mining company will handle the export itself under prevailing national regulations and according to the agreements it has with buyers. Botswana, in partnership with De Beers, ships all of its diamonds to De Beers. BHP Billiton, operator of the first Canadian mine, sold 35 per cent of its early production to De Beers. Today it markets everything it produces through its own facility in Antwerp. If a diamond is found by an illicit miner in Sierra Leone or Angola or the Congo, he will probably sell it to the boss of the gang he works with, who may pass it on to a local dealer, who in turn can legitimize it and take it to the capital city for resale and export. Or it may fall into the hands of an itinerant trader who will take it across the border into Guinea or to the Central African Republic, or Ghana, where it will change hands again and be legitimized. Or it may find its way into a parcel of diamonds that is carried by rebel soldiers to a buyer across the border. A dealer may fly the diamonds straight to Brussels, walking past customs officials – if there are any – and boarding a train to Antwerp. There, any one of a dozen buyers might take what he offers. The price will depend on the quality of the goods, the assessment of risk, and whatever discount is currently being levied on diamonds without papers.

And then there is Dubai. Once a dusty little emirate with almost none of the oil and gas enjoyed by its neighbours, it was known historically for pearl exports and a notoriously unregulated trade in gold. Today Dubai is a very different place, a capitalist dream on steroids as someone once called it, where a night in the royal suite at the world's only seven-star hotel costs upwards of $4000. In today's Dubai the trade in rough diamonds is big. Between 2003 and 2008, rough diamond imports increased by 170 per cent, to more than two billion dollars. And the mark-up on exports in 2008 was 43 per cent. In other words, just over two billion dollars worth of rough diamond imports turned into three billion dollars worth of rough diamond exports. Apart from some sorting and repackaging, no value was added to these diamonds: no cutting, no polishing, no jewellery, nothing.

So what, as they say, is up? Several things. One is that Dubai importers are making sharp deals on their purchases in Africa. To use a mining analogy, one might say that Dubai gets the diamonds and Africa gets the shaft. But there is more to it than that. A lot of the trade has to do with transfer pricing and the concealment of profits – in countries like India – for the purpose of tax avoidance. Sell cheap (to yourself) in Dubai and lose money at home where taxes are high; resell in Dubai where taxes are low, and your profits soar. Belgium has lost a significant part of its diamond trade to Dubai in recent years, not least because of its tough anti-money laundering laws and its crackdown after 2003 on conflict diamonds and other illicit goods. Dubai has tilted the diamond playing field in ways that have not yet been fully understood.

Whether a diamond reaches the market through fair means or foul, through Antwerp, Dubai or Mumbai, it will take about two years between the day it comes out of the ground, and the day it is sold in a jewellery shop. It may have passed through half a dozen countries and been the subject of a dozen trades. It may have been carried through a steaming jungle by a rebel courier, or dug out of solid rock in the frozen Siberian wasteland. It may even have passed through the digestive tract of the digger who found it, eager to conceal it from someone at the next bend in the pipeline. If you have recently purchased a diamond, there is a three in five chance that it came from Africa, and nine chances out of ten that it has travelled to both Antwerp and India. Until the Kimberley Process Certification Scheme was initiated in 2003 (about which, more later) there was one chance in four that it had been stolen at some point on its journey through the pipeline, or that it had been used by someone to launder money or evade taxes. While those possibilities have declined, they still exist.

There are, in essence, only two primary markets for rough diamonds: De Beers, and the rest. Through its own mines and its agreements with other companies, De Beers today controls the sale of about 45 per cent of the world's output. Although this is much less than at most times over the last hundred years, half is still enough for De Beers to retain the control it wants over supply and price. Most of the rest of the market for rough diamonds is found in Antwerp, once the centre of the industry's cutting and polishing business, but now more a centre for trading than anything else. More than 80 per cent of the world's rough diamond production finds its way through Antwerp, because in addition to what is taken there independently of De Beers, the city is home to half of De Beers' sightholders.

Many of these sightholders and Antwerp-based trading firms are no longer Belgian, although diamonds still represent, at seven percent, one of Belgium's largest exports. The shops and offices crowded along Pelikaansstraat and Hoveniersstraat house the representatives of mining firms like BHP Billiton, and buyers from countries as far afield as Israel, India, Thailand and the United States, eager to feed their own cutting and polishing industries. By far, the largest diamond processing country in the world today is India, where three quarters of a million people or more, depending on the state of the economy, cut and polish diamonds. Nine out of every ten diamonds are processed in India, representing more than three quarters of the world's diamonds by value. At almost $14 billion in annual sales, diamonds are India's largest single export.

About one fifth the size of the Indian industry, but more than double the size of the next in line – Russia and South Africa – Israel is the world's second largest processor of diamonds. The Israeli industry began in the 1930s during the last years of the British Mandate in Palestine, and for a few years it thrived, in part because of special allocations of rough diamonds from De Beers. After the Second World War, however, things changed. The Belgian government wanted to reassert the primacy of Antwerp, and De Beers wanted diamonds from the Belgian Congo. Israel was caught in the squeeze, leading the government to foster a domestic diamond cutting industry and encouraging Israelis to go to Africa themselves to make their own deals independently of De Beers and Antwerp. Growth was in large part due to support provided by the government in the form of soft loans in foreign currency, generous subsidies and favourable tax treatment. Things changed in the 1960s and 1970s, as the Israeli industry began to take off. De Beers could no longer ignore it, nor could it afford to have a major going concern operating outside the family. In return for allocating diamonds to Israel, De Beers required the Israeli industry to guarantee purchases from De Beers, an effort aimed at damping down independent buying activity in Africa.

Other countries, especially in Africa, are hopeful of emulating the Israeli experience, at least in a small way. The governments of Namibia and Botswana have used the leverage of their diamond mines to press De Beers into partnerships and supply arrangements with fledgling cutting and polishing industries. The governments are keen not just to create jobs and ancillary industries, but to build foreign exchange earnings. This is not an exclusively African concern. When diamonds were discovered in Canada, the Government of the Northwest Territories – an under-populated and under-developed part of the country – aimed to encourage the creation of diamond-related industries. It set its sights on the potential for cutting and polishing. There was already a small cutting and polishing industry elsewhere in Canada, but nothing in the north. The establishment of such an industry presupposes a steady supply of rough diamonds, and at the beginning of negotiations BHP Billiton was opposed, intending to sort and sell all of its diamonds in Antwerp, or to De Beers in London. Negotiations became difficult until the Territorial Minister of Resources threatened to impose a mining tax 'that would choke a mule'. This was an offer that BHP Billiton could not refuse, and the company agreed to make as much as 10 per cent of its production, by value, available to local firms for cutting and polishing. Four small firms were subsequently established, but only one survives.

These and similar efforts in other diamond producing countries are treated with considerable disdain by the rest of the industry, including De Beers. Nicky Oppenheimer is particularly derisive. 'The South Africans have a viable cutting industry,' he says, 'but it has taken them 70 years to establish. Look at what it cost the South African government over those 70 years – look at the subsidy the government had to invest to create 1,500 jobs in South Africa. The return will be a complete disaster. Show me a single producing country other than South Africa which has a viable cutting industry attached to it. Maybe Russia, but even here I wonder if they have accounted properly.'[2]

One way of maintaining a viable cutting industry in a country where labour costs are steep is to concentrate only on high quality diamonds. There are an estimated 200–300 skilled cutters and polishers in the United States. Over 60 per cent of what they produce comes out at more than two thousand dollars per carat (wholesale), significantly higher than the average Indian output of $27 a carat. The value added (or, rather, the value and the *cost* added) in the United States obviously reflects a market for higher quality gems. The high end of the US market expends the greatest amount of money, while the lower end of the market accounts for the greatest number of diamonds.

About half of the world's diamond jewellery is sold in the United States every year. The US is therefore a significant part of the diamond pipeline. But the diamond pipeline does not end on the fingers of fiancées and the earlobes of the hip hop generation. Second-hand diamonds represent the distant end of the market, an area that is not much reflected in advertisements offering ideas of value, foreverness and eternity. There is a reason. Used diamonds do not hold their value very well. Take the case of the 'Elizabeth Taylor Diamond'. In the mid 1960s, Harry Winston bought a 100 carat diamond from De Beers and had it cut into a 58-facet, 69.42 carat jewel which he sold to Harriet Annenberg Ames for $500,000. Mrs. Ames thought better of the purchase after spending $30,000 in insurance premiums each year, just to keep it in a safe. She asked Harry Winston to take it back, but he declined. It finally wound up in a Parke-Bernet auction catalogue in October 1969, and was bought by Cartier for $1,050,000. Mrs. Ames got $868,600 after taxes and commission, and Cartier sold it five days later to Elizabeth Taylor for $1,100,000. The diamond changed hands on a plane flying over the Mediterranean in order to avoid further taxes. A decade later, Elizabeth Taylor tired of the diamond, announcing a sale price of $4 million and a fee of $2,000 per viewing in order to cover the insurance costs associated simply with showing it. At that price there were no viewers, and she finally sold it to a dealer for a reported $2 million. Given the levels of inflation in those oil-crisis years, not to mention the cost of insurance, Ms. Taylor probably took a hefty loss on the transaction.[3]

Most buyers of diamond jewellery are not, of course, in this league. But further down the diamond chain, resale values can be even worse. Journalist

Peg Hill investigated the Toronto market and discovered that price and value are two different things, and that they exist as much in the eye of the beholder as they do in the real world of diamond dealers. Hill took a family heirloom diamond dinner ring, appraised six years earlier for insurance purposes at $4,950, for a new appraisal by the same jeweller. The appraisal came in at $5,500 – not great at 11 per cent in six years, but an appreciation, nevertheless. But when Hill tried to sell the ring, she learned more. The appraising jeweller told her that he would take the ring on consignment and use $5,500 as the asking price. But Hill would get only $2,800 of that – if it sold. About half of the consignment jewellery, she was told, sells within a year. The rest does not. A tour of several pawnbrokers drew offers ranging from $800 to $1,200; not very good in relation to the jeweller's offer but it was cash on the barrel-head, with no wait. Hill's problem was the same as Liz Taylor's: most jewellery just doesn't appreciate in value.[4] Where dealers are concerned, loose polished diamonds have probably held their value over the past ten years. For individuals it is a different matter. They buy at retail prices, but if they sell to dealers, they will get only wholesale, taking a 30 to 40 per cent cut in the process.

Nobody, not even De Beers, has ever seriously promoted diamonds as an investment, although with the 2009 recession, some in the industry pulled out their calculators. Why was gold such a good investment, increasing in price by a factor of four in only nine years, while diamonds were not? Scrap gold, mainly in the form of old jewellery, represents something between 30 and 50 per cent of newly mined gold, but diamonds simply do not come back to the market. An estimated 4.5 billion carats were mined in the 135 years after 1870, with an estimated retail value today of something like $1 trillion. But most of these diamonds are still out there somewhere because, as industry watcher Chaim Even-Zohar puts it, 'diamonds have proven a pretty lousy investment throughout the years.'[5]

Finally, there is the issue of stolen diamonds – not the illicit rough diamonds that are the primary subject of this book, but the diamonds and jewellery stolen from upstairs bedrooms, jewellery shops and in major heists at airports, or on 47th Street and Hoveniersstraat. These find their way back into the pipeline and are likely to do so at significant discounts, discounts which have the effect, if the volume is high enough, of depressing the price of legitimate goods. This was likely the case with diamonds stolen from 109 of the 189 safety deposit boxes in the basement vault of the Antwerp Diamond Centre in February 2003.

Thieves had done this before, stealing $4.55 million worth of diamonds from the Antwerpsche Diamantkring in 1994. This time the take was higher, perhaps $100 million. In August 2009, a heist at Graff Diamonds in London's Mayfair reportedly netted the thieves £40 million, Britain's largest jewellery robbery of all time. Diamonds, of course, are only worth stealing because sooner or later they *can* be reintroduced into the diamond pipeline – plumbed for recycling, no doubt, to some of the same people they were stolen from in the first place.

CHAPTER 5

ANGOLA: ANOTHER DISTRACTING SIDESHOW

[De Beers'] purchases of diamonds on the open market in Antwerp, Tel Aviv and in Africa, helped by the establishment of buying offices in Angola, were at higher levels than the previous year, owing mainly to the larger quantity of Angolan goods coming onto the market in the second half of 1995.
    – Chairman's Statement, *De Beers Annual Report,* 1995

Among the African colonists, Portugal was the first to arrive and the last to go. A contemporary of Columbus, the great Portuguese explorer Vasco da Gama reached Angola as early as 1498. Before long, a mutually beneficial trading relationship had changed into a predatory demand for slaves to service the plantations and mines of Portugal's growing colony in Brazil. Throughout most of the 18th century there were as many as a million Africans working on Brazilian sugar plantations, and many of them had come from Angola as slaves. In all, it is estimated that three million African slaves left for the Western Hemisphere through Angolan ports.

By the end of the nineteenth century the Brazilian colony was gone, but Portugal – one of the smallest and weakest countries in Europe – controlled an African empire twenty times its own land mass. The winds of political change that started to blow across Africa in the 1950s seemed to have no effect on Portugal. Angola was an essential source of raw material, minerals, coffee – and land for Portuguese settlers. In 1940 there were about 44,000 Portuguese in the colony; by 1960 the number had grown to 179,000. In 1952, before he became Prime Minister of Portugal, Marcello Caetano summed up the Portuguese position and attitude: 'The natives of Africa must be directed and organized by Europeans, but are indispensable as auxiliaries. The blacks must be seen as productive elements organized, or to be organized, in an economy directed by whites.'[1]

Part of this organization – without much in the way of education or health services to back it up – centred on the diamond industry. Diamonds were first discovered in Angola in the north-eastern Lunda Province in 1912, and in 1917 the *Companhia de Diamantes de Angola* (DIAMANG) was formed to begin mining in earnest – mainly in Lunda Province and in the Cuango Valley to the west. Ownership was shared between Portuguese, British, Belgian and American investors. The early diamonds were mainly alluvial, but over 300 kimberlite pipes were subsequently identified, the most productive at Catoca in Lunda Province. Angolan diamonds vary in quality, but a relatively high proportion are gemstones. Diamonds were therefore an important part of the colony's output, and in time they became both a cause of unrest and a means to control it. In 1947, DIAMANG had 17,500 African workers, of whom almost a third were provided 'by intervention of the authorities' in a *corvée* of forced labour. Wages paid in cash and in kind typically averaged 830 angolars a year, about $25.[2]

Serious civil unrest began during the 1950s, and a full-fledged war for independence broke out in 1961, shaped and fought by three different armed guerrilla movements. The first, the MPLA *(Movimento Popular de Libertação de Angola)*, had Marxist roots, and was quick to spread its revolt across the north of the colony. The second, the *Frente Nacional de Libertação de Angola* (FNLA), drew its support from the newly independent Congo and later from China. Both movements took their strength from particular ethnic groups, as did a third. In 1966, one of the FNLA leaders, 31 year-old Jonas Savimbi, broke away and created his own movement, UNITA *(União para la Independencia Total de Angola)*, with Marxist overtones appropriate to any self-respecting African liberation movement in the 1960s. For several years, however, neither Savimbi nor his movement were taken seriously. Long-time Angola watcher Basil Davidson wrote in 1972 that 'Reports by Finnish, Italian, West German, and OAU observers in eastern districts, as well as those of the present writer, were unanimous in concluding that UNITA had become, by 1970, little more than another distracting side show.'[3] Whether this was actually true at the time or just wishful thinking, it proved over time to be very, very wrong.

By 1966, diamonds were providing Portugal with five percent of the colony's revenue, and had become a major factor in paying for a war that would continue for another eight years. It was a 1974 military coup in Lisbon, however, not the direct impact of war, which led to Angolan independence the following year. Among the liberation movements, there was a scramble. Savimbi recognized the importance of the moment, dropping his recently adopted pro-China Maoist rhetoric in favour of a pro-West, multi-racial stance. An early four-way transition agreement between the three liberation movements and Portugal fell apart almost before the ink was dry. Moscow, alarmed at both American and Chinese support for the FNLA, increased its support to the MPLA, which also received assistance from Cuba in the form of training, money, weapons and combat troops. South Africa entered the fray, sending direct military support to UNITA and ordering its army across the border into Angola. Amazed by the lack of resistance, the South African forces raced towards the capital. In response, the Cubans cobbled together a hurried airlift, and the two sides – the MPLA backed by Cubans, and UNITA backed by South African troops – met in battle on the outskirts of Luanda. It was as much luck as military prowess that gave the day and the ultimate victory to the MPLA. When Independence Day arrived in November 1974, the MPLA had occupied Luanda and was, therefore, the *de facto* Government of the People's Republic of Angola. The South African Defence Force withdrew from the country, and the war for independence ended. Diamond wars, however, lay ahead.

The new war that began in 1976 was in large part a proxy fight between the Soviet bloc and the West, with Cuba and South Africa scampering alongside their respective mentors. In the immediate post-independence period, the MPLA government strengthened its position with large infusions of Soviet equipment and military personnel. Cuba also provided assistance in the form of equipment and troops – 4,000 in 1978, rising to 21,000 by 1981. Under the Carter administration, the US provided limited indirect support to UNITA, but there was also assistance from China, France and Morocco. South African aid to UNITA was guaranteed because of growing MPLA support for liberation movements in Southwest Africa (SWAPO) and in South Africa (the ANC). With the election of Ronald Reagan, US and South African military support for UNITA increased, as did Soviet and Cuban assistance to the MPLA. By 1985, there were 950 Soviet officers and 45,000 Cuban troops in Angola. The writing, however, or at least some writing, was on the wall. Zimbabwean independence and South Africa's gradual acceptance of the idea of Namibian independence signalled new winds of change. Cold War aid continued but there was growing pressure for peace talks. A 1988 agreement finally saw the beginning of the end of foreign troops. Fighting continued, but far away in Berlin, a wall that served as a metaphor for almost five decades of trouble in Africa was collapsing. More talks became imperative for both MPLA and UNITA, and a 1991 cease-fire led eventually to elections the following year.

Savimbi fully expected to win those elections. When he lost, the war resumed. By now, however, bereft of their Cold War allies and unencumbered by interference from formerly apartheid South Africa, both the MPLA and UNITA focused greater attention on domestic resources for weaponry: oil and diamonds. UNITA had begun exploiting diamonds in the 1970s, and in 1984 it overran key diamond areas in the Cuango Valley, exporting about $4 million worth of gems that year. That was only the beginning. In 1985 it attacked the state-owned *Empresa Nacional de Diamantes de Angola* (ENDIAMA) diamond sorting facility in Andrada (now Nzaji), seriously reducing government exports. By 1993, UNITA had taken most of the best diamond areas, and by 1996 it was exporting a staggering $1 million worth of gems every day.[4] For its part, the government depended on lucrative sales of oil. Peace talks and another cease-fire, combined with the arrival of thousands of UN peacekeeping troops, did little to keep the warring factions apart, although by 1998 it was abundantly evident that the aggressor and the party with the least genuine claim to legitimacy was UNITA.

An arms embargo had been established in 1993, and in 1997 further sanctions froze UNITA bank accounts and prohibited the travel of senior UNITA officials. Violence and brutality escalated nonetheless, and in the middle of 1998, recognizing at last the importance of diamonds to the war's continuation, the UN Security Council placed a worldwide ban on the purchase of diamonds from UNITA, or from UNITA-controlled areas. Only diamonds certified by the government of Angola could now be traded legally.

After 37 years of war, this was the proverbial too little, too late. By then, as many as 300,000 Angolans had died in battle, and hundreds of thousands more had died indirectly. Millions were displaced and the country's infrastructure, seriously underdeveloped at independence in 1975, had been completely destroyed. Two hundred thousand people had been disabled by land mines, more than two thirds of the population lived on less than a dollar a day, and three children out of ten died before their fifth birthday. And yet amidst the carnage, conflict continued, and the commercial channels funnelling UNITA diamonds out to world markets and bringing weapons back in were among the few things still actually running in Angola.

Unable to function, the last UN peacekeepers withdrew in 1999, leaving Angolans to their own devices. It was obvious, and not just to UN peacekeepers, that the sanctions were not working. And it was obvious that a conflict, funded in the past by Cold War rivalries and external supporters was now being funded by natural resources. At the centre of it lay the country's diamonds. After independence, the MPLA government had nationalized DIAMANG and created a new enterprise, ENDIAMA (*Empresa Nacional de Diamantes de Angola*), with De Beers contracted to manage the country's mines, a relationship that lasted for several years. Through the 1990s, however, UNITA exercised continuing control over significant parts of the diamond areas, affecting formal production and government revenues, and taking what it needed for itself. During cease-fires there was increased formal mining carried out by registered companies, combined with 'informal' mining carried out by diggers – *garimpeiros*. Some of the diamonds derived from this informal mining were sold legally through government channels, some were sold through UNITA, and some were smuggled out to the Congo and elsewhere in well-established, traditional diamond smuggling operations. In good years, ENDIAMA might be expected to export $200–300 million, although this was well under half of what was actually being mined. In bad years, such as 1993, the total was less than $35 million.[5] Although UNITA represented the biggest drain on government diamond revenues, there was also a high level of Angolan army collusion with smugglers, and even with UNITA.

During its most lucrative years, UNITA ran a sophisticated mining, sorting and marketing operation. It operated a 'ministry' of natural resources and used a variety of techniques to extract diamonds. In some cases it was able to run standard, labour-intensive diamond mining operations over wide areas and for long periods of time. In other areas it engaged in hit-and-run mining, staying in an area as long as it was safe and then moving on. In other cases it would simply raid diggers and companies in government-held areas. For a time, UNITA also operated a formal sales structure, and it even held tenders at its Andulo headquarters until 1999.

With the advent of UN Security Council sanctions, a polite fiction developed: governments providing or allowing arms shipments to UNITA would now observe the arms embargo; companies buying UNITA diamonds would stop; fly-by-night aircraft conveying weapons to Angola would be grounded; offending bank accounts would be examined by accommodating governments in Europe and elsewhere, and where appropriate, closed. Sitting at the large table in the UN Security Council Chamber crafting a text on sanctions may have been satisfying for the authors. But after so much war and the billions of dollars spent on arms, it was unlikely that words committed to paper in New York would ever convey much to Jonas Savimbi and his supporters.

The fact that the Security Council emperor had few clothes was proclaimed at the end of 1998 by the British NGO Global Witness in a groundbreaking report on Angolan diamonds: *A Rough Trade: The Role of Companies and Governments in the Angolan Conflict.* The report did not diminish the political and social issues involved in the Angolan war, nor did it exclude oil from the equation. But it laid much of the responsibility for the deaths of an estimated half million people during the 1990s squarely at the feet of the world's diamond industry, and it blasted the willing disregard of UN sanctions by the governments of diamond trading and purchasing countries. *A Rough Trade* stated that 'since 1992, UNITA have consistently controlled 60–70 per cent of Angola's diamond production, generating US$3.7 billion in revenue, enabling them to maintain their war effort. UNITA's diamonds,' the report said, 'reach the major international markets through a worldwide diamond industry that operates with little transparency or scrutiny from the international community.'[6]

And Global Witness pointed the finger at De Beers, whose annual reports during the 1990s boasted of the company's ability to mop up 'open market' Angolan diamonds – those not marketed through the state diamond company, ENDIAMA. *A Rough Trade* reprinted excerpts from De Beers' own annual reports. In 1992, De Beers' Chairman stated, 'That we should have been able to buy some two thirds of the increased supply from Angola is testimony not only to our financial strength but to the infrastructure and experienced personnel we have in place.' In 1993 he spoke of measures taken 'in the second half of 1992 to restrict sales while at the same time making substantial purchases of diamonds (mainly Angolan) on the open market'. And in 1995 he spoke of 'the substantially increased production of Angolan diamonds – mainly the higher value gem qualities – coming on the outside market, of which the [De Beers] CSO has successfully bought up about two-thirds.' In 1996 he referred to 'the increasing outflow of Angolan diamonds to the major cutting centres, much of which De Beers was able to purchase through its outside buying offices.' The 1996 De Beers Annual Report went on to say that outside buying in 1996 'reached record levels, largely owing to the increases in Angolan production. Angolan diamonds tend to be in the categories that are in demand, although in the main, these buying activities are a mechanism to support the market.'

A better term might have been to *protect* the market, because at an average of half a billion dollars worth of diamonds each year between 1992 and 1998, UNITA's spoils represented almost ten percent of world production. This could have had a seriously destabilizing effect on prices, had De Beers allowed it to fall into other hands.[7]

The Global Witness report also said that Belgium bore significant responsibility for sanctions busting because of Antwerp's open market for diamonds, and it blamed the Angolan government for sloppy management of its certification system. The UN Security Council called Global Witness staff to New York early in 1999, and for the first time in history, an NGO provided the august body with a briefing on an international crisis. The Security Council, all too aware now that its decisions were being ignored, decided in May 1999 to establish an independent panel of experts to look into how the sanctions were being violated, who was violating them, and what could be done.

When the UN Panel of Experts on Angola finally reported in March 2000, it corroborated Global Witness's analysis of the Belgian situation. Its report said that 'The extremely lax controls and regulations governing the Antwerp market facilitate and perhaps even encourage illegal trading activity.' It went on to say that 'The Belgian authorities have failed to establish an effective import identification regime with respect to diamonds. Nor has any effective effort been made to monitor the activities of suspect brokers, dealers and traders – virtually all of whom appear to be able to travel freely and operate without hindrance.'[8] 'Smuggling is not risky,' one African diamond courier said. 'I have been doing it nearly my whole life. My contacts will guarantee free passage at the airport at home, and once you're on the plane, the job is done. I am never checked for diamonds when I enter Belgium. To sell my diamonds, I just go to one of the diamantaires in the Pelikaanstraat and present myself at the counter with my batch of stones. The diamantaires are always friendly and take me to a room in the back and serve me something to drink. They even offer to arrange for a place for me to stay in Antwerp.'[9]

But the diamonds did not all go straight from UNITA-controlled territory in Angola to Antwerp. Many made stops along the way, and the UN report was notable for being the first to 'name and shame' sitting heads of government for their complicity. Diplomatic etiquette – or perhaps more pointedly, diplomatic hypocrisy – had made such revelations impossible in the past, but Angola Sanctions Committee Chairman Robert Fowler was disgusted by the flagrancy with which sanctions were being flouted. Canada's Ambassador to the United

Nations, Fowler had served as Deputy Minister of Defence and had advised three Canadian Prime Ministers on foreign policy. He had not gone to the United Nations to sit on his hands. He understood, as did others, that after so many years of war and so many toothless resolutions, the UN's reputation was on the line. One of those named in the report (although how much he was shamed remains a moot point) was Burkina Faso's President Blaise Compaoré, who personally provided a safe haven for transactions between UNITA and Antwerp-based diamond dealers. President Gnassingbé Eyadéma of Togo, Africa's longest serving head of state, provided a similar safe haven in return for a share of the loot. And until his overthrow, Mobutu Sese Seko did the same. For Jonas Savimbi, these were business arrangements, nothing more, nothing less. For Compaoré, Mobutu and Eyadéma, it is hard to imagine that they were anything more than business arrangements either. While there was no love lost between Mobutu and the Marxist MPLA, cash usually trumped all other considerations. For Compaoré and Eyadéma, money was everything.

UNITA also moved diamonds through South Africa, Namibia and Zambia, where controls were lax or nonexistent. In Zambia, buyers handed out leaflets at gas stations in border towns, offering to pay 'highest prices' for diamonds and gold. Once valued and cleared by the Zambian Mines and Development Department, the diamonds were effectively laundered and on their way to the legitimate market. Other diamond traders from the Congo, Zambia and elsewhere were licensed by UNITA to travel in UNITA-held territory in order to buy UNITA-approved diamonds. They paid fees as high as $35,000 a month.[10]

Weapons are larger and more cumbersome than diamonds, but they were not much more difficult to bring in than diamonds were to send out. First, however, they had to be obtained. With the collapse of the Soviet Union and the end of the Cold War, Eastern Europe was awash in cheap armaments, and ironically Savimbi was able to purchase weapons that might once have been destined for his enemy, the MPLA. He bought from a variety of sources, mainly in Ukraine, Moldova and Bulgaria. Arms brokers based in the United Arab Emirates, Cyprus, Panama, Gibraltar, Britain, Israel and the Bahamas made the deals, and weapons going in followed some of the same routes used by diamonds going out. Blaise Compaoré provided Burkina Faso end-user certificates and trans-shipment stops. Phoney Togolese and Guinean end-user certificates were also used. Mobutu Sese Seko provided transit stops and forged paperwork for years, and Paul Kagame, President of Rwanda after the genocide, also assisted because like Jonas Savimbi, he hated Laurent Kabila,

Mobutu's successor. Planes loaded with supplies also took off from South Africa's Lanseria Airport, with flight plans for Zambia. As soon as they entered Zambian airspace, however, they changed course for UNITA headquarters at Andulo in central Angola. Flights from Europe stopped variously at Khartoum, Goma, Niamtougou in northern Togo, and Nairobi, with final destinations given as the Congo, Tanzania and other uncontroversial places.[11]

There was no shortage of small airlines, phoney registrations and false flight plans. Three airlines of note were Air Cess, Trans Avia and Air Pass, all owned by one Viktor Anetolyevich Bout. A report prepared for the Security Council in 2001 described Bout as a former Russian air force officer, strongly thought to be connected to Russian organized crime, and the operator of the largest fleet of Antonov aircraft in the world.[12] Bout was only 34 at the time, but he had several passports and was supplying military equipment to a variety of conflicts throughout Africa. Viktor Bout, who will appear again in this book, based his companies in the United Arab Emirates and registered his aircraft in countries that were all too willing to sell their name for a few dollars: Liberia, Central African Republic, Swaziland, Equatorial Guinea, Congo-Brazzaville. In 2002, Bout was finally banned from entering the United Arab Emirates and a Belgian arrest warrant was issued for money laundering and criminal conspiracy involving arms trafficking, diamonds and currency counterfeiting. Bout retreated to Moscow where he was given high-level political protection. 'Maybe I should start an arms-trafficking university and teach a course on UN sanctions busting,' he told a reporter in August 2003.[13]

The Security Council expert panel on Angola was reconstituted as a 'monitoring mechanism' in 2000, and continued to report through 2001 and 2002. Its reports are illuminating. De Beers had by then halted all purchases from the 'outside market' – not just in Angola, but everywhere. Despite this change, and despite the 'naming and shaming' of the first report, UNITA diamonds continued to find their way into the legitimate trade: at least $300 million in 1999 and $100 million in 2000. They were now better disguised and took new routes, but the laundering was facilitated by a vast network of shell companies, created by established buyers in Europe, Israel and the United States. UNITA diamonds were moved through convenient tax havens where record keeping was lax, and they were declared as originating in countries that were nothing more than a transit stop. Rwanda and Uganda, for example, countries with no diamonds of their own, were declared as the origin of gems going to Antwerp. In 2000, Tanzania – which does have diamonds of its own – exported $1.7 million worth to Belgium, according to the Tanzanian Ministry of Mines. The Belgian Ministry of Economic Affairs, however, recorded imports from Tanzania worth $11.5 million that year.[14] The average run-of-mine value of Tanzanian diamonds is about $140 per carat, but the Belgian import figures recorded almost $600 a carat, an indication that something was rotten in the states of either Tanzania or Belgium. The bulk of these diamonds, at least by value, could not possibly have been Tanzanian.

The rotten state of Zambian diamond exports was even more apparent. The government of Zambia told Security Council monitors in 2001 that no diamonds had been officially exported from Zambia since the end of 1998, and that it did not believe that there was any significant smuggling of diamonds through its territory. Zambia itself is not a diamond producer. But between February and May 2001, the Government of Belgium recorded diamond imports from Zambia valued at $13.3 million, with an average per carat value of $373.[15]

A more specific case was uncovered in 2002. One of the largest underground diamond dealers in Angola, Jose 'Chico' Francisco, had sold illicit Angolan diamonds to an Antwerp dealer, through a middle man in the Central African Republic, whom he knew as 'C. Van Tures'. A UN report said that between January and September 2000, Van Tures exported 50,000 carats, worth $18 million, to Limo Diamonds on Antwerp's infamous Pelikaanstraat. The value, at $360 a carat, was significantly higher than the average $140/carat produced in the Central Africa Republic. Another $10 million worth of Van Tures' exports to Limo were said to be from Zambia. When cornered by UN monitors, Limo officials said they had never met Van Tures, and that they could not account for the sources of the diamonds he provided. They said they knew nothing about the value of diamonds produced in one African country or another. They had simply bought $30 million worth of diamonds from someone they had never met, because he was able to provide high-quality goods.[16]

The UN monitors were appalled by the continuing flow of illicit diamonds from Angola into the legitimate trade. In October 2001, they reported that while UNITA exports had declined, something between $1 and $1.2 million worth of diamonds were being smuggled out of Angola each day, representing between $350 and $420 million in a year – in brazen defiance of an embargo which prohibited all exports except those certified by the government. The monitors said that the primary responsibility for intercepting diamonds mined in defiance of the Security Council embargo clearly lay with governments, and yet huge volumes – representing five per cent of world trade – were reaching markets across the world without difficulty. And few illicit Angolan goods were being intercepted anywhere. 'No diamond dealer,' the monitors said, 'has claimed to have witnessed Angolan gems being traded on any diamond bourse. These diamonds seem to vanish into thin air after leaving Angola. How is this possible, given the magnitude of the trade, which is close to the output of Australia or Namibia? Perhaps more importantly, why is it possible for diamonds to vanish?'[17]

The answers were simple enough. A large part of the trade in rough diamonds had always been illegal. And because governments did not care, they did not bother to address the issue. Consequently they had few mechanisms and little expertise to deal with the problem. On occasion it had fallen to De Beers to grapple with large and specific problems of diamond smuggling in order to protect world prices – as it did in the 1950s in Sierra Leone and Liberia, and as it did during the 1990s when it tried to buy up the river of 'outside diamonds' flowing from Angola. It was this illicit, smuggler-ridden underbelly of the diamond industry that permitted the creation of conflict diamonds. Jonas Savimbi did not need to invent smuggling routes, nor did he apply any pressure to diamond buyers. Many were already buying stolen goods, and nobody cared.

When the war resumed in 1998, UNITA no longer controlled the best diamond mining areas in the Cuango Valley, where 90 per cent of the stones were gem quality. It did carry out mining and raiding operations throughout the country, but its diamond revenues were in clear decline from 1999 onwards. Then, in February 2002, Jonas Savimbi – now 67 and no longer the sure-footed young rebel of the 1960s – was unexpectedly caught in an ambush in Moxico Province. Flies swarmed over his bullet-riddled body when it was displayed for reporters, lying on a broken table under a large tree. With him, he had one suitcase containing diamonds and another filled with dollars. UNITA issued a statement: 'Anyone who thinks the ideals of UNITA died with the leader is mistaken. UNITA is a cause.' But UNITA fighters had been living an increasingly difficult existence, and when the offer of a cease-fire came from the government, UNITA collapsed.

With the end of UNITA as a cohesive fighting force, Angola faced new diamond challenges. One was, and remains, the Angolan army and its officer corps. Some officers had become used to running their own illicit mining operations; others had long been used to doing side deals with traders inside and outside the country, and even with UNITA. The government tried to get a grip on some of this by creating the Angolan Selling Corporation (Ascorp) in 2000. In an effort to end the leakage, Ascorp was given a monopoly over all diamond buying and exporting in Angola, and with increased vigilance, the new company quadrupled government diamond revenues in a year. This resulted, at least in part, not from better control, but from a better spread between the prices paid by Ascorp and what the company was able to realize on the international market. In other words, by virtue of its monopoly position, Ascorp simply lowered the prices it paid for rough diamonds. In the short run this increased profits, but in the longer run it simply pushed diamonds back into the illicit stream and out into other countries where dealers are willing to pay higher prices.

The creation of Ascorp grew out of a rivalry between De Beers and one Lev Leviev, a rivalry that is still far from resolution. De Beers interests in Angola are not new, but in 1990 the stakes were raised with the signing of a new agreement underpinned by a $50 million dollar development loan to ENDIAMA. The war, however, meant that De Beers could not prospect in many of its new concessions. For its part, ENDIAMA lost money and then failed in its loan repayments. De Beers was caught completely off guard by the creation of Ascorp, an offspring of SODIAM, a wholly-owned subsidiary of ENDIAMA. SODIAM took half of Ascorp on behalf of the government, and Lev Leviev took a large part of the other half for himself, essentially cutting De Beers out of the picture and providing himself with sole rights to all Angolan exports.

Leviev is a phenomenon. The scion of a prominent Jewish family in Tashkent, Leviev immigrated to Israel in 1972 when he was 16, and apprenticed in a diamond polishing factory. In some ways he has never looked back, although in fact, he is constantly looking back. And going back. He has been President of the Russian-Israeli Chamber of Commerce and has close ties to senior government officials, including Vladimir Putin. A philanthropist, his diamond empire comprises polishing factories in Russia, Israel, Armenia, India, China and South Africa. In 1996 he acquired control of Africa-Israel, one of the largest companies in Israel, and he owns or controls dozens more. One is a Hong Kong-based company named Welox Ltd., which made the deal with Ascorp. By the end of the 1990s, Leviev had a large and vertically integrated diamond operation, which ran from exploration and mining to cutting, polishing and retailing. His sales of rough and polished diamonds were said in the mid 2000s to be in the neighbourhood of $3 billion annually, undoubtedly a worry for De Beers, whose DTC sales in 2004 were $5.7 billion. In 2005 Leviev exported a stunning $601 million worth of diamonds from Israel alone, making him responsible for almost two per cent of the country's entire exports and once again the leading diamond exporter in that country by a wide margin.*

By 2003, the best laid plans of the Angolan government and its clever Ascorp monopoly arrangement were already in tatters. The blame was laid not on a pricing structure that penalized miners – often impoverished *garimpeiros* living in unhealthy and dangerous surroundings – but on the *garimpeiros* themselves. The government decided that illicit foreign miners, most of them from the Democratic Republic of the Congo, were a threat to Angola's sovereignty and its territorial integrity – not to mention the hoped-for profits from the new marketing system. A forced expulsion plan was devised, and here the government showed just how effective it could be when it suited. *Operation Brilhante* expelled an estimated 260,000 foreign citizens from Angola over an 18 month period under conditions widely criticized for their brutality. The vast majority of those expelled were *garimpeiros* and their families, pushed into forced marches that were accompanied by rape, death and the administration of emetics and laxatives aimed at finding every last diamond before the aliens were driven across the border.

Many of the expelled Congolese drifted back into Angola, however, driven by poverty and the lure of diamond wealth. So each year, with the regularity of clockwork, *Operation Brilhante* or a similar brutal exercise by another name is repeated, complete with robbery, rape, beatings and forced marches back to the border.

In the Angolan government's view, there should be no more *garimpeiros*; there should be only companies and employees. Those who want to dig should work for the companies that were expected to take up mining leases everywhere, when the war ended. Until the economic downturn of 2008, many new companies did arrive, and no doubt they will return. The diamonds will

---

* By 2009, however, the Leviev 'genius' seemed to have evaporated, not least because of huge investments in the American sub prime mortgage market. Leviev was forced to restructure the enormous debt he had accumulated, while the value of Africa-Israel, which had made huge profits during the early part of the decade, fell by 95%.

still be there. But among Angola's many problems, two or three stand out. The first is that over the years the Angolan government has mortgaged itself to the eyeballs. In order to finance the war, it borrowed against current and future oil revenues. Not even the IMF can say whether the estimate of $9.5 billion in accumulated debt is even remotely accurate.

Therein lay the second problem: the government's almost complete lack of transparency on matters financial. This opacity, in turn, attempted – although not very well – to mask a bigger problem: massive corruption. A leaked IMF report calculated that between 1997 and 2001, an estimated $1 billion a year had disappeared from Angola's balance of payments. With the end of hostilities, little changed. Transparency International has placed Angola near the bottom of its corruption index for several years. On a scale of one to ten, where countries like Denmark, New Zealand, Sweden and Singapore rate a nine or more, Angola scored only 1.9 in 2008, down from a 2 in 2004. This was a higher rating than Haiti, Sudan and Myanmar, but only fractionally so in a heated contest for last place.

The ability of the Angolan elite to milk the country's diamond resources is, in fact, limited only by its imagination. One of the most blatant examples is the requirement that foreign investors 'partner' with a local company. These 'joint ventures' are neither partnerships nor are they 'joint' except that the local company gets to take between 5 and 25 per cent of the project, while contributing next to nothing. Take for example a company called *Lumanhe Extração Mineira, Importação e Exportação*, sometimes known as 'the general's company' because five of the six principals hold the rank of general in the Angolan army. The company, which took a 15 per cent share in diamond projects at Chitotolo and Cuango, netted $5 million in 1997, rising to $22 million by 2006. In ten years, the generals' cumulative net income, after taxes, reached an astonishing $120 million, or $2 million, per general, per year.[18] By 2008, companies like Lumanhe were taking more than 30 per cent of Angola's diamond industry profits, in return for doing nothing. Or rather, for getting out of the way.

'The end of the war in Angola means that, right now, the main institution in the country is corruption,' wrote Rafael Marques, a Luanda journalist jailed by the government for his views. 'The system is rotten to the core, and until you change the entire system, nothing will change.'[19] The government reaction to such charges, whether from dissident journalists or the IMF, is lawsuits, contracts for PR firms to help burnish the country's image, and outpourings of hurt denial. 'We do not deserve the labels that certain foreign entities are trying to place on Angolan institutions and the country's foremost officials,' said the secretary-general of the ruling party. Those, he said, 'that do not wish to make any efforts to help Angola consolidate peace should at least keep quiet, instead of trying to discourage those that have shown a great humanist spirit, and are doing their best to save lives.'

◆

The full extent of Angola's tragedy may never be known. Between the 1960s and 2002, a million or more people died and two generations lived in abysmal poverty and fear in a country blessed with great wealth and abundant natural resources. A Marxist, then a Maoist supported by China, Jonas Savimbi later transformed himself into a darling of the Central Intelligence Agency and then became a brutal warlord who depended for much of his career on white supremacist South Africa for his survival. Writing about the overwhelming waste, *Washington Post* journalist Jim Hoagland said that by imposing their ideological conflicts onto Africa's post-independence struggles, Washington and Moscow had wasted resources, lives, time and their own moral authority in distant struggles they never bothered to understand.[20]

A skilled and charismatic guerrilla leader, Savimbi finally ended his days trading diamonds with criminals, a sordid caricature of the freedom fighter he once aspired to be. Ronald Reagan gave him stinger missiles and called him Africa's Abraham Lincoln. And Jean Kirkpatrick, Reagan's UN Ambassador, once toasted Savimbi this way: 'Linguist, philosopher, poet, political, warrior; Savimbi has admirers the world over, and I have long been one of them. He is one of the few authentic heroes of our time.'[21]

CHAPTER 6

LIBERIA AND THE LOVE OF LIBERTY

Once elected and in charge of the machine, why then, I'm the boss of the whole show.

– Edwin Barclay, President of Liberia, 1930–1944[1]

The love of liberty brought us here. So reads the motto of Liberia, found in a scroll beneath the national crest. The crest depicts a sailing ship, recalling the arrival in 1822 of the country's first settlers, freed slaves from America. They named their first settlement 'Monrovia' after the fifth President of the United States, and when they proclaimed the Republic of Liberia in 1847, they invoked in its name the central theme of their enterprise: freedom. Never colonized, Liberia was the first independent republic on the African continent. But its ties to the United States remained strong. Liberia's government was based on the American system, with a House of Representatives and a Senate. The currency eventually became the US greenback, and the flag was a copy of Old Glory with a single star instead of many.

But the freedom the settlers invoked was restricted mainly to those who had travelled on the sailing ships from America, and their descendants. Those who already lived in the land that became Liberia were regarded as something beyond the pale by the Americo-Liberians. Over the ensuing century, they received few benefits from the new state, which in any case did not extend to its present borders until late in the nineteenth century. Indigenes were not given the vote until after the Second World War, and it was not until 1963 that the colonial style administration of the interior was scrapped, bringing the entire country under a common system of government.

Financially, Liberia was a shaky proposition from the outset. The government obtained its first usurious loan from a London bank in 1870, and debt-wise, it never looked back. By the end of 2001, Liberia's external debt stood at $2.6 billion, over 80 per cent of it borrowed from the World Bank, the International Monetary Fund, the African Development Bank, and a collection of rueful 'donor' governments. Ninety percent of the debt was in arrears, and the government was unable to meet even the most basic payments.[2] In an attempt to raise funds of a different sort in 1926, President Charles King made an arrangement with the Firestone Rubber and Tire Company, the first of many bad deals negotiated between Liberian leaders and foreign companies, always under the watchful eye of the US government. Firestone obtained a 99 year lease on a million acres, turning it into the world's largest rubber plantation, and causing some to nickname Liberia, unkindly, 'the Firestone Republic'. Much of the labour for the rubber plantations was a form of indenture, often so brutal that the army – the Liberian Frontier Force – was required to ensure its continuation, at one time causing the issue and the question of Liberia's continued independence to be raised in the League of Nations.

Liberia's trafficking in diamonds stolen from Sierra Leone became a concern to the pre-independence colonial government in Freetown, especially after a diamond rush in the 1950s triggered massive smuggling of the country's gems through Monrovia. Monrovia's attraction to smugglers included Liberia's porous borders, a see-no-evil attitude on the part of the government, the US dollar – which by then was legal tender in Liberia – and the relatively higher, untaxed prices offered by dealers who established offices there in order to buy smuggled diamonds. In the 1950s, it was estimated that 20 per cent of all stones reaching the world's diamond markets were smuggled from Sierra Leone.[3]

Liberia itself has relatively negligible diamond potential, probably not more than about 150,000 carats a year. In 1987, before officialized laundering began in earnest, the country exported an all-time high 295,000 carats at an average value of $37 per carat – a small amount of relatively low quality goods. By then, prospectors and diamond experts had all but given up on future investments. Where diamonds were concerned, Liberia had become little more than a staging ground where fictional mines acted as a cover for the laundering of vast amounts of diamonds smuggled from other countries, mainly Sierra Leone.

The True Whig Party, formed in 1869, ruled Liberia without interruption until its leadership was extinguished in a bloody massacre 111 years later. Its most prominent leader was a lawyer, William Tubman, who served as President from 1944 until his death in 1971, perfecting an already well-established tradition of cronyism, patronage and corruption, oiled by an 'Open Door' economic policy which welcomed any and all foreign investment. Royalties and taxes on the resulting business enabled Tubman to extend his patronage, and to bring larger areas of the country into the political and economic ambit of more modern times. The changes were largely cosmetic, however. Uprisings in what Americo-Liberians called 'the hinterland' may have ended in the 1930s, but Liberia remained a seriously underdeveloped country, with education and health services beyond Monrovia provided largely by foreign missionaries, international voluntary organizations and foreign aid agencies.

Tubman's successor, William Tolbert, attempted limited reform. Seen as tokenism, the effort aggravated fledgling opposition groups and student radicals inspired by independence movements across Africa. This in turn served to alienate members of his own conservative ruling elite. As historian Stephen Ellis put it, by the 1970s 'Liberia could no longer be convincingly described as the beacon of hope to black people the world over, the only independent negro republic, but was looking more like a corrupt and ramshackle neo-colony, managed on behalf of the US government and the Firestone Rubber Company.'[4]

Riots in Monrovia in April 1979, sparked by an increase in the price of rice, unleashed a fury of grievance. The US, wary of new left-tilting attempts by Tolbert to appease the opposition, distanced itself from the shaken government, signalling to dissidents, perhaps, that it would not intervene if a sudden change were to take place. It did, a year later. Seventeen soldiers launched a coup on the night of April 12, 1980, disembowelling President Tolbert in the Executive Mansion and executing 13 senior members of his government ten days later in front of celebratory crowds on a Monrovia beach. By the time the 'beach party' was over, Master Sergeant Samuel Doe, young, inexperienced and illiterate, had emerged as Head of State and co-chairman of the so-called People's Redemption Council.

Although Doe and his clique spoke of freeing Liberians from the yoke of oligarchy and tyranny, they soon found themselves dependent upon the Americo-Liberian elite that had managed the country and its financial affairs over the previous century and a half. Doe did bring some of the young anti-Tolbert 'progressives' into the government, but few of them lasted. And the United States, rekindling Cold War tensions at the start of the Reagan administration, took a renewed interest in Liberia. The US needed an ally in West Africa where CIA listeners and listening equipment could be located, and where US arms flights on their way to UNITA rebels in Angola could refuel. It also needed an ally to offset the generous and multifarious blandishments being made at that time by Libya's President, Muammar Gaddafi – towards students, radicals and any potentially friendly government in the region. In Samuel Doe the US got all this and more. At the height of Doe's popularity in Washington, the American embassy in tiny, decrepit Monrovia had more staff than any other in sub-Saharan Africa.

By 1984, the facade of liberation and development had fallen from the Doe regime, with enemies and friends alike finding themselves at the wrong end of firing squads. That year, Doe accepted the offer of a state visit to Libya. What followed could be seen as a cheap parody of *The Mouse that Roared,* were it not to have such tragic consequences. A high-level State Department visit to Monrovia was arranged on short notice, followed in quick succession by cash, long-term development assistance and advice on removing political dissidents from positions of any influence. 'Libya was important,' a senior State Department official later said. 'We told Doe: this is the wrong thing to do. It might give these guys a foothold in the region. With regard to Libya, we bought Doe off. There was a direct link [between aid and foreign relations].'[5]

Uneducated he may have been, but Doe was willing to learn. He became an avid student of the behaviour of his predecessors and some of his contemporaries in other countries. He made himself the centre of a web of economic manipulation and corruption which firmly cemented his control and his personal wealth. As a harbinger of things to come, he managed the Forestry Department Authority himself, which collected logging fees independently of the Ministry of Finance. He did business with contractors as diverse as Thai generals involved in Cambodian timber, and companies associated with private armies in Lebanon.[6] He introduced a Liberian dollar – nicknamed the 'Doe dollar' – and then manipulated currency exchange rates. He inflated the civil service rolls, and skimmed money from imports of petroleum, agricultural products and food aid. As in the Congo, official exports of rubber, iron ore and timber dropped, and large international commercial firms gave way to smaller companies dominated by Lebanese expatriates and the Americo-Liberian elite.

These were much better able than bigger companies to conceal their transactions, often using diamonds as a portable and non-traceable hard currency. Diamonds, in fact, were central to Doe's manipulation of money and international relations. Having given up the Libyan connection in return for US favours, he then played the Lebanese card for Israeli favours. The Israeli government, concerned that Sierra Leonean diamonds were being smuggled via Monrovia to finance factions in Lebanon's civil war, provided military assistance and fostered commercial links in the logging industry as a way of buying friends, information and influence.

By 1988, however, Doe's brutality, corruption and mismanagement had reached a pitch that was hard, even for his staunchest external supporters, to stomach. He met the Pope and was fêted at the White House by Ronald Reagan, who referred to him as 'Chairman Moe', but with the winding down of the Cold War and a fast-diminishing US need for an Angolan staging base in Liberia, Doe was no longer of great interest. As with Tolbert a decade earlier, the US now stepped back and watched as the forces of Doe's destruction gathered.

One of these forces was manifested in a young Liberian with an economics degree from Bentley College in Massachusetts. To earn money, Charles Taylor had worked variously for a company called Sweetheart Plastics and as a department store salesman during his years in the US. He had also engaged in anti-Tolbert student politics. At age 31 in 1979, he was arrested briefly as part of a group that occupied the Liberian mission to the United Nations during a visit by President Tolbert. Back in Liberia, Taylor found himself after Doe's coup in charge of the General Services Agency. The GSA, charged with the allotment of government property, was a milch cow and a valuable learning opportunity for a young man with ambition. Taylor, however, did not ascribe to Doe's idea that Doe alone should control the dairy, and he was accused on various occasions of skimming resources for himself and for his own little coterie. He absconded to the US only days ahead of an arrest warrant, which was followed soon afterwards by an extradition request. In May 1984 Taylor was incarcerated in the Plymouth County House of Correction near Boston, where he spent 16 months awaiting extradition to Liberia for embezzlement.

The trial, however, never happened because Taylor simply escaped, returning to West Africa to begin exploring possibilities for what would soon become a war against Samuel Doe. Oddly, Taylor had been represented during his incarceration in the US by former US Attorney General Ramsey Clarke, who should perhaps have known better, but who had the political acuity to understand how and why Taylor's 'escape' might have been arranged. 'Doe was very necessary to the United States,' he posited, 'and they wanted to thin out Doe's opposition in the US by getting Taylor out. The CIA wanted deniability. Charles escaped from jail, came to Staten Island, then went to JFK airport and flew to Europe direct. Friends got him out. I don't think he escaped. I think he went to people who wanted him on that adventure. And the US government couldn't accuse Charles of escaping if they actually helped him escape.'[7] But if the US government colluded in Taylor's escape in order to protect Doe, it made a big mistake.

Taylor began his rampage to power on Christmas Eve 1989, having taken generous advantage of precisely what the United States feared: Libyan largesse. He had spent the four years after his time in the Plymouth County House of Correction drumming up support from various factions of the Liberian diaspora and travelling across West Africa looking for official backing. Much of this, as well as training in Libya, was underwritten by Muammar Gaddafi. Gaddafi had also supported Blaise Compaoré, a Burkinabe military officer who assassinated Burkina Faso's President, Thomas Sankara in 1987. Once in power himself, Compaoré became a staunch backer of Taylor's newly-formed National Patriotic Front of Liberia (NPFL), providing it with a base, end-user certification for weapons, diplomatic passports, training, men and money. Ivorian President Houphouët-Boigny, godfather of President Tolbert's son, Adolphus, had never forgiven Samuel Doe for the young man's death during the coup. He too was willing to provide Taylor with assistance, tacit and otherwise. This included an operating base in Côte d'Ivoire and transhipment facilities from Burkina Faso.

Taylor might have won his war against Samuel Doe early, had it not been for the intervention of a West African Peacekeeping force, the Economic Community of West African States (ECOWAS) Monitoring Group (known as ECOMOG), which arrived in Liberia in August 1990, securing Samuel Doe's hold on Monrovia if little else. Later that year, however, Doe was captured by one of Taylor's rivals, Prince Johnson, and hideously tortured before being murdered. Nevertheless, the war continued for seven more years, taking the lives of 60,000 to 80,000 people directly, and bringing to an end the concept of Liberia as a nation in anything but name.[8]

After the death of Samuel Doe, the brutality of the war escalated, and Taylor was forced to take a leaf from the book on economics that had provided so many useful lessons for Samuel Doe. While Monrovia may have eluded him, much of the country's interior, along with the ports of Greenville and Buchanan did not. His first successful export was timber, sold through consortia of foreign companies and syndicates of Liberians and Lebanese traders based in Liberia, and just across the border in Ivory Coast. He also made deals for rubber and iron ore, and then turned his attention increasingly to diamonds. According to one estimate Taylor was able to trade goods worth about $100 million annually between 1990 and 1992,[9] but this was small in comparison with what was to come.

Taylor's approach to the diamond trade was two-pronged. On the one hand, he gave his war against Doe a vicious tribal flavour, depicting West Africa's ubiquitous Madingo traders as Doe collaborators. Historically, Madingos had controlled much of the region's cross-border diamond smuggling, and this now fell neatly into Taylor's own hands as those Madingos who remained alive and were able, fled the areas under his control. Secondly, he fostered a surrogate 'revolution' in Sierra Leone, helping to establish the Revolutionary United Front (RUF) under the leadership of another Gaddafi graduate, Foday Sankoh.

The story of the RUF and Sierra Leone is told in Chapter 7, but Sankoh's *modus operandi* in Sierra Leone, beginning in 1991, was essentially the same as Taylor's. Operating from bases in Liberia, he and a rag-tag gang of disaffected Sierra Leoneans, backed by more professional Liberian fighters, created havoc in the Sierra Leonean countryside, setting their sights squarely on the economic opportunities presented by the diamond fields of Kono District, less than a hundred kilometres from their primary base in Liberia. Throughout the 1990s, the RUF channelled millions of dollars worth of diamonds through Charles Taylor's laundering machinery, obtaining the funds it needed for its own war, and providing Taylor with a generous percentage to fund his own. Between 1994 and 1998, over 31 million carats, worth US$1.96 billion – enough to pay off most of the Liberian national debt – were recorded at Belgian customs as Liberian.

Between 1990 and 1997, the rump Liberian government sitting in Monrovia was incapable of providing official export cover for any diamonds whatsoever. Any diamonds reaching world markets and said to be Liberian during this period were either exported by Taylor and his associates, or they originated elsewhere and were simply laundered under the Liberian name. Finally, ECOMOG tired of keeping Taylor out of Monrovia, and the world acceded to an election that only he would be permitted to win. After 1997, as the principal resident of Monrovia's Executive Mansion, Taylor and his government could have taken greater official responsibility for the inexplicably large volumes of diamonds going to Belgium. There was a brief attempt at this in 2000, when a phony diamond rush was created at Paynesville, near Monrovia. This might have been used as an explanation for at least some of the diamonds leaving the country, had anyone believed it. Absent that, however, it seemed more plausible to deny everything. In 2000, the Liberian government informed a UN Expert Panel that official Liberian diamond exports had totalled only 8,000 carats in 1998, valued at $800,000, against $269 million worth of diamonds imported that same year into Belgium as Liberian. There were similarly divergent figures for 1999.[10] Taylor's reluctance to end the confusion stemmed in part from the fact that while he had inadvertently sustained an arrangement that allowed others to parade falsely declared 'Liberian' diamonds past dozy Belgian customs inspectors, he still needed his own laundry service for stolen Sierra Leonean diamonds. But there was more to it than that. Even after he was elected President, Taylor needed what the International Monetary Fund euphemistically refers to as 'off budget' income.

As President of a UN member nation, one which aimed to participate in the international monetary and trading system, Liberia had to respect certain conventions and obligations. One was visits from the IMF, to which Liberia – courtesy of past presidents and IMF officials – owed over $600 million. While the IMF failed to notice the diamond connection, it did note continuing irregularities in the logging industry and in the country's most lucrative breadwinner: the use of Liberia as a flag of convenience for companies, airlines and shipping firms. In a 2002 report, the IMF spoke of the 'retention by the supervising agencies of significant revenue from the shipping registry and logging assessments and the usage of very sizeable resources for security purposes.' What this means in simpler language is that 'Budgeting has become dysfunctional, tax incentives for large projects are granted on an *ad hoc* basis, the procurement system is weak, there are no apparent rules or oversight for purchases by the military, and income reported by Liberia's shipping registry does not match with receipts recorded by the Ministry of Finance.'[11] Even simpler language would have used words like 'embezzlement', 'fraud' and 'theft'.

There may have been no '*apparent* rules', but there were certainly rules, all devised and managed by Charles Taylor. Global Witness reported in 2001 that at least seven out of the 25 logging companies operating in Liberia had direct links with arms suppliers or with funding and provisioning Taylor's military machine. It reported as well, that an estimated $130 million worth of timber had been exported in 2000, while only $6.7 million in revenue had been recorded.[12] Somewhere between those two numbers was the split between Taylor and the logging companies.

The UN Security Council Expert Panel reporting on Sierra Leone in December 2000 recommended an embargo on Liberian timber exports, arguing that the off-budget proceeds from timber, along with diamonds, was helping to finance Taylor's military support for the RUF. France and China, however, objected to the inclusion of timber sanctions in the draft Security Council resolution. It was argued that this would hurt ordinary Liberians. A subsequent UN Expert Panel on Liberia was charged with a more detailed examination of the issue. Two weeks before it could report in October 2001, however, Secretary General Kofi Annan submitted a separate report to the Security Council, prepared on his behalf by the UN Office for the Coordination of Humanitarian Assistance (OCHA). This report said that timber sanctions would cost 10,000 'relatively well-paid jobs' in Liberia, they would deprive the government of important tax revenue (to be used, *inter alia*, for the renovation of a college in Maryland County), they would shut down secondary industries, and they would negatively affect the construction and maintenance of 'most of the roads in remote areas of Liberia'.[13] Typical of a traditional, and some might say myopic humanitarian focus, the report failed to mention the long-term economic impact of clear cutting, the embezzlement of funds and the use to which they were being put, or the environmental impact of the broad logging roads cutting wide swathes through virgin forest lands. The report – written by people thinking primarily of the generalized sanctions in Iraq at the time – simply repeated Liberian government claims, exaggerating the potential job loss by a factor of at least two.

The report echoed the crocodile tears that had been shed earlier in the year by China and France, concerned about the economic impact of a timber ban on 'ordinary Liberians'. Coincidentally, 50 per cent of official Liberian timber exports in 2000 went to China, and 26 per cent went to France. 'Of course we import timber from Liberia, but that is not our concern; we just want to find a proper balance between humanitarian issues and the possible link between natural resources and arms,' a Chinese official said,[14] without spelling out what that 'proper balance' might be. Similarly, a French official at the UN said 'we are completely open to imposing sanctions on timber (and rubber), if the link with arms is proved.'[15]

The Expert Panel that reported two weeks after the Secretary General's OCHA report offered considerable proof. And it recommended that the IMF should commission a detailed report on revenue from timber concessions in order to determine more clearly the discrepancy between official and unofficial revenue from timber exports. It recommended a UN ban on round log exports starting in July 2002, encouraging local operators to diversify into wood processing before that date. No action was taken. Taylor would later admit that he accepted millions of dollars into a personal bank account at the time – but not, of course, for personal gain. 'This covert account was used to buy arms,' he said.[16]

The Security Council did, however, ban all diamonds said to be 'Liberian' from the international trade, with effect from May 2001. Not all of the billions of dollars worth of diamonds ascribed to Liberia by Belgian importers during the 1990s originated in Sierra Leone. But something between $25 million and $125 million per annum did, with a likely $70 million in 1999 alone.[17] These were all conflict diamonds. The mark-up between what a West African digger received and what a rough diamond fetched in Antwerp could be as much as five hundred to one thousand per cent, leaving plenty of margin in between for the various handlers, whether dealers, or RUF and NPFL personnel wielding machetes and Kalashnikovs. It is possible, therefore, that a billion dollars worth of Sierra Leonean diamonds were laundered through Liberia during the 1990s, providing significant amounts of money for the purchase of weapons and the prosecution of two brutal wars, one in Liberia and the other in Sierra Leone, with occasional excursions into Guinea.

The Guinea operation was, in fact, intended to be Act Three in Charles Taylor's long-running and repetitive West African power play. In September 2000, Sierra Leone's RUF attacked several Guinean border towns due south of the capital, Conakry. The area had become home to tens of thousands of Sierra Leonean refugees who had fled the RUF wars inside Sierra Leone, and this cross-border attack did two things. First, it wreaked havoc among the refugees and created an overnight humanitarian disaster. The RUF might have gone further had their radio appeals to Liberia for more ammunition been answered. But these attacks were a feint, intended to draw the Guinean military away from the main target area further east. In January 2001, the RUF attacked Guinea through an area known as the 'parrot's beak', aiming at the diamond-rich areas around Macenta in the Forest Region of the country. Caught off guard, the Guinean military at first fell back, leaving yet more Sierra Leonean refugee camps exposed, and turning the situation into what UN High Commissioner for Refugees, Ruud Lubbers, called, 'the world's worst refugee crisis'.

In promoting the RUF incursions into Guinea Taylor had two objectives. The first was the political and military destabilization of Guinea, an ally of Sierra Leone, supplier of troops to ECOMOG, and home to many Liberian insurgents who were making occasional but not very effective raids into Liberia. The second was the diamond fields of Macenta, with estimated reserves of 25 million carats worth well over $2 billion to anyone with the time and resources to exploit them properly. Guinea, hardly a paragon of diamond rectitude, had for years been an alternative channel for smuggled Sierra Leonean diamonds and for stones from a variety of other places as well. Between 1995 and 1999, for example, Guinea registered exports of $113.5 million worth of rough diamonds to Belgium, while Belgium recorded imports worth $461.3 million.

As the RUF troops were razing the Guinean border town of Guékedou and heading on towards Kissidougou and Macenta, Guinea did something that the Sierra Leone government had been unable to do when rebels first appeared there: it fought back. It used everything in its arsenal: cannons, jet fighters, ground troops, and it stopped the incursion in its tracks. It had help from the UN Security Council, which in March had given Charles Taylor two months to demonstrate that he was no longer supporting the RUF. Taylor blinked, but the threatened UN sanctions were imposed nevertheless, and his Guinean operation came to a close.

By the middle of 2002, Taylor seemed to be on the defensive but, as Chapter 9 will demonstrate, the proverbial fat lady had not yet picked up her sheet music. By that summer, Taylor's five years in power had resulted in the arrest, torture, rape and execution of a wide range of unarmed critics: journalists, human rights activists, students and political leaders. Amnesty International released more than a dozen reports on atrocities committed by government armed forces and police in 2001 alone. His armed Liberian enemies, now calling themselves Liberians United for Reconciliation and Democracy (LURD), were pushing him back towards Monrovia, just as he had pushed Samuel Doe. But Taylor was writing a fourth act to his regional play. Beaten back from his western and northern borders, he now looked eastward, to Côte d'Ivoire.

Once an exemplar of African stability and economic development, Côte d'Ivoire had fallen on hard times economically and politically after the death in 1993 of its first post-independence president, Felix Houphouët-Boigny. Faltering cocoa and coffee prices, and a wobbly return to multi-party democracy after years of one-man rule, led to the country's first military coup in 1999. Côte d'Ivoire had been critically important to Charles Taylor in providing a base for his first attacks on the Doe government. Houphouët-Boigny had given him other support, including ports from which he could export stolen Liberian timber. The new Ivorian military leader, Robert Guei, was similarly supportive of Taylor. But Guei, hard pressed by the international community, convened elections in 2000 and, to his surprise, lost. For two years, the Ivorian military, riven by tribal disputes and angry at cutbacks initiated by the civilian government, stewed. Then, in September, 2002, a military revolt erupted. Robert Guei was an early victim, shot dead by loyalist troops. But the dissidents managed to hold key towns in the north and west of the country, and what looked like a momentary hiccup on the country's return to normalcy turned into a civil war.

This was not just Charles Taylor's cup of tea; it was a full-blown tea party fully catered by the Liberian President. Within weeks, the disgruntled Ivorian military were joined in their struggle against the central government by new groups of fighters that nobody had heard of before, all gaining strength, weapons and men from Liberia and farther afield. By early 2003, the fighting on Liberia's borders, as well as inside the country had displaced almost half the population, making it a humanitarian tragedy of immense proportions, while in western Côte d'Ivoire, 750,000 people had fled their homes.

Deprived of diamond income from Sierra Leone, Taylor continued to plunder the Liberian rainforest in order to fuel his war machine. Vast swathes of virgin tropical hardwood went under the axe, and timber exports grew to pay for weapons that continued to flow, despite the UN arms embargo.[18] In May 2003, two and a half years after France and China had prevented a UN ban on Liberian timber exports because of the impact it might have on 'ordinary Liberians', the Security Council at last took action, preventing Charles Taylor from exporting any more of Liberia's remaining forests. Thousands of 'ordinary Liberians', not to mention thousands of ordinary Ivoirians, Guineans and Sierra Leoneans had died in the interim.

Six years after the momentary possibility of peace that followed Taylor's election, the country remained consumed by war. Having devastated Sierra Leone and brutalized Guinea, Taylor's contagion was at work in Côte d'Ivoire. Hundreds of thousands of refugees languished in camps while others remained on the move. Sierra Leone hosted the largest UN peacekeeping force in the world. Human Rights Watch, describing Taylor's increasingly desperate fight against rebels inside Liberia, said that government forces had 'committed war crimes and other serious human rights abuses, including summary executions of scores of civilians, widespread rape of girls and women, and looting and burning of villages.'[19] The same, they said, was true of LURD forces, 'although to a lesser extent'. At about the same time as Human Rights Watch was issuing its report, Taylor was awarded an '18 karat solid gold Peace Medal' by the Union of African Karate Federations Zone III for 'his numerous contributions to peace and sports in the sub region'. The Liberian Karate Federation told him, 'You have chosen the path of peace, Mr. President, and history will smile favourably on you.'[20]

◆

The Liberian Karate Federation notwithstanding, history will not smile favourably on Charles Taylor. But as LURD and other rebel forces closed in on Monrovia in the summer of 2003, fate did. In July 2003, while US President George Bush was on a week-long goodwill tour of Africa, the Liberian government and both rebel movements appealed to the United States for peacekeeping troops. With US media attention focussed briefly on Africa because of the President's trip, the pressure for American action was great. After days of silence the President finally ordered a naval task force to head for Liberian waters. The humanitarian situation in Monrovia was grim. Food and water had all but disappeared, and most relief agencies had fled. 'Everybody is trapped, it doesn't really matter which direction you go in,' one foreign visitor to Monrovia told IRIN, the UN news service, as forces loyal to Taylor traded automatic arms fire with rebels in the background. 'This is a people being slowly starved to death,' he added. 'There are no food supplies coming in and there is no rice left. There is very little food and there is rain coming down. There are appalling sanitary conditions. People are very sick...'

The United States, with its long historical attachment to Liberia, could have earned tremendous goodwill through an engagement in Liberian peacekeeping. And while the job of pacifying Liberia would not have been quick or easy, Liberia was not Somalia, and it was not Vietnam or, for that matter, Afghanistan or Iraq. Nevertheless, it was not until August 11 that the first international peacekeepers finally arrived, none of them American. With a U.S. naval flotilla lying offshore, it was Nigerians and other West Africans who finally stepped ashore. In fact when a handful of US marines did land, their job was only to beef up security at the American embassy, where civilians had been laying out the bodies of dead children for media effect.

A deal was finally brokered between Taylor and his antagonists. In return for a safe haven in Nigeria, Taylor agreed to step down 'in the interest of peace'. The safe haven was important, because a UN-backed Special Court for Sierra Leone had indicted Taylor for war crimes and crimes against humanity, and the last thing he wanted in early retirement was a trial in front of an international war crimes court. As with other deals arranged to 'facilitate peace' in West Africa, this one reeked. Taylor was going down, one way or the other, and could easily have been arrested by the UN peacekeeping forces he had invited into the country. Instead, he was given a podium in the presence of other African leaders to make a speech about peace, and to tell his traumatized people, 'By the grace of God, I *will* be back.' In the BBC and CNN footage, the President, bedecked with medals and the sash of office, appears to weep. In fact, however, everything had at last collapsed, even his own private generator, and the apparent tears were only sweat, induced by heat, his costume and – perhaps – humiliation.

Taylor would sweat a bit more in the years to come, as call after call was made by Amnesty International, Human Rights Watch and others for his expulsion from Nigeria and a handover to the Special Court. Nigerian President Obasanjo steadfastly refused, despite Taylor's continued long-distance meddling in Liberian affairs. And although there were occasional postures of outrage from members of the Security Council, that august body could never quite summon the will to demand that Nigeria hand him over. Taylor, it was surmised, perhaps knew too much, and it would be unpleasant for Nigeria, the United States and others from whose largesse he had benefited, to have him 'tell all' in open court. Whatever ideas there are about ending the impunity of African tyrants, the process did not look as though it would start with Charles Ghankay Taylor.

◆

In January 2006, 67-year old Ellen Johnson-Sirleaf took office as the President of Liberia, following elections supervised by a full-blooded UN peacekeeping force with a budget that year of $760 million. Johnson-Sirleaf had three major distinctions to her credit. She was the first truly democratically elected leader in the country's history. Second, she was the first woman head of state in African history. And third, she inherited one of the worst debt loads on the continent. Liberia's external debt, all negotiated by one thug after another – more than half of it with 'aid' agencies like the IMF, the World Bank, the African Development Bank and others – was in the neighbourhood of $3.8 billion. Liberia's debt-to-export ratio was more than 2,700 per cent at the end of 2004, about 18 times higher than what is thought by the IMF to be 'sustainable'.[21] This is a bit like saying that Liberia was in 18 times worse financial trouble than the average country on the verge of bankruptcy.

Earlier, in 2002, De Beers Chairman Nicky Oppenheimer said that it had been 'with horror that we learned some years ago that some diamonds were being used to fund the conflict in some strife-torn African states'.[22] This was a little disingenuous. What De Beers doesn't know about diamonds is not worth knowing. It is, and was always well known throughout the diamond industry that Liberia never had diamonds worthy of the name, and that for almost half a century it had been nothing more than an *entrepôt* for illicit goods. Liberia had, after all, been the primary centre of attention during the 1950s for De Beers' International Diamond Security Organization. Nobody much cared, however, as Liberia began to slip beneath the waves of corruption, brutality and war, much of it fuelled by diamonds. Certainly nobody in the industry raised an alarm, a query or even an eyebrow as billions of dollars worth of diamonds entered the legitimate trade as 'Liberian'. Each year, Belgium's Diamond High Council recorded the statistics as though they were perfectly respectable, and after the issue was raised and made public by the Canadian NGO Partnership Africa Canada in January 2000, it took another 16 months for the UN Security Council to finally take the action that could have been initiated much earlier by the industry itself, had it not grown fat and complacent on corruption.

CHAPTER 7

SIERRA LEONE: DIAMONDS IN THE RUF

'First they killed my mother, then they killed my father, then they killed my auntie. Then they put my arm on the ground and the man took the cutlass and chopped it once. He chopped it again and the second time my arm fell off. He told me to go find Ahmad Tejan Kabbah and Kabbah would give me a new arm.'

– Testimony of Damba, an eight year old girl, May 2000[1]

Through the 1990s, a war in the tiny West African nation of Sierra Leone grew into a tragedy of major humanitarian, political and historical proportions. Diamonds fuelled a conflict that destabilized the country for a decade. The Revolutionary United Front (RUF) rebellion that began in 1991 was characterized by banditry and horrific brutality, wreaked primarily on civilians. It is recorded that 75,000 people – most of them civilians – lost their lives, but the number is probably much higher. Rebel butchery left thousands of women, men and children without hands and feet, disfigured physically and psychologically for life. Children were forced into combat and sexual slavery. At different times during the crisis, as many as half of Sierra Leone's people – more than the entire population of Kosovo – became displaced or were refugees. Schools, hospitals, government services and commerce ground to a halt in all but the largest urban centres. Mineral resources which should have been available for development were used instead to finance war, robbing the potential beneficiaries and an entire generation of children, putting Sierra Leone dead last on the United Nations Human Development Index.

Africa's first modern state, Sierra Leone was founded by black Nova Scotians –
freed slaves – over 200 years ago. A weak post-independence democracy was
subverted in the 1960s and 1970s by corruption and despotism. Economic
decline and military rule followed. It is hard to say who did the most damage
to Sierra Leone after it achieved independence in 1961. Vying for top spot is
Foday Sankoh, a charismatic sociopath who styled himself 'Corporal' Foday
Sankoh, recalling his days as a minor coup plotter in the Sierra Leone military.
He is also said to have been a photographer, but by the late 1990s he was
spending more time in front of the camera than behind it. After a stint in
Benghazi learning the arts of revolutionary warfare from teachers assigned by
Muammar Gaddafi, Sankoh created the Revolutionary United Front (RUF),
and spent most of the 1990s at the head of an army of drug-addled killers who
murdered and mutilated the civilians he said he wanted to liberate from the
clutches of tyranny.

A second candidate for most destructive is Charles Taylor, the Liberian
warlord. Taylor had financed the early stages of his own warpath by selling
timber. But diamonds soon proved more lucrative. Taylor backed Sankoh's
fledgling Revolutionary United Front, giving it a Liberian base, weapons, and
an outlet for whatever it could steal in Sierra Leone. The RUF trademark was
grisly: horrific rape was commonplace, and RUF 'soldiers' chopped the hands
and feet off civilians, often small children. As a terror technique, it had no
rival in clearing the country's alluvial diamond fields, providing the RUF and
Taylor with a highly rewarding money machine.

The third candidate would have to be Siaka Stevens, a former police
constable and trade unionist who founded a political party in the 1960s, the
All Peoples Congress. Eventually he became the country's Prime Minister and
then President. In 1985, after 17 years of mismanagement, corruption and
brutality, he retired with a fortune in ill-gotten gains, setting the stage for the
country's horrific implosion.

But Sierra Leone's tragedy, which is intimately linked to the diamond
trade, goes back further in time. Until diamonds were discovered in 1930,
and for some years afterwards, the colony was a drain on the British colonial
exchequer. Development spending was kept to a minimum, and control
over the interior was manifested by a manipulative power- and tax-sharing
arrangement with local chiefs. As late as 1921, there were only five colonial
administrators living beyond the Freetown peninsula. And in Kono District
where the first diamonds were discovered, there were virtually no colonial

investments in health, education or other developmental infrastructure until the waning days of the British administration.

Until the end of the 19th century, the commercial and administrative life of the more robust Freetown colony was dominated by Creoles, anglicized descendants of the freed slaves who had returned to Africa in the early 1800s from North America and Britain. In an effort to curtail the growing influence of this potentially disruptive political class as the interior was beginning to open up, the colonial authorities sought alternatives. One was even greater empowerment of up-country chiefs. Another was the encouragement of an alternative commercial class. This appeared in the form of a newly arrived group of Lebanese immigrants, refugees from the tyranny and poverty of the collapsing Ottoman Empire. The first Lebanese arrived in Freetown in 1893, and by the turn of the century there were 41 in the city. The first were Maronite Christians, but they were soon overtaken in number by Shi'ite Muslims arriving from the impoverished areas of South Lebanon.

The Lebanese proved to be astute entrepreneurs, and as their numbers grew they quickly eclipsed the Creole commercial class, moving up-country wherever opportunity presented itself. With the construction of a narrow-gauge railway and feeder roads, they became major investors in the transportation business, which provided further opportunities for commerce, collusion and eventually control in the retail and produce trades. The first Lebanese trader arrived in Kono District hot on the heels of the diamond discovery in 1930, two years before the appointment of a colonial officer, and well ahead of the Sierra Leone Selection Trust (SLST), which was eventually to mine the diamonds.

In minimizing direct control over most of the country, the British colonial authorities had, by the time of independence, created the appearance of a national infrastructure without investing huge sums. As a result, the writ of the central government was only wafer-thin. Police, courts, army and civil servants were a veneer on the surface of colonial life, more prominent in Freetown than elsewhere, and weaker with every mile away from the capital. It was essentially a system of tributors: of chiefs, Lebanese entrepreneurs and a handful of foreign companies willing to collect or pay taxes to the centre as long as they were given a significant measure of freedom in the periphery.

Where diamonds were concerned, the stage was set for a power clash early on. In 1935, the colonial government gave SLST – a subsidiary of the Consolidated Africa Selection Trust (CAST) and part of the giant Selection Trust Ltd. mining empire – exclusive prospecting and mining rights over the entire country for a period of 99 years. In return, the company was to pay income tax at the rate of 27 per cent on its profits, an amount later increased to 45 per cent. At the beginning, corporate control over the diamond fields was a relatively simple matter, and in the immediate post-war period, the system seemed to work well. Between 1948 and 1952, SLST paid over £3 million in taxes, making it the jewel, so to speak, in the colonial crown. But the Kono diamonds and those subsequently found farther south at Tongo Field were mainly alluvial. This meant that they could be mined without a great deal of equipment or investment, and theft became more and more problematic. Lebanese traders rapidly assumed the role of provocateurs and middle men, moving illicitly mined diamonds out of the country in dozens of ways, but mostly through Monrovia, the capital of Liberia. During World War II, Graham Greene worked for the British Secret Intelligence Service in Sierra Leone, making it the setting for one of his best books, *The Heart of the Matter*. The 1948 novel chronicles the travails of a guilt-ridden British colonial police officer struggling with corruption, diamonds and Lebanese smugglers. One passage is telling: "'Oh, the diamonds, diamonds, diamonds,' Yusef wearily complained. "I tell you, Major Scobie, that I make more money in one year from my smallest store than I would in three years from diamonds. You cannot understand how many bribes are necessary.""[2]

By the early 1950s, more and more illicit miners were moving into Kono, leading to a general breakdown in law and order, and threatening to overwhelm the entire SLST operation. Pass laws and police campaigns to expel 'strangers' – 'Operation Parasite', 'Operation Stranger Drive' – had little impact. By 1956, there were an estimated 75,000 illicit miners in Kono, one of the reasons De Beers hired Sir Percy Sillitoe to create the International Diamond Security Organization. As described in Chapter 1, this cloak and dagger operation – ostensibly about preventing diamonds from reaching Soviet H-bomb factories – had as its real purpose a change in post-war colonial currency regulations, allowing De Beers to offer better prices in hard currency in Sierra Leone. It was, in a sense, a last-ditch effort to stem the flow of smuggled goods, estimated to be as much as half of the colony's entire annual output.

For a while it worked, but other innovations also contributed to its success. SLST's lease was cut to a more realistic 450 square miles, reducing the territory that had to be policed. And an Alluvial Mining Scheme was created, giving indigenous miners access to diamonds in the rest of the country.

With independence in 1961, however, new pressures developed. Siaka Stevens, Minister of Mines during the colonial twilight, had supported corporate control over the diamond industry. Now, in charge of his own opposition party in an independent Sierra Leone, he devised a populist platform, agitating against foreign ownership of the principal diamond resource, advocating a socialist welfare state, and whipping up popular sentiment against SLST. In 1968, seven years after independence, he at last gained the Prime Ministership, and set about creating ways to keep the job forever. Diamonds were part of the plan.

Henneh Shamel was part of a wealthy Shi'ite family from South Lebanon. Since the 1930s the Shamels had been heavily involved in gold mining, and latterly in diamond mining and smuggling. Shamel had been an ally of Stevens during his early political years, but by 1969 they were no longer friends. In November of that year, a spectacular daylight robbery at Hastings Airport near Freetown saw $3 million in SLST diamonds disappear in a little less than ten minutes. Shamel was arrested and charged with the crime. But the evidence against him was weak and in 1970 a judge acquitted him. Stevens nevertheless had him deported, probably on the advice of his new Afro-Lebanese associate, Jamil Sahid Mohamed. Jamil, as he was known, had a ten carat diamond pedigree, having spent six months in jail in 1959 for illegal possession of diamonds. He now began to work with Stevens to take control of the diamond industry. In 1971, Stevens created the National Diamond Mining Company, taking over 51 per cent of SLST's shares and effectively nationalizing the company. Jamil bought 12 per cent of the government shares, and SLST's control – and its shipments of diamonds – began to slip precipitously. In 1984, a company controlled by Jamil bought the remaining shares of SLST, and the official diamond industry all but disappeared into the pockets of Jamil Sahid Mohamed and his mentor, the Prime Minister of Sierra Leone. From a high of over two million carats in 1970, official diamonds exports fell to 48,000 carats in 1988.

In the years before his retirement in 1985, Siaka Stevens suborned the judiciary, corrupted the army and destroyed the police force. This was not difficult, as they had never been strong. In their place he created a new security apparatus designed more to protect himself and his investments than anything else. It was a 'shadow state': a country within a country, where nothing was quite what it seemed.[3] Stevens also turned Sierra Leone into a one-party state, made himself executive president, and then bludgeoned all political opposition into submission. Once he had sidelined SLST, the

Lebanese became increasingly involved in the formal diamond trade, or what was left of it. From the late 1970s to the early 1990s, Lebanon's civil war played itself out in microcosm in Sierra Leone. Because the various Lebanese militia needed financial assistance, Sierra Leone's diamonds came into play as a kind of donor base, an informal tax on behalf of one faction or the other. This was of great interest to Israel, not least because part of the Sierra Leonean Shi'ite community actively supported the AMAL faction, which on the one hand fought against Israel's greatest enemy, Hezbollah, and on the other was Syria's main ally against Israel. It could not have been lost on Israel that the leader of AMAL, Nabih Berri, had been born in Sierra Leone and was a boyhood friend of Jamil, the most influential man in the country's diamond business.

It was largely through Berri that Iran became interested in Sierra Leone, building a large cultural centre in Freetown and making the country its main base in West Africa. This further agitated Israel, which had been trying unsuccessfully to restore ties with Sierra Leone, broken during the Arab-Israeli war of 1967. In a dramatic move, Jamil persuaded Stevens' successor, Joseph Momoh, to invite Palestinian leader Yasser Arafat for a state visit to Freetown in 1986. In Freetown Arafat offered several million dollars to Momoh in exchange for a training base for his PLO fighters, an offer which Momoh, warned by aides, turned down.[4] This was the beginning of the end of Jamil's power in Sierra Leone. Lobbyists began to prod Momoh towards stronger ties with Israel and an end to Lebanese dominance. In 1987, Momoh announced that he had foiled a coup plot involving Jamil, his own Vice-President Francis Minah – a close associate of Jamil – and a few lower ranking soldiers and police. Minah was tried for treason and hanged. Jamil, out of the country at the time, remained in self-exile for the duration of Momoh's tempestuous regime.

The foiled 'coup' allowed Momoh to create his own partnerships. Israel, long anxious to get the Lebanese away from Sierra Leone's diamond wealth, was an obvious alternative. One of the first investors to arrive was the Russian-born Shabtai Kalmanovitch and his Israeli-based enterprise, the LIAT construction and Finance Company. Commercially speaking, however, LIAT did not amount to much. Most of its contracts were with government, and many projects, announced with much fanfare, never got started. Kalmanovitch's main interest was diamonds, and perhaps drugs. Among other things, Kalmanovitch set up a diamond buying office in Freetown. At first, the partnership appeared to benefit the diamond industry, and exports increased by 280 per cent in late

1987. Illegal production and exports however, did not decrease accordingly, and it was discovered that Kalmanovitch was using Sierra Leone to circumvent United Nations weapons, diamonds and gold embargoes on South Africa.[5]

While in Sierra Leone, Kalmanovitch brought in other money launderers, drug traffickers and arms dealers, all scrambling to gain access to diamonds. In 1986, Marat Balagula, considered a 'godfather' of the Brighton Beach Russian mafia, found a soft landing in Sierra Leone with Kalmanovitch. Balagula, who had degrees in mathematics and business, was considered one of the initiators of the Russian mafia franchise in Antwerp, sometimes called the 'red mafiya'. He and Kalmanovitch became involved briefly in importing gasoline to Sierra Leone, in a deal reportedly backed by fugitive American businessman Marc Rich and guaranteed by the Luccheses, an old-time American crime family.[6]

Two others, Boris 'Biba' Nayfeld, another Brighton Beach mobster, and Rachmiel 'Mike' Brandwain who was active in the Antwerp underground, met with Kalmanovitch and Balagula in Freetown in 1987. Brandwain at that time ran a small electronics store in Antwerp and was involved in tax-free export transactions with Eastern Europe. Before his trip to Sierra Leone, he had been released on bail after being charged with a gold smuggling deal between Luxembourg and London. He was also involved in intercontinental money laundering and smuggling, including heroin trafficking and diamonds. Brandwain's story ended when he was shot to death in 1998 in a parking lot in Antwerp, near the diamond district where he kept his headquarters.

Boris Nayfeld eventually went to prison in the United States for heroin trafficking between Thailand and New York. Balagula also went to prison in the US, for credit card fraud and for neglecting to pay $85 million in taxes on the sale of almost a billion gallons of fuel.[7] Shortly after the 1987 Sierra Leone meeting, Kalmanovitch was arrested in London on an American warrant. Following jail time for forged cheques, a foray into South Africa and some Israeli prison time as a Soviet spy, he eventually became owner of the highly successful Spartak Moscow women's basketball team. No longer a forger, sanctions buster and spy, Kalmanovich had now become an 'oligarch'. Then, in 2009, his past finally caught up with him. While negotiating a Moscow traffic snarl, he and his Mercedes were riddled with semi-automatic gunfire. Neither survived. Such were the investors who infested Sierra Leone's diamond economy in the 1980s.

By 1991, Momoh was desperately seeking new foreign firms to generate revenue in the climate of corruption and economic free-fall over which he presided. Joint ventures proliferated, most of them leading nowhere. The RUF war began that year, and from the outset, the rebels attempted to cut Momoh off from the Kono diamond fields. In April 1992, he was overthrown in a military coup. Led by 27-year old army captain Valentine Strasser, the National Provisional Ruling Council (NPRC) came to power on a promise to end corruption. The real news in Strasser's arrival lay not in his commitment to reform, although this is what he too promised the IMF, but in a further looting of the country's diamond resources.

Foday Sankoh began his war on Sierra Leone in March 1991. But as the RUF interest in diamonds came into focus, Foday Sankoh remained a cipher. Few knew what he looked like and nobody knew exactly what he wanted, aside from power. Vague tales about fighting for justice and democracy emerged from the forest with released captives, and in 1996 an RUF pamphlet appeared, *Footpaths to Democracy*. In it, the RUF talked about its struggle against the 'raping of the countryside to feed the greed and caprice of the Freetown elite and their masters abroad', and it spoke of a 'liberation theology consistent with our pride in ourselves as Africans.'[8]

British anthropologist Paul Richards saw the RUF in 1996 as a 'coherent movement' populated to a large extent by 'youngsters' whose 'political project cannot be ignored'. He characterized the rebel leadership 'as an excluded intellectual elite', whose violence was 'an intellectual project in which the practical consequences have not been fully thought through.'[9] The RUF was a response to a crisis of modernity, a breakdown in traditional patrimonial relationships.

Many Sierra Leoneans saw it a little differently. Social historian Ibrahim Abdullah charts the development of two streams of young men who eventually converged into the RUF leadership. The first were violent, unlettered thugs, many of whom had learned their trade doing the dirty work for Stevens, Momoh and other politicians for whom violence was the answer to every question. The second was a group of self-styled 'radical' students at Fourah Bay College who schooled themselves in their opposition to Siaka Stevens and his successor by listening to Bob Marley and Peter Tosh, smoking dope, and reading – of all things – the 'Juche Idea' of Kim Il Sung and the Green Book of Muammar Gaddafi. Although there were smatterings of Marcus Garvey and Frantz Fanon in their studies, the students were essentially cut off from serious radical ferment elsewhere, and in their Fourah Bay hothouse they developed odd ideas. Several were sponsored to attend annual Green Book celebrations in Libya, travelling there via Accra and then returning to recruit others. In all, three, or perhaps four dozen Sierra Leoneans travelled to the training camps at Benghazi for insurgency training. Some were students, some were unemployed youth, and one was an older man who had spent seven years in prison for his part in a 1971 coup plot, 50 year-old ex Corporal Foday Saybana Sankoh.

It is said that Sankoh first met Charles Taylor at Gaddafi's secret *al-Mathabh al-Thauriya al-Alamiya* – World Revolutionary Headquarters – in Benghazi. Certainly he would have met Liberians there, men from Burkina Faso and a whole host of putative African revolutionaries. Gaddafi recruited a rogue's gallery of such types during the 1980s. He provided training, money and succour for Laurent Kabila, fighting against Mobutu Sese Seko in the Congo. He provided support to Blaise Compaoré, who murdered his closest friend, the President of Burkina Faso, taking the job for himself. He gave training and support to Kukoi Samba Samyang, who subsequently attempted a coup in The Gambia, and he sent 600 troops in a vain effort to support the collapsing Ugandan tyrant, Idi Amin. He supported the IRA in Northern Ireland, the Basque ETA in Spain, West Germany's Baader-Meinhof Gang and the Moro Islamic Liberation Front in the Philippines. As historian Stephen Ellis puts it, the Libyan World Revolutionary Headquarters became, in the 1980s, 'the Harvard and Yale of a whole generation of African revolutionaries.'[10]

Whatever ideology the RUF may have had when it began, it vanished as Sankoh put his 'revolution' into practice. The few intellectuals who returned to West Africa from Libya with him were soon stood up against a wall and shot, eliminating any challenge to authority. Charles Taylor, using the services of young Sierra Leoneans in his Liberian war at the time, turned some of these and some of his own fighters over to Foday Sankoh for his initial efforts. After that, the RUF 'recruited' its own fighters inside Sierra Leone, kidnapping children and forcing them to commit atrocities against their families and villages in order to make sure that they could never go home again. They were given drugs and socialized into a culture of violence and murder. A mixture of gunpowder and cocaine known as 'brown-brown' was rubbed into scrapes on their foreheads, giving them wild thoughts, including the idea that they were immune to bullets. They were given red tablets and white tablets, and crack, which they called 'blueboats', and they were injected with 'medicine'. Soon they were no longer 'youngsters', they were 'child soldiers', a term which fails to convey a sense of the monsters they had become. Girls were taken too, to become porters and sex slaves. 'How revolutionary is a revolutionary movement which slaughters and terrorizes the very people it claims to be liberating?' asks Ibrahim Abdullah.[11] The short answer is 'Not very.' Their revolutionary tract *Footpaths to Democracy* lifted phrases straight out of the writings of Mao and the Guinean freedom fighter, Amilcar Cabral. The RUF had no real ideology beyond a desire for power. It had no ethnic grievance or following. Land was not an issue, nor was religion. Unlike the wars in Angola and the Congo, its fight was devoid of Cold War undertones, and eventually it was consumed by its own astonishing violence.

By 1995, the RUF were in firm control of the diamond fields of Kono District and Tongo Field. Diamonds had become a central bank for the RUF, and mining was carried out through a system of forced labour. Diggers were permitted to share in what they found, courtesy of a 'two pile' system. But the diggers were closely watched by armed RUF guards, and the better diamonds were always seized. The diamonds were then transported to RUF headquarters at Buedu, near the Liberian border, and from there they were taken to Monrovia. Arms, brokered by Charles Taylor through a network of international criminals, were driven and sometimes airlifted by helicopter back to the RUF.

Despite a UN arms embargo, Taylor was able to obtain weapons from a variety of sources. Some came from his old mentor, Muammar Gaddafi. Some were supplied by Victor Bout, who used Liberian registry numbers on some of the aircraft he used to fly weapons around Africa. Another source was a thickset thug with a penchant for dope and prostitutes. Leonid Minin was born in the Ukraine, and after the fall of the Berlin Wall, he became involved in a wide range of criminal activity: stolen works of art, arms trafficking and money laundering. His association with Charles Taylor centred on arms and diamonds. Although huge volumes of weapons are available for purchase around the world, most governments take care to ensure that sales are properly documented, or that there is a good enough cover to allow for credible deniability. Such was the design in a shipment of arms that arrived in Ouagadougou, the capital of Burkina Faso in March 1999. The shipment included anti-tank weapons, surface-to-air missiles, rocket propelled grenades and launchers, 715 boxes of weapons and cartridges and 408 boxes of cartridge powder.

The weapons were ordered by the Burkina Faso Ministry of Defence from the state-owned Ukrainian company, Ukrspetsexport, through a Gibraltar-based company, Chartered Engineering and Technical Services. Although an end-user certificate was issued for Burkina Faso, this is not where they stayed. Burkina Faso's President, Blaise Compaoré, a beneficiary of the Benghazi academy and a staunch supporter of both Charles Taylor and Foday Sankoh, had some of the weapons trucked southwest to Bobo Dioulasso. These, and the boxes remaining in Ouagadougou, were then transhipped to Monrovia, courtesy of Leonid Minin. Minin had flown to Monrovia in a leased BAC-111 on March 8. He and Taylor created a fiction that this was an executive passenger jet, with virtually no cargo capacity. Indeed, the plane was a passenger aircraft; it still bore the colours of its previous owner, the Seattle Supersonics basketball team. Over the next two weeks, the plane made four trips to Ouagadougou and three to Bobo Dioulasso, each time picking up weapons. Several trips were required, because the plane, in fact, did not have a large cargo capacity. The crates of weapons were distributed under the seats and in the aisle, and some were even strapped into the passenger seats like travelling basketball players. On March 31, the plane few back to Europe for other duties, carrying a lighter but more valuable cargo of diamonds.[12]

A West African peacekeeping force – ECOMOG – had used Sierra Leone as a rear base in Liberian operations, starting in 1990, but its predominantly Nigerian troops did not become directly involved in Sierra Leone operations until the middle of the decade. ECOMOG officers and what was left of the Sierra Leone army were regularly accused of collusion in looting and diamond smuggling. Soldiers by day, rebels by night, they were sometimes called 'sobels'. The Nigerians were also accused of brutality and human rights violations, charges not hard to believe in such a brutal war. A girl named Sia tells her story: She was kidnapped by the RUF when she was eleven, after seeing her sister killed in front of her. An RUF commander made her his 'bush wife' and she was regularly raped by his men. Sometimes she was sent to villages the RUF planned to attack, to sleep with Nigerian soldiers and obtain information. 'I was a spy,' she says. 'I gave them sex and they gave me information. And then we would kill them.' As she became a trusted member of the RUF, she was assigned to 'cuttings' as she calls them – chopping the hands off other children. And she became a fighter. 'They knew I would be a good soldier, so they began training me with weapons training, manoeuvres, how to kill close up with a pistol. They gave me two pistols for close range. I always saw the people before I killed them. I checked if they were dead, then I gave them another shot in the head if they weren't.'[13]

Besides ECOMOG, the only force strong enough to keep the RUF away from Sierra Leone's second and third cities, Bo and Kenema, was a traditional hunters' society, known as the *kamajors*. Originally organized by local chiefs for village protection, they were reorganized into what became known as the Civil Defence Force, and for a time they numbered more than 20,000 men, more than the RUF and the army combined. But by 1995, even they were in difficulty.

Its back to the wall, the failing government of Valentine Strasser made a deal with one of the scavenging junior mining firms that had arrived at the end of Joseph Momoh's Israeli experiments. DiamondWorks was, in 1995, a company incorporated in Canada and listed on the Toronto Stock Exchange with a head office in Vancouver. In fact it was managed from London, with operational headquarters in Johannesburg. Its Vancouver presence gave it access to Canadian stock exchanges where, like many other junior mining firms, it spent more time mining for shareholders than diamonds. DiamondWorks owned Branch Energy, a company listed in the shadowy registers of the Isle of Man. In turn, Branch Energy had a close relationship with a private South African military firm, felicitously named 'Executive Outcomes'. Branch Energy introduced Strasser to Executive Outcomes' founder, Eeben Barlow, who not long afterwards imported 200 mercenaries, air support and some sophisticated communications equipment. Within a week they pushed the RUF back from Freetown. Having few of the logistical, professional or political constraints that encumbered ECOMOG, they cleared the diamond fields within a month, scattering the RUF like a train of soldier ants disturbed by a boy with a stick. A few weeks later, Branch Energy was given a 25 year lease on diamond concessions in Kono.

Amidst the ensuing charges and counter-charges, DiamondWorks and Branch Energy denied human rights abuse and they denied any corporate connection between themselves and Executive Outcomes. Human rights organizations, political scientists, ethicists and many Western governments pronounced themselves shocked at the derogation of sovereign responsibilities to mercenaries, and at what looked like a possible protection racket: mining leases for body bags. 'Executive Outcomes Must Go!' howled the Freetown dailies, now that the RUF threat had diminished and the idea of protection from self-serving white mercenaries seemed less appealing. And less necessary. 'Executive Outcomes Must Go!' was a refrain echoed by a newly chastened RUF, suddenly willing to sit at the peace table and talk like sane men.

In some ways, 1996 was a pivotal year for Sierra Leone. The military, under pressure from the public and donor agencies to hold elections, sated from a five year binge at the money trough and disgraced by their own incompetence, finally gave in. Elections were held in March and a former United Nations official, Ahmad Tejan Kabbah, was elected President. Kabbah took over peace negotiations that had already begun with the RUF in Abidjan, and in November, a peace accord was finally signed. As part of the deal, Executive Outcomes was sent packing. Then, six months later, soldiers raided Freetown's notorious Pademba Road prison and released 600 inmates. Among them was a Major, one Johnny Paul Koroma, who in short order declared himself head of state. Tejan Kabbah and his government fled to Conakry in neighbouring Guinea, and Koroma set about creating a coalition government with the RUF.

Foday Sankoh had been caught napping by the coup. Visiting Nigeria when it occurred, he was promptly jailed by the Nigerian authorities. Leaderless or not, however, the RUF now dispelled any remaining doubt about their nature. For six months, Johnny Paul Koroma's Armed Forces Ruling Council (AFRC) and the RUF presided over a systematic reign of terror. Judges, journalists and members of Kabbah's parliament were tortured and murdered. Looting and rape became commonplace. Government offices ceased to function, banks remained closed and normal commerce came to a halt. People starved. Among his innovations, Chairman Koroma appointed as 'Chief of Defence Staff' an RUF hooligan named Sam Bockarie, who liked to be called 'Mosquito' or 'Maskita'. A former diamond digger, hairdresser and disco dancer, Bockarie was also a bloody killer and Foday Sankoh's right hand man.

Interviewed in Buedu in 2000 by Steve Coll of the *Washington Post*, Bockarie comes across as narcissistic, dangerous and unbalanced. 'I am a good looking man,' he says, contradicting the evidence of photographs. 'I like good living.' After a lengthy peroration on the war, he tells Coll, 'You know, I really admire myself.' Bockarie had become Foday Sankoh's most ruthless general, a man whose reputation for murder and mayhem had spread throughout the country and beyond. Aware that he might eventually face some sort of retribution, Bockarie denied human rights abuse in a backward sort of fashion. 'I don't believe in innocent killing in the field,' he said. 'I have no outlaw record. If soldiers have raped, I have executed them. If soldiers have dropped arms, I have disciplined them. Those are the only two crimes I have committed.'[14] Those two – execution and 'discipline' – and countless attacks on civilian targets over a decade; those two and a series of bloody murders within the

RUF itself; those two and the theft of millions of dollars worth of diamonds which he often carried personally to the offices of Charles Taylor and his cronies in Monrovia.

In February 1998, ECOMOG – embarrassed by the coup and chased out of Freetown – finally summoned the strength to force the AFRC and the RUF to abandon the city. President Kabbah returned and the AFRC dissolved. But the RUF did not. Issa Sesay, one of the RUF commanders, escorted Johnny Paul Koroma to the relative safety of Buedu, and was dismayed to discover that the Chairman had been concealing a bag of diamonds to help pave his way to a better life elsewhere. 'This information came as a surprise to me,' Sesay wrote in a report to Foday Sankoh. He 'found it hard to believe that at a time when we were trying to put the fighting men under command and control and provide the necessary logistics to halt our retreat and move forward, J.P. Koroma would keep diamonds for his own use and flee, leaving us with a problem that he had created.' Johnny Paul was, in fact, lucky to get away with his life. The RUF murdered diggers for so much as looking sideways at a diamond.

By the end of 1998, the RUF was again in the ascendant, even though their leader, recently transferred from Nigeria, was incarcerated in a Freetown jail. ECOMOG had continued its ineffectual attempt to solve the problem, but over the years it had suffered serious casualties. Somewhere between 800 and 1200 Nigerian soldiers had lost their lives, and the effort was said to be costing Nigeria a million dollars a day. Then, in January 1999, the RUF attacked Freetown with a vengeance. They razed parts of the city as the Nigerian soldiers fled to the west, and for two weeks they searched for civil servants, politicians and civil society leaders, killing many on the spot. By the time ECOMOG beat them back, 6000 civilians lay dead, and 2000 children were missing. Nigeria had had enough. The newly elected civilian government in Lagos announced that it would pull its troops out of Sierra Leone within six months. This much-touted 'African solution to an African problem' was falling apart.

In fact ECOMOG was an experiment, one that Western governments hoped might relieve them of responsibility for dealing with Africa's wars. The United States was particularly reluctant after Somalia to be drawn into another African conflict, and although President Clinton had stood at the Kigali airport in Rwanda after the genocide there, saying 'Never again', he didn't mean it. The UN – controlled by the five permanent members of the Security Council: Britain, Russia, France, China and the United States – had failed in Somalia; it had done little more than run away from Rwanda, and it was about to pull its peacekeepers out of Angola where there was no peace to be kept. Sierra Leone was thus caught between Scylla and Charybdis – between a big rock and a very hard place. The days of the lacklustre ECOMOG were numbered, but there seemed little prospect of a United Nations peacekeeping force to take their place. Faced with an impossible situation, Tejan Kabbah bowed to growing international pressure to make another peace arrangement with the RUF. There could never be a military solution, he was told; the solution had to be political.

What then occurred must go down in the annals of international diplomacy as one of the most stunningly cynical and disgraceful episodes of all time. Jesse Jackson, 'Special Envoy for the President and Secretary of State for the Promotion of Democracy in Africa' had already been to Freetown and Monrovia. In 1998 he had urged President Kabbah to 'reach out' to the RUF in order to make peace. Somehow, presumably, this would 'promote democracy'. Now, prominent members of the Congressional Black Caucus in the United States became involved. Many were close to Charles Taylor, and some were thought to be beneficiaries of his largesse. New Jersey Representative Donald Payne wrote to Kabbah, urging negotiations. 'Successful negotiations must be without precondition and include the permanent release of Mr. Foday Sankoh,' Payne wrote.[15] Under direct personal pressure from Jesse Jackson and American State Department officials, and with a rapidly dwindling military capacity to resist the RUF, Kabbah finally agreed to a cease-fire. He released Foday Sankoh who joined him for negotiations in Lomé, the capital of Togo. There, over a marathon 45-day negotiating session, US officials and others helped to broker a peace deal. What resulted, on 7 July 1999, was a blanket amnesty for all RUF fighters. In addition, the RUF was given four ministerial posts in Kabbah's government and vice presidential status was conferred on Foday Sankoh. As icing on the cake, he was also made head of a new commission to oversee the country's diamond resources.

The RUF had demonstrated that butchery paid off. Instead of being punished, they were rewarded, and they were assisted in the process by the most powerful government on earth. At precisely the same moment that NATO was spending billions of dollars to save Kosovars from human rights abuse, much worse atrocities were being generously rewarded in Sierra Leone. Instead of going to prison, Foday Sankoh was made vice president. As a prize for eight years of diamond theft, he was put in charge of the country's entire mineral wealth. Assistant US Secretary of State Susan Rice bragged at the time that 'the US role in Sierra Leone ... has been instrumental. With hands-on efforts by the president's special envoy Jesse Jackson, Ambassador Joe Melrose, and many others, the United States brokered the cease-fire and helped steer Sierra Leone's rebels, the Kabbah government, and regional leaders to the negotiating table.'[16]

UN officials as well as representatives of ECOWAS and the British government had also participated in the negotiations. But when UN Special Envoy Francis Okello sought permission from New York to initial the deal, someone at UN headquarters woke up to the words 'absolute and free pardon and reprieve to all'. The UN High Commissioner for Human Rights, former Irish President Mary Robinson, objected, and Okello was instructed to append a handwritten note saying that the UN did not acknowledge the application of the amnesty to 'acts of genocide, crimes against humanity, war crimes and other serious violations of international humanitarian law.' Given what happened in the ensuing months, it was just as well. There were no such compunctions in Washington at the time, but six months later a US State Department Spokesman, Philip Reeker, would say that 'The United States did not pressure anybody to sign this agreement... We neither brokered the Lomé peace agreement nor leaned on President Kabbah to open talks with the insurgents... It was not an agreement of ours.'[17]

Reeker had good reason for trying to distance the US from the Lomé agreement. Apart from its grotesque rewarding of criminality, the deal was destined to fail. Peter Takirambudde of Human Rights Watch said that the agreement represented 'a major retreat by all the parties – the UN, the Clinton Administration, the others. For the rest of Africa, where there are rebels in the bush, the signal is that atrocities can be committed – especially if they are frightening atrocities. The lesson to other rebels is that half measures will not do.'[18]

As part of the agreement, the United Nations Security Council at last agreed to send a peacekeeping force to replace the departing Nigerians. The first contingent began to arrive at the end of 1999, and for a while, a fragile near-peace prevailed. In November 1999, however, Sam Bockarie said 'I'm envisaging another serious battle in Sierra Leone. I told all my men to clean all their barrels and wait.'[19] It didn't take long. A month later, a dispute between Bockarie and Foday Sankoh erupted in a firestorm of bullets and blood in Buedu. When it was over, eight of Mosquito's senior aides lay dead, allegedly by his hand, and the 35-year-old Mad Max general disappeared into the forests of Liberia. Foday Sankoh, now free of internal dissension, could relax in his newfound role as chairman of the mineral resources commission. But as he set about making deals for his personal enrichment with the stream of eager foreign businessmen who began arriving at his new Freetown offices, he kept a close watch on the UN peacekeeping force. The United Nations Mission in Sierra Leone (UNAMSIL) was gathering in strength and was gradually deploying into the countryside. Sankoh had been given complete authority over Sierra Leone's diamonds, and he was not about to let any army but his own pitch its tents in the diamond fields.

The clash came at the beginning of May 2000 when a force of 500 Kenyan and Zambian peacekeepers was stopped near the rebel-held town of Makeni. In a sudden test of willpower, eight peacekeepers lay dead, and five hundred were kidnapped, spirited away into the bush along with their vehicles and military hardware. Surprised as the soldiers may have been, the Security Council was even more astounded. The first test of UN resolve after its pullout from Angola looked like it might be the last. As diplomats again evacuated Freetown amidst rumours of a final RUF push, the world's media poured in and their reports streamed out. Why, they asked, had UNAMSIL been comprised only of troops from developing countries: India, Zambia, Bangladesh, Kenya, Jordan? Why had they arrived so ill-equipped? Why had they not fought back? Why were there no troops and weapons from countries more practised in the arts of war? The answers were self-evident. They were the same answers to the same questions asked a year earlier when Kosovo was getting so much attention and Sierra Leone none: nobody cared. Sierra Leone was of absolutely no strategic interest to anyone except Charles Taylor, the RUF and the diamond trade. Uganda's foreign affairs minister said it clearly enough: 'When it is Kosovo, you are there in one minute and you spend billions... When it is Africa there are all sorts of excuses.'[20]

Several factors contributed to ending the embarrassing rout. First, the British government acted quickly, sending a battalion of paratroopers and five warships. Within days they had stabilized the panic in Freetown and secured the main roads leading out of the city. Then, on May 7, there was a massive public demonstration outside Foday Sankoh's house in Freetown. Tens of thousands of civilians, enraged over the rewards showered on the rebel leader, exasperated by the continuing conflict, and fearful that the UN peacekeeping mission might collapse, gathered outside the hillside building on Spur Road. It was a peaceable crowd but it was noisy, and Sankoh's supposedly unarmed guards lost their nerve. Without warning, they opened fire, killing 17 civilians. Then they scattered. Sankoh hopped over a back wall and escaped, but he was captured a few days later and jailed. There is a photograph of him in a taxi with his gleeful captors, his bewildered face pressed against the glass. It was later discovered that the RUF had stockpiled weapons throughout the city, and had planned a coup that would have taken place within a matter of days.

In the two years that followed, much changed. The kidnapped UNAMSIL troops were released in due course, having been moved to Liberia and flown to Monrovia under the protection of Charles Taylor, who now posed implausibly as a peacemaker. UNAMSIL numbers were increased to 17,000, making it the biggest UN peacekeeping operation in the world, although there were still only token troops from Western nations. A UN Security Council Expert Panel was commissioned to examine the relationship between diamonds and weapons in Sierra Leone and it provided convincing evidence of Charles Taylor's direct complicity in moving diamonds out of Sierra Leone, and weapons in. The Security Council slapped a global embargo on all Liberian diamonds, and placed a travel ban on Charles Taylor, his family, his cabinet, and a wide range of Liberian civil servants. The existing arms embargo was tightened, and as a result, the RUF – on a major rampage through the end of 2000 – was gradually starved of ammunition.

Its last major adventure was an invasion of Guinea in September 2000. Distracting the Guinean government with attacks on refugee camps south of Conakry, RUF troops launched a major incursion on border towns in the east. The invasion was intended to be a repetition of Taylor's own invasion of Liberia in 1989 and Sankoh's invasion of Sierra Leone in 1991. It was thought that if the rebels could rout the Guinean forces and take control of the diamond areas around Macenta, they could deprive the government of the funds it would need to fight a prolonged war. At the same time, they could obtain the resources they would need for themselves. For Charles Taylor, this proxy war was important, because Guinea had long harboured anti-Taylor Liberian dissidents, and if the attacks succeeded, he could kill several birds with one stone. They did not succeed, nor did he. Guinea threw all of its firepower against the invaders, obliterating them. Once more on the defensive, the RUF agreed to a cease-fire in Sierra Leone. But this time it was different. It was now clear that Foday Sankoh was not going to be released to sit at any negotiating table. It was also clear that whatever destruction they might cause in the interior, the RUF would never be allowed to march on Freetown again. UNAMSIL, renewed in its mandate, bolstered in both numbers and equipment, and backed by no-nonsense British paratroopers, would not permit that to happen. And Charles Taylor, now under the brightest international spotlight of his career and deprived of at least some means of income, blinked.

In January 2002, Ahmad Tejan Kabbah declared the war to be officially over. In May that year, an election was held and Kabbah was returned in a ballot that was probably the most open and fair since independence, 41 years before. The new peace deal established a UN-backed Special Court, a hybrid of the ones established to deal with Rwandan and Yugoslavian war crimes. Based in Freetown, it was supported by a team of prosecutors and judges from a wide variety of countries, including Sierra Leone. It began its formal deliberations in December 2002, with a three year mandate to try those most culpable of human rights violations and war crimes. Its first indictments were issued in March 2003. Foday Sankoh was charged, along with his erstwhile 'Battlefield Commander', Issa Sesay, and the absent Sam Bockarie. Johnny Paul Koroma was also charged, on the run again after another apparent coup plot backfired only days before the indictments. In due course, Charles Taylor too would be charged. In announcing the indictments, the Special Court's Prosecutor, David Crane, quoted Robert Jackson, Chief US Prosecutor at the Nuremberg war crimes trial: 'We are able to do away with tyranny and violence and aggression by those in power against the rights of their own people only when we make all men answerable to the law.'

In addition to the Special Court, a Truth and Reconciliation Commission was established, as a means of dealing with the many individuals and atrocities that the court could not. UNAMSIL began to reduce its numbers at the end of 2002, and finally withdrew at the end of 2005. By then, however, there were 15,000 UN peacekeepers in Liberia, only minutes away from Freetown by helicopter, should they be required.

Where diamonds were concerned, the changes too were remarkable. For almost 20 years, official diamond exports had been negligible. During the time of Siaka Stevens, the industry had been so seriously debased that most diamonds were exported unofficially, to the benefit of corrupt government officials and the country's wide circle of Lebanese diamond dealers, ready and willing to buy anything that sparkled. During the RUF years, some diamonds were sold by rebels to Lebanese traders and others on the government side of the line, but most went out through Liberia. In 1999, Sierra Leone exported only $1.5 million worth of diamonds. By 2000 official exports increased to $11 million. The following year, exports reached $26 million, and in 2005 they totalled $142 million, more than in any year over the previous two decades. Taxes were paid, and the government, responding to an idea from Sierra Leonean NGOs, agreed to return some of the tax money to the chiefdoms where the diamonds were mined. Much remained to be done, however, and the challenges in creating an international diamond regulatory scheme are told in Chapter 12. For a while longer, Charles Taylor would remain at the helm in Liberia, making plans for better days and other opportunities. At his side – until Taylor decided he no longer served a purpose – was Sam Bockarie, no doubt in awe of his own abilities and countenance until the end. But after thirty years of appalling government and a brutal conflict that had lasted twice as long as the Second World War, Sierra Leoneans began to feel that they had turned a corner.

CHAPTER 8

PRESIDENT MOBUTU'S GHOST

Listen to the yell of Leopold's ghost
Burning in Hell for his hand-maimed host.
Hear how the demons chuckle and yell
Cutting his hands off down in Hell.

– Vachel Lindsay, *The Congo*, 1914

The Congo's unhappy engagement with modern times can be divided into four periods. During the first, from the late 1870s until 1908, the country's current borders took shape under the administration of the 'Congo Free State'. Anything but free, this 'state' was the personal fiefdom of Belgium's King Leopold II. The second period was one of direct colonial rule from Brussels. Forced to assume responsibility for the colony after Leopold's mismanagement became an international scandal, the government of Belgium supposed that its mandate might last forever.* As late as 1955, when the ubiquitous

---

* 'The Congo' has been through many name changes. While under the direct control of Leopold, it was known as 'The Congo Free State'. Under the control of Brussels, it became the 'Belgian Congo'. At Independence it was renamed the 'Democratic Republic of the Congo'. As part of an 'authenticity' program, President Mobutu renamed the country 'Zaire' in 1971, and his successor, Laurent Kabila, re-christened it the 'Democratic Republic of the Congo' (DRC) in 1998. 'Zaire' has been avoided in this text wherever possible, in order to avoid confusion. The term 'Congolese' refers to this country. The DRC's neighbour to the northwest – a former French colony – is known as the Republic of Congo. The capital of the Republic of Congo, Brazzaville, lies directly across the River Congo from Kinshasa, which is the capital of the DRC. In this chapter, the Republic of Congo is mostly referred to as 'Congo-Brazzaville'.

winds of change were beginning to blow across Africa, Brussels still believed that independence was decades away, rather than the mere 60 months that remained. The third period, a 37-year stretch from independence in 1960 until 1997, was mostly dominated by a single man – Joseph Désiré Mobutu. At the age of 29, Mobutu became army chief of staff, and within eight weeks of independence had dismissed the country's president and prime minister amidst a scramble of plots, counter-plots and Cold War intrigue that would set the stage for decades of chaos, corruption and conflict. The fourth period began in 1997 when the Mobutu regime buckled under the weight of its own corruption. Mobutu left behind a country described best by what it was not than by what it was, a place on the map of Africa defined more by the borders of its nine neighbouring countries than by the ability of its remaining administration to do anything more than forage, pillage and plunder.

Diamonds, the foundation on which a modern-day Congo might have been constructed, were instead a curse. They were at the centre of the country's problems, almost from the day they were discovered in 1907. It is possible, in fact, that Leopold II would never have relinquished control of his 'free state' had he understood the extent to which diamonds were spread – not far below the surface – across vast swathes of territory bordering the French colonies to the north, and in the lands bordering the Portuguese colony of Angola to the south.

Leopold was vain, greedy and ambitious, and he was nothing if not an entrepreneur. Styled 'King of the Belgians' at his coronation in 1865, Leopold had dreamt of the benefits and glories of empire since his youth, once depicting his small country – one fifth the size of Florida – thus: '*Petit pays, petites gens*'. Mesmerized by tales of explorers returning from Africa, and dismayed by the Belgian parliament's lack of interest in the wealth and power that might flow from potential colonies, Leopold hit on one of the most original plans for empire in the sorry annals of colonialism. Focusing on the vast unexplored stretches of central Africa, he set himself up first as a patron of exploration and then as a great humanitarian, determined to rid the continent of Arab slavery, and to civilize the heathen. In 1876 he hosted a grand 'geographical conference' in Brussels, bringing together the world's foremost explorers, geographers and humanitarians. Leopold's presentation was brilliant. He told his audience that, 'To open to civilization the only part of our globe which it has not yet penetrated, to pierce the darkness which hangs over entire peoples is, I dare say, a crusade worthy of this century of progress.'[1] The upshot was the creation of the International African Association, a philanthropic organization which in the ensuing years became the front for a very different kind of penetration.

Leopold engaged the great African explorer, Henry Morton Stanley, to plant his flag – a gold star on a blue background – wherever he could. Stanley, who had found the long-lost missionary, David Livingstone in 1871, now concluded one of the century's most significant feats of exploration, taking three years to cross the entire African continent from Zanzibar to the Atlantic Ocean and the mouth of the Congo River. Having written extensively about the horrors of the Arab slave trade, he became Leopold's pretext for empire, as well as his instrument. When the Berlin Conference was inaugurated in 1884 to draw up the definitive colonial map of Africa, Leopold's vast territory had been staked out, and his expressed objective, to make the Congo a free trade zone, was enthusiastically accepted by the other colonial powers.

But Leopold had something else in mind. Trade, like the state, would not be free. It was intended primarily to benefit the King of the Belgians, now presiding over a territory 77 times larger than the Kingdom itself. Ivory, tropical hardwood, palm oil and minerals were the primary *raisons d'être*, extracted by companies that were given generous concessions over vast territories. A private army, the *Force Publique*, was created to enforce Leopold's order and to ensure adequate supplies of labour for the building of roads and a railway into the interior. The worst excesses centred on rubber, which became increasingly important as a new century dawned and the automobile industry began to develop. Villages were given quotas for the production of rubber from wild vines in the country's forests. Failure to meet targets brought down the wrath of the *Force Publique*, which raided and destroyed entire villages, killing men, women and children. A harbinger of things to come in Sierra Leone, Leopold's men taught recalcitrant villagers a lesson that was not lost on their neighbours: they chopped off their hands.

The cost to the people who lived in Leopold's empire was enormous. A Belgian government enquiry in 1919 estimated that from the days when Stanley began to plant Leopold's flag, the population of the Congo had been reduced by half. Adam Hochschild, author of *King Leopold's Ghost*, explains how this was achieved, and what it meant in numbers. First, people died from outright murder – war made by the *Force Publique* and others on innocent civilians. More died from starvation, exhaustion, exposure and the spread of disease. The estimate of those who died or fled during those first years of Belgian influence is estimated in several studies at ten million people, and in one at a staggering thirteen million,[2] a human rights crime of genocidal proportions.

The scandal took more than a decade to emerge and to become a force strong enough to disengage the Belgian king from his stranglehold on the Congo. Even so, the price was high. The Belgian government assumed 110 million francs worth of debt, much of the money borrowed earlier from the government itself and never repaid. A further 45.5 million francs was devoted to various projects that Leopold had started, including a massive royal palace at Laeken. And another 50 million francs was for Leopold himself, 'as a mark of gratitude for his great sacrifices made for the Congo'.[3] Most of the funds were expected to come not from Belgian taxpayers, but from the Congo itself.

With the departure of Leopold, little actually changed in the Congo. Plantations gradually supplanted the harvesting of wild rubber, but forced labour continued, accompanied by cycles of uprising and brutal repression. Copper, zinc, gold, tin and diamond mining grew – all becoming important to the allied effort during World War I and even more important during World War II. Most of the uranium in the Hiroshima and Nagasaki bombs was mined in the Congo. All colonial production was accomplished with forced labour, which grew to as much as 120 days per man per year during World War II. By then, the biggest of the Congo's golden eggs were copper and diamonds. Diamonds, found in alluvial and kimberlite deposits in vast stretches of land around Kisangani, Mbuji-Mayi and Tshikapa, were nominally controlled by the *Société Internationale Forestière et Minière du Congo* (Forminière), founded in 1906 under Leopold's auspices. By 1929, the Congo had become the world's second largest diamond producer after South Africa, although the bulk was industrial rather than gem quality.

Until the 1930s, there was little demand for poorly crystallized diamonds. They were known as 'bort', and apart from their use in the polishing of gem quality diamonds, they had limited value. But in the 1930s, Krupp, the powerful German industrial complex, developed a tungsten carbide alloy that was stronger than steel. The only material hard enough to cut and shape it was diamond, and suddenly De Beers had a new product: the 'industrial diamond'. Because such diamonds were available in the Belgian Congo by the ton rather than by the carat, Sir Ernest Oppenheimer knew he had to gain control of the Forminière production. 'Forminière,' he wrote to his son Harry, 'will dictate the post-war politics of the diamond trade. By controlling the Congo production, De Beers will maintain its leading position in diamonds.'[4]

De Beers negotiated a deal with Brussels. In return for all of the Forminière production – sold to a De Beers subsidiary in London – De Beers would provide the Belgian diamond cutting and polishing industry with the bulk of its gemstones. To cement the arrangement, De Beers also bought shares in a Belgian firm, Beceka, which owned controlling shares in Forminière.

In 1953, the Belgian Congo produced five per cent of the world's zinc, seven per cent of the world's copper, half the world's uranium, 80 per cent of the world's cobalt and 70 per cent of the world's industrial diamonds, along with a goodly proportion of gem quality stones. It was also the world's largest rubber producer. A measure of the colony's value to Belgium can be seen in its export statistics. In the mid 1950s, its annual exports totalled over $3 billion, compared with only $60 million from British Kenya.[5] Although the colony boasted an enviable infrastructure, which in some ways rivalled that of other colonial territories, it was patchy and selective. It was built almost solely to support the extractive industries and enclave operations that were managed exclusively by Belgians, centred primarily on copper, diamonds and agriculture. Forced labour ended only with independence. When the Belgian flag was finally lowered in 1960 after more than 50 years of direct Belgian rule, there were only 17 Congolese university graduates.[6]

It is perhaps not surprising that the first political ructions in the newly independent country should have erupted around minerals. Within seven days of independence, the army mutinied, leading almost immediately thereafter to the secession of mineral-rich Katanga province. The country's mercurial new Prime Minister, Patrice Lumumba, called for UN help, but when the peacekeepers' limited mandate restrained them from halting the rebellions, he called for assistance from an all too willing Soviet Union. Within weeks, a thousand Soviet 'technical advisors' had arrived, further dividing the country and giving its newly-appointed army chief, Joseph Mobutu, reason to sack both Lumumba and the country's president. This happened less than 60 days after the precipitous Belgian pullout, and less than nine months after negotiations for independence had started in Brussels. So panicked was the US government by the sudden arrival of Soviet advisors, and by the spectre of a return to power by Patrice Lumumba, that President Eisenhower himself is said to have sanctioned the execution of the ousted Prime Minister.[7] Five years of rebellion, secession, reintegration and confusion followed, until October 1965, when Mobutu stepped in again, this time taking control decisively, and for good.

Mobutu inherited little that he might build upon in terms of state infrastructure. The country was politically fractured; there was little law and less order. And the police force, army and judiciary had virtually no experience of loyalty, independence or democracy. Rather than building on the crumbling foundations he found, Mobutu took a short cut to the consolidation of power, one that would become popular among other African leaders in the 1960s and 1970s. Systematically and ruthlessly, he bypassed the formal trappings of the modern state, creating his own in their image. He subverted the army and police, putting men in charge who were loyal to him; loyal because they were directly dependent on him for the fortunes they accrued. He changed his cabinet as the year changes seasons, appointing, sacking and reappointing men until they understood that they owed fealty to only one person. To maintain his legion of sycophants, Mobutu needed cash, and for much of the first ten years of his reign, what the economy did not produce, lenders – the World Bank, aid agencies and private banks – did. In 1971 he embarked on an 'authenticity' campaign, aimed at looking forward, away from the colonial era. He renamed the country and the river that defines it 'Zaire', and he renamed himself Mobutu Sese Seko, becoming 'The Guide', 'The Helmsman', 'Father of the Nation'. Two years later he inaugurated a new campaign, this time 'Zaireanization', under which all foreign-owned businesses were handed over to 'sons of the country'. Farms, plantations and industries were confiscated and handed out to the faithful, with Mobutu himself taking the cream off the top.

But Zaireanization coincided with the 1974 oil crisis and with precipitous drops in the price of copper and coffee. This reduced the booty and converted an economy with good possibilities into one with significantly fewer. Corruption and mismanagement went into overdrive. When Mobutu nationalized the copper giant *Union Minière* in 1967, it produced as much as 70 per cent of the country's export earnings. Renamed Gécamines, it went into a long, slow decline. From a peak annual production of 550,000 tons, it dropped to 200,000 tons by the beginning of the 1990s, and in 1997 it produced less than 38,000 tons of copper. (By 2008 production had fallen to only 12,000 tons.) Not all of the proceeds were 'lost'; they were simply lost to the national economy and whatever they might have contributed to the development of the country. Taxes, forward selling, phony concessions, inflated payrolls, smuggling and outright embezzlement ensured that for many years into its decline, Gécamines was able to continue lining the pockets of the president and his cohorts. When Gécamines' cobalt production was similarly despoiled, diamonds remained.

The diamond sector was more difficult for Mobutu to plunder because much of it was found in the Kasai provinces where he had less political control than elsewhere. And while the world price of diamonds was more stable than that of copper, this was due almost exclusively to the work of De Beers. Through the 1960s and 1970s, De Beers had a monopoly on the purchase of Congolese diamonds, produced mainly by the mining giant, *Société Minière de Bakwanga* (MIBA), the successor to Forminière. To gain greater control himself, Mobutu first nationalized MIBA, including the part owned by De Beers. Then, in 1981 he ended the De Beers purchasing monopoly, deciding to market the diamonds through a consortium of three firms, one in London and two in Antwerp. Between the nationalization in 1973 and the cancellation of its buying monopoly in 1981, De Beers continued to purchase what MIBA produced, although MIBA's output fell dramatically, from 13.4 million carats in 1973 to only 8.7 million carats in 1979. These were mainly industrial diamonds. Better goods simply found their way across the river to Brazzaville and to other cities beyond Mobutu's reach, where the welcome mat was always out.

When Mobutu ended the De Beers monopoly, however, polite fictions about who was really in charge fell away. De Beers retaliated by dumping huge quantities of Congo-quality industrial diamonds onto the world market, reducing the price to less than a dollar a carat and making it impossible for Mobutu's newfound friends to do business with him. Within two years, the Congo had signed a new deal with De Beers.

Where diamonds were concerned, Mobutu was like a hound after a bitch in heat. Unable to break De Beers, he took another tack. In 1983, he 'liberalized' the diamond sector, allowing for the creation of an entirely new class of diamond exporter, dependent on him for licenses and privilege. With the discovery of new alluvial diamond fields in Oriental province, artisanal diamond production increased, rapidly outstripping the production of MIBA. In the 1970s, small miners accounted for less than a quarter of the Congo's diamond production but by 1986 they represented 64 per cent of the total. This was in part because MIBA, like Gécamines, was being looted by a Mobutu crony, Jonas Mukamba. At the height of his powers, Mukamba was estimated to be skimming between $1.5 and $2 million a month from MIBA on Mobutu's behalf.[8]

Most Congolese economic statistics are untrustworthy and provide little more than indicators, or orders of magnitude. This is especially true of diamonds, which always find the path of least resistance to the best price. Mobutu might insert his henchmen into the system and pay lower prices in order to realize a better return in Antwerp. But the diamond flow would rapidly alter course, with better stones showing up in the buying offices of De Beers and others, conveniently located across the river from Kinshasa in the capital of the former French colony, now the Republic of Congo, Brazzaville. Or they might surface in Bangui, capital of the Central African Republic. Or in Burundi or Zambia or Angola or any other place offering a better price. So MIBA's stated production in 2000 of $76 million worth of diamonds, compared with 1983 production of $47 million, looks good, but in fact it means very little. The value of diamonds in either year might have been deflated by smuggling, theft or embezzlement, or it might have been inflated by diamonds from Angola or somewhere else, brought into the country illicitly. Or the figures, produced by various government agencies, might be completely and utterly fictitious, fabricated in the overheated minds of miscreant officials attempting to mollify the World Bank or the IMF, or the country's kleptocratic president.

Mobutu's survival owed itself in part to his genius for corruption and manipulation. But there was another factor which added to his longevity and to the suffering of the Congolese people: the Cold War. Until the fall of the Berlin Wall, Mobutu remained a staunch ally of the Western world, a steadfast bulwark against inroads of communism into Africa. He had proven his mettle in his dismissal of Lumumba, and he did it again when he provided a base for UNITA rebels (and their American backers) fighting against the Marxist government of Angola after 1975. He also provided a route out of Angola for UNITA gems, becoming one of the first purveyors of conflict diamonds. He visited the White House as an honoured guest of almost every president from John F. Kennedy to George Bush *père*. He wooed France and its '*francophonie*' giving diamonds as a personal gift to President Giscard d'Estaing and actually repaying debts owed to companies in which d'Estaing's family had interests. He bribed Belgian officials and made way in his later years for increased Belgian business in the Congo. Diamonds were always the centrepiece. And he ensured whatever access he could for all of his 'allies' to cobalt and other strategic minerals.

As a result, the US, France and Belgium were ready to assist Mobutu with troops or an airlift whenever there was a rebellion that needed quelling. And all provided lashings of aid money. Between 1975 and 1997, the country received more than $9 billion in foreign aid from the World Bank, the IMF and a cross section of bilateral donors. Failed projects, disappearing cash and financial crises notwithstanding, the aid money kept flowing. The country agreed to reform after reform, adjustment after structural adjustment, and its debt was rescheduled nine times between 1976 and 1989. But the money kept on coming. 'He played us and his environment like a Stradivarius,' said Chester Crocker, former US assistant secretary of state for Africa. 'He would play us off against the French, the French against the Belgians, the CIA against the State Department.' [9] Crocker's feigned wonderment is not a little ingenuous. The French, the Belgians, the CIA and the State Department were each as good at playing the Mobutu Strad as its owner.

With the end of the Cold War, however, the Stradivarius lost its tone, and one by one the donors closed their cash registers. As the country disintegrated around him, Mobutu hunkered down in the palaces he had purchased in Europe, and at Gbadolite in Équateur province. There, at the most garish of his palaces, musical fountains still greeted guests who were flown in on chartered Boeings and the occasional Concorde. He and his cronies now invested more of their energies in the informal economy and a clandestine, overlapping trade in guns, drugs, diamonds and money laundering. As always, rough diamonds remained at the centre of this, because in a world of vanishing friends and disappearing markets they retained their value, and there were always outsiders eager to buy. The diamonds really did look as though they might be forever. The continuing war in Angola provided an ongoing opportunity for weapons sales and a continuous incoming supply of diamonds to augment the dwindling opportunities for predation at home. In Mobutu's last years, diamonds represented almost one third of the country's formal exports, but that was only half of the story. Official diamond exports in 1995, for example, were worth $331 million. But Belgian diamond imports from the Congo that year totalled $646 million. [10]

The end for Mobutu began on 6 April 1994 when a plane carrying the presidents of Rwanda and Burundi was shot down near Kigali, the capital of Rwanda, signalling the start of the Rwandan genocide. In three months, almost a million Tutsis and moderate Hutus were dead at the hands of their Hutu neighbours. Amidst the carnage and bloodlust, the rebel Rwandese Patriotic Front stepped up its advance on Kigali. Fearing retaliation from a victorious Tutsi army, vast numbers of the Hutu population fled, more than a million men women and children crossing the borders into neighbouring countries. Almost half wound up in the Congo, in camps dominated by former Hutu generals and militia, still armed and still dangerous.

A standoff of sorts existed for over two years. Aid agencies maintained the camps, giving cover and succour to *genocidaires* and to Hutu militia who conducted armed raids across the border into Rwanda. For Mobutu it must have been a bewildering time. As his own resources and power ebbed against the backdrop of his pillage and his defunct alliances, his generals and other entrepreneurs were at last able to make their own deals with arms merchants, aid agencies and diamond smugglers. Finally, the new Rwandan government and its primary African backer, Uganda, had enough. When a group of Congolese rebel organizations announced the formation of the Alliance of Democratic Forces for the Liberation of Congo-Zaire (AFDL) at the end of 1996, Rwanda and Uganda assisted with weapons, troops, logistics and cash.

Aiming to keep whatever friends he could, Mobutu continued to provide Angola's UNITA rebels with arms, end-user certificates, transit points and other favours in return for diamonds. Inbound weapons flights from Eastern Europe regularly stopped at Kinshasa or at Mobutu's personal lair, Gbadolite, on their way to rebel-held territory in Angola. It is not surprising, therefore, that in January 1997, Angola, tired of Mobutu's continuing support for UNITA, joined the onslaught on the Helmsman. Zambia, Zimbabwe, Eritrea and Tanzania assisted as well, with weapons or staging bases for Mobutu's antagonists.

Mobutu's army, rotten to the core, fell back without engaging the rebels, looting as it retreated. The AFDL, led by long-time rebel leader Laurent-Désiré Kabila, took the diamond towns first: Kisangani in March 1997, Mbuji-Mayi in April, then Lubumbashi. In May, Western embassies contacted Kabila to urge a more rapid advance into Kinshasa, fearing a complete power vacuum and a breakdown in whatever law and order was left. Amidst the chaos, the Father of the Nation flew out. His exit was arranged by his last diamond co-conspirator, Joseph Savimbi, who sent an ancient Ilyushin cargo plane to airlift Mobutu and his grasping family to their final exile.

In his last years, Mobutu had presided over a virtually non-existent formal economy. The government printed money and raised salaries, but it collected little in the way of taxes to cover its expenses. Inflation ran at 4,500 per cent in 1993, and 10,000 per cent in 1994, levelling off at 657 per cent in 1996. When he finally left the following year, the foreign debt he had incurred stood at $12.6 billion, and two thirds of it was in arrears. Five years later, the debt remained, growing at more than $52 million a month because of unpaid interest. Like King Leopold, Mobutu had used the Congo as a personal plaything, enriching himself and his cronies. Like Leopold, he left behind a crippling debt made up of criminally thoughtless loans from 'investors' and the foreign governments and international aid agencies that had condoned and encouraged his predatory mismanagement. As in Leopold's case, ordinary Congolese citizens were somehow expected to dig themselves out of a political environment based almost entirely on corruption, and to pay back loans that had done little more than increase their misery.

Laurent Kabila, whose troops marched into Kinshasa on 15 May 1997, had begun his political career as a young, anti-Western Marxist rebel, fighting against Mobutu's army in the early 1960s. He attracted the attention of other revolutionaries and for a time was joined by Che Guevara, then on a sales mission to market Cuban-style revolution. Guevara, however, was unsuccessful in the Congo, recording in his diary his disgust with Kabila's cowardice. Others noted Kabila's predilection for women and alcohol. By the time Kabila resurfaced in the 1990s, questions of booze, women, cowardice, Marxism and anti-Western attitudes no longer arose. The world wanted only a replacement for Mobutu. Kabila's consuming interest was in power and the wealth that might be derived from it. In order to finance his march to Kinshasa, Kabila sold diamond and other mineral concessions left, right and centre, signing contracts with companies as eager for profits as himself. One such arrangement gave America Mineral Fields important cobalt and diamond concessions. A lot of cash and Kabila's use of a company plane helped clinch the contract.

In power, however, Kabila renounced that deal and many others, as well as all of the mining agreements made by Mobutu in his final scramble for cash. New deals and new concessions would, after all, yield new income. But they would not yield much in the way of investor confidence. Plans for an independent central bank were soon cancelled, and currency reform collapsed. As before, money was printed rather than earned. Relatives, cronies and former Mobutu henchmen were appointed to key positions, and political parties were banned. Kabila scrapped all references to 'Zaire', re-christening the country the Democratic Republic of the Congo. And he junked Mobutu's green flag, bringing back a version of King Leopold's yellow star on an azure banner.

Kabila soon learned that name changes, currency manipulation and extortion have their limitations, especially in an economy where there is only one hard and fast currency, diamonds. And so his attention turned, as had Mobutu's, to that one constant. In 1998 he began a series of 'reforms' in the diamond sector, aimed at increasing his control and the revenues that would derive from it. He banned foreigners from diamond mining areas and he required traders to pay a $25,000 performance bond along with their taxes – in advance. He required dealers to sell through a Kinshasa bourse, which had a membership fee of $3 million. He halted the sale of diamonds in anything but the local currency, which was all but worthless. The outcome was as swift as it was predictable. Diamond sales through official channels dropped by one third, from $451 million in 1998, to only $290 million in 1999. At the same time, other exports fell even more dramatically. As a result, the collapsing diamond sector actually represented a higher proportion of national exports in 1999 than it had in 1998. Something had to be done.

Flailing about for a solution, Kabila hit on an idea that made matters even worse. In 2000, his government revoked all previous diamond export arrangements and awarded a diamond export monopoly to a single company, the subsidiary of an Israeli firm, International Diamond Industries (IDI). Large sums of money changed hands, and Kabila's Minister of Mines enthused about the new arrangement: 'This is the optimum way for the Congo diamond production to be marketed in a transparent manner that will inspire trust and confidence...'[11] It did nothing of the sort, possibly because IDI knew that it would have a matter of months, if that, to make its investment back before the government changed its mind yet again. One of the few ways of doing that was to squeeze as much profit as possible out of the price it paid for diamonds. In a monopoly situation, it would have been possible for IDI, theoretically, to reduce the purchase price significantly. But given the levels of corruption in the wider diamond world, given the levels of corruption in the Congo, given the porosity of African borders, and given the constant demand and steady world price for good gemstones, the only real monopoly game in the diamond industry was run by De Beers, not IDI.

The day the IDI arrangement came into effect, already depressed Congolese diamond exports plummeted. Depending on whether you believe the statistics of the Central Bank or the official diamond exporting body, exports fell from a monthly average of $20 million to either $3.7 million or zero. Congolese diamond imports into Belgium – always significantly different in volume for a variety of reasons, including smuggling and false invoicing – dropped by half, from $50 million in September to $24.6 million in November. While the Belgian import and Congolese export figures bear no resemblance to each other – a result of massive corruption at both ends of the chain – they indicate what happened when Kabila introduced his monopoly: it simply flushed the diamonds into other streams.

The closest and most accessible was a short boat ride away, directly across the Congo River from Kinshasa, in the capital of the Republic of Congo, Brazzaville. Once the hub of French Equatorial Africa, Brazzaville had become the capital of an under-populated, mineral-poor country that was destined to spend part of its post-independence years under a Marxist regime which imported Cubans, Russians, North Koreans and a lot of red bunting. Left in destitution after 80 years of French colonial rule, Congo-B saw nothing in diamonds, if not opportunity. Like Monrovia's role in laundering Sierra Leonean diamonds, Brazzaville provided a useful outlet for buyers and sellers of diamonds emanating from the other side of the river. By the 1990s, this small country with almost no diamonds of its own had become a source of huge volumes of gems. In 1996 it actually accounted for one tenth of the entire world diamond production. While Mobutu might have thought himself lucky to be able to export $347 million worth of diamonds officially that year, Belgium actually imported almost twice that value – $612 million worth – from tiny, penurious, diamond-free Brazzaville.

With the arrival of Kabila, official exports from Kinshasa picked up momentarily, until the new president began implementing his larcenous policies. In 1998 and 1999, Belgium imported very few diamonds from Brazzaville, but when the IDI monopoly was negotiated, the impact was immediate. In August 2000, the value of Brazzaville diamonds imported into Belgium was zero. The following month, when the IDI monopoly went into effect, it jumped to $18 million, and the month after that it doubled to almost $40 million.

As noted elsewhere, all of these statistics must be consumed with more than a grain of salt, as none is reliable except as a general indicator of corruption and predation. What the statistics also demonstrate is that nothing could stem the flow of diamonds to the waiting arms of the international diamond industry, the showrooms of Cartier, Tiffany and Zales, and the fingers of millions of fiancées throughout the industrialized world. The statistics were never hidden, and it was no secret to the diamond industry that major exporting countries like Liberia and the Republic of Congo produced no diamonds worthy of the name. The traders who bought diamonds from these impoverished developing countries knew beyond doubt they were dealing in goods that were stolen, smuggled or used for tax evasion. Belgian import authorities and those in other countries like Israel and the United States had to know they were aiding and abetting corruption and criminal behaviour. The World Bank, the IMF, other lenders and donor agencies examining the national accounts of these countries also knew that something was wrong. And yet nobody said a word about it. Ever.

And because nobody said or did anything, the diamond industry sank further into squalor and corruption. Other countries, seeing the industry's lack of interest and control, decided this was a bandwagon worth boarding. Only fifteen months after assuming the Congolese presidency, Kabila found himself in a proxy fight with his erstwhile allies, Rwanda and Uganda. Dismayed by Kabila's acceptance of Hutu extremists into his new army, Rwandan army units attempted a coup in Kinshasa and then retreated to offer their support to new rebel movements that had sprung up, determined to topple Kabila. Kabila called on Zimbabwe and Angola for assistance, and once again the country was at war. The initial motivation on all sides had to do with security. Having rid themselves of Mobutu, Uganda and Rwanda were not prepared to see Kabila support *genocidaires* in the Congo. Zimbabwe used the Southern Africa Development Community security pact as its justification for supporting a member nation against rebel armies. And Angola supported Kabila because UNITA had fallen into bed with one of the rebel movements, the *Rassemblement Congolais pour la démocratie* (RCD), laundering Angolan diamonds out of Kisangani as though they had been mined in the Congo. But all of these countries were soon deeply engaged in mineral exploitation.

Resources have always been of interest to invading armies. Caesar's legions carried the riches of the known world back to Rome. Napoleon's armies did the same for France. Some of the fiercest fighting during World War II focused on the oil fields of the Caucasus, and the first Gulf War was almost exclusively about oil. Colonialism was founded on resources available for the taking across far-flung empires. So it is not surprising that African armies sent to 'help' a neighbour might become involved in more mercenary activities.

The armies that allied themselves with Kabila and those that sided with his enemies were no different. During 1998 and 1999, the phenomenon was more chaotic than organized. A UN expert panel described the approach: 'Between September 1998 and August 1999, occupied zones of the Democratic Republic of the Congo were drained of existing stockpiles, including minerals, agricultural and forest products and livestock. Regardless of the looter, the pattern was the same: Burundian, Rwandan, Ugandan and/or RCD [rebel] soldiers, commanded by an officer, visited farms, storage facilities, factories and banks, and demanded that managers open the coffers and doors. The soldiers were then ordered to remove the relevant products and load them into vehicles.'[12] By the middle of 1999, the methodology was becoming more systematic, more targeted, and considerably more sophisticated. Both Rwanda and Uganda set their sights on the diamond town of Kisangani, often clashing with each other directly, or through the various rebel movements that acted as their proxies, shifting allegiance at the drop of a diamond. The cost to Congolese civilians was enormous.

Uganda and Rwanda both appointed 'governors' of the territories they occupied, and a welter of small air cargo companies emerged to ferry loot back to Kigali and Entebbe. Many of these companies, and the banks that sprang up in Kigali and Kisangani, had owners or shareholders closely related by blood or politics to the Presidents of Uganda and Rwanda. And they taxed the 'exports' of their allies, the rebel movements fighting against Kabila. The *Rassemblement Congolais pour la Démocratie* (RCD) was headed by strongman Jean-Pierre Bemba, whose father had been a cabinet minister in Mobutu's government and then in Kabila's. In 2000 the RCD attempted to demonstrate its capacity for governance by keeping records of what it exported, recording diamond shipments by five companies worth almost four million dollars. Three companies exported gold, and eleven were involved in shipping out coltan. Coltan – columbite-tantalite – is a metal ore in high demand because of its excellent conductivity from the communications and aerospace industries. Coltan-based capacitors are used in most cell phones, laptops and pagers, and at one point during the war it was fetching $400 per kilogram. Over one 18-month period, Rwanda exported $250 million worth of coltan, a mineral not found within its borders.

The diamond records, like all records in the Congo, represent only the tip of an iceberg, with the most realistic 1999 estimates of stones moving through Kisangani pegged at $70 million.[13] The volume would probably have been even higher had Ugandan and Rwandan forces not clashed three times in a single year for control of the diamond fields, eventually dividing the territory and the booty. Both countries were recorded as the source of several million dollars worth of diamonds entering Belgium each year between 1998 and 2001, even though neither country produced diamonds of its own, and neither had what could be called a 'legitimate' diamond business.

Perhaps the most cynical of the looters was Zimbabwe, which had helped Kabila to power, staying with him through his many travails. The help came with a price tag, however. One part of the deal was a $53 million commercial contract between Kabila and Zimbabwe Defence Industries for military equipment and supplies. Another was the supply of Congolese power from the Inga hydroelectric dam, used to resuscitate ailing Zimbabwean industries and paid for in fast-declining Zimbabwe dollars, a significant boon for a debt-ridden economy in serious economic trouble. Congolese copper was shipped out to stoke Zimbabwe's smelters, and the head of the Zimbabwean army, General Vitalis Zvinavashe, obtained military contracts from the Kabila government for his own trucking firm. Diamonds, however, were on everyone's mind. General Zvinavashe and Job Whabira, Permanent Secretary in Zimbabwe's Ministry of Defence, along with the heads of two Zimbabwean parastatals, formed a company they named Operation Sovereign Legitimacy (OSLEG), as if just one of the words – 'sovereign' or 'legitimacy' – was not enough to cover the larceny. The supposed goal was to make the Zimbabwean military operation in the Congo financially sustainable, a completely new approach to military plunder. Zimbabwe's Defence Minister, Moven Mohachi, explained it this way: 'We saw this as a noble option. Instead of our army in Congo burdening the treasury for more resources, which are not available, it embarks on viable projects for the sake of generating the necessary revenue.'[14] The noble option was extended, arranging with COMIEX, a Congolese parastatal, under the name of COSLEG, to export millions of dollars a month worth of diamonds.

Because it had neither the capital nor the expertise to exploit the available mining concessions, however, COSLEG went into partnership with a subsidiary of Oryx Natural Resources Ltd., a company registered in the Cayman Islands. According to a UN Expert Panel, together they formed a company named Sengamines, which obtained the rights to two of the Congo's richest diamond concessions, previously owned by MIBA, without due regard for legal requirements.[15] This was essentially a payback from Kabila to Zimbabwe for its military assistance. Oryx, which had a chequered career of lawsuits against its detractors, was accused in 2002 by the UN Expert Panel of being a front for Zimbabwean military investments in the Congo. It was, *inter alia*, said to be laundering diamonds from Sierra Leone and Angola, and smuggling diamonds out of the Congo. In response, Oryx invited the UN Panel to repeat the allegations in a public forum, beyond the legal protection offered by the UN. It said that the allegations were 'completely baseless' and it went on to state that the company had 'a strong commitment to helping local communities by building schools, roads, and bridges. It provides fresh water, donates food and anti-malaria drugs, and is working with the World Health Organization to develop a tsetse fly eradication program.'[16]

Like King Leopold and Oryx, many, it seems, went to the Congo only to do good. And some of them did very well. In fact Oryx had little commitment to anything and within a couple of years it had vanished. Namibia, which along with Zimbabwe provided Kabila with military support, was another do-gooder. Although the Namibian government denied allegation for two years, it was finally forced to admit in 2001 that a Namibian firm – 'August 26 Holding Congo' – was exploring for diamonds in Tshikapa. August 26 Holding Congo was a subsidiary of a Namibian parastatal, formed under the 1990 Namibian Defence Act by the Ministry of Defence.

Further north, the Central African Republic (CAR) was also involved in a diamond laundering scheme of considerable complexity. The government of Ange-Félix Patassé, who became president of the country in 1993, was insecure from the start, surviving various uprisings and coup attempts over the following decade, and finally succumbing to a military takeover in 2003. Although nominally supportive of the Kabila government, Patassé's regime owed its survival during intense fighting in 2001 to an intervention by Jean-Pierre Bemba's new rebel alliance, the *Mouvement de libération du Congo* (MLC). Bemba purchased supplies in and through Patassé's capital, Bangui, paying in whatever form of currency he could dig up. The obvious result was a considerable difference between official CAR diamond exports – in the neighbourhood of $90 million per annum – and imports into Belgium from Bangui, which averaged as much as $150 and $200 million a year between 1995 and 2001. In 2000, official exports totalled 461,000 carats, while importers in Antwerp and elsewhere racked up imports from the CAR of 1.3 million carats.

The haemorrhage of diamonds out of the Congo (and sometimes into the Congo from Angola) must have been as big a disappointment to Laurent Kabila as his failure to get a serious grip on the political, military and economic affairs of the country. Having studied the Helmsman at a distance for so long, he may have thought it was going to be easier than turned out to be the case. Kabila had another surprise coming to him: just 32 months after his army had entered Kinshasa, he was shot dead, under circumstances that to this day remain unclear.

Kabila's son, Joseph, became President of the Congo on the death of his father in January 2001. As before, negotiations, rebel alliances and foreign intrigues shifted and changed, re-forming like clouds in a summer sky. The likelihood of any peaceful power sharing seemed as remote as it ever had throughout the Congo's tragic and bloody history, with complete meltdown forestalled only by the arrival of a UN peacekeeping force, ramped up to almost 19,000 troops and civilians by 2005.

In March 2001, an American humanitarian organization, the International Rescue Committee, released a report that was eerily reminiscent of a 1919 enquiry conducted by the Belgian government. The 1919 report estimated that some ten million people had died during the first 40 years of Belgian association with the Congo. The IRC estimated that in a 32 month period between August 1998 and March 2001, 2.5 million more people died than would have been the case under normal circumstances. Most of the deaths resulted from disease and malnutrition brought on by the fighting, although 350,000 people had been killed in the conflict. The IRC knew that the numbers it presented were so high that they would invite scepticism. 'Nonetheless,' the report stated, 'the statistics... are based on a survey that was carefully conducted by a widely respected epidemiologist following rigorous scientific procedures. And while the exact precision of the numbers may be subject to discussion, there can be no doubt that the survey reveals a humanitarian crisis of staggering proportions.'[17] In April 2003 they issued a new report, boosting the number to 3.3 million, and in January 2008 they revised the numbers upward again, to 5.4 million deaths – the worst human calamity since World War II.[18]

Leopold's ghost, burning in hell for the theft and amputations, the massacres and misery he visited upon the Congo, must be crying out in three part harmony with the ghosts of Mobutu Sese Seko and Laurent Kabila. If there is justice in the netherworld, the three of them surely have an enormous backup choir of cronies, enablers and 'business partners' – those who encouraged and made deals with them, those who loaned them money, those who bought their misappropriated rubber, their copper, their cobalt and their coltan. And their diamonds.

CHAPTER 9

ENTER AL QAEDA

We Shi'a have nothing in common with these crazies [Hezbollah] – we drink whiskey, gamble and enjoy life – it's just a few young idiots and some deal-makers who should know better. Why should we want to fight the Jews? Because Tehran tells us to? Who the hell do they think we're selling our diamonds to?

– Lebanese Diamond Dealer in Sierra Leone[1]

Being a 'UN Expert' is no simple thing. Towards the end of my six-month stint on the UN Expert Panel that examined the connection between diamonds and war in Sierra Leone, I began to think we should title our report to the Security Council, 'Everyone is Lying'. Our five-person panel travelled together, in smaller groups, and individually to a dozen countries in Africa, to the Ukraine, Dubai, India and all across Europe in search of illicit diamonds, the people who bought and sold them, and their connection to guns, sanctions-busting and war. The trail was winding, badly marked, and it often had to be traversed in utter darkness. Many times a promising lead would simply gutter out, a dead-end of wasted time, effort and plane tickets.

In September 2000, in a dingy office at Sierra Leone's Defence Headquarters, I interviewed a number of intelligence officers about the RUF, the progress of the war, and diamonds. The conversation was like many – wary and anecdotal, without much new information. Then, someone spoke out of turn. A young officer revealed that he had been with the RUF for several months at their headquarters at Buedu. His position had been overrun, and to save himself, he pretended to join them. Eventually they trusted him, and he had access to all of the top leaders: Issa Sesay, Ibrahim Bah (a 'real general' from Burkina Faso) and a woman named Isatu Kallon, whose nickname was 'Sensitive'.

In the early RUF days, according to the officer, Issa Sesay gathered diamonds from various digging sites and gave them to Sensitive for transmission to Guinea, Liberia and Côte d'Ivoire. For a time, another woman named Monica ('who had a beautiful voice') was Charles Taylor's diamond representative in Kono District. Colonel 'Jungle Jabba', Dennis 'Superman' Mingo and a dozen others moved in and out of the camp. Amidst all this, the soldier told me that he had been with the RUF general, Sam 'Maskita' Bockarie, on various occasions when he had spoken by satellite phone with someone far away named 'Carlos'. Bockarie asked Carlos repeatedly about weapons, promising diamonds in return. Carlos, the man with the guns, was thus a direct link between diamonds and weapons trafficking. It was important to learn his real identity. 'Maybe he was an American,' the soldier said. He spoke 'with an accent' – not much of a clue in a world where everyone speaks with some kind of accent. Carlos had planned to visit Buedu and did make it to Monrovia, apparently on a private jet. He then travelled to Gbarnga, Charles Taylor's up-country lair and the jumping-off spot for weapons deliveries to the RUF. Carlos brought the weapons, and he left with diamonds. That was all the young soldier knew. But no additional amount of questioning in Freetown, or later in Monrovia, shed any more light on the mysterious Carlos.

At the time, the US television program 60 *Minutes* was planning a segment on diamonds, and our Panel had run into two of the producers on various occasions – in Pretoria, Freetown and London. For UN inspectors, dealing with the media can be a tricky business. Journalists want 'the story', and they want it now, and we had been warned to be very careful in anything we said to reporters. But good journalists were often ahead of us on the trail and they could provide important markers. This happened accidentally in a casual conversation with one of the 60 *Minutes* producers, when the name Nicholas Karras cropped up. I had never heard of him, but I immediately put two and two together: Carlos; Karras! West Africans too, speak 'with an accent', and it would have been easy for the soldier or for me to get the names mixed up.

I was in Jerusalem interviewing diamantaires, Israeli government officials and assorted soldiers of fortune when I obtained a cell phone number in London for Karras. I made a cold call. Maybe he took the call because it was from Israel; maybe he agreed to meet me a week later in London because I was 'from the Security Council'. Whatever the reason, we met on a perfect George Smiley kind of night: cold, rainy and dark (it was night, after all). He wanted to meet at his 'club' – the 9th floor Peak Club at the Carlton Towers Hotel in Kensington, because he wanted a public place where his security people could 'keep an eye on things'. Like me, I supposed. One of his bodyguards intercepted me as I entered the club, and another watched from a gallery above as Karras and I talked.

Nicholas Karras, a heavy-set American somewhere in his late 40s, told me he was president of Anaconda Worldwide Ltd – 'Mining Precious Commodities' it said on his card – headquartered in London, with an office in South Africa. He said he had been working intensively in Sierra Leone for a couple of years, and he placed a lot of emphasis on his philanthropic efforts there – support for hospitals, computers for school kids and such like. He said he was providing diamond miners with equipment and supplies, and he worked with chiefs in several villages where diamonds were mined. He said he had assisted senior government people with plane tickets so they could travel to Europe on business, 'repair their cars' and so on. He did not provide cash, and where his charitable work was concerned, he always gave it directly, 'not through the government'.

The conversation was largely one-sided as he rambled from tales of his good works to the subject of diamonds, war and bad publicity. He said he had 'never, never' been in Liberia, hated the RUF, had never dealt in weapons, and was increasingly nervous about growing attention to his efforts to corner the diamond market in Sierra Leone. He had already made one shipment of diamonds under the country's new certification system, and this had attracted unwanted media queries. He spoke about offers from De Beers and said that *Esquire* was doing an article on him for the January 2001 issue. He said the RUF were bandits and criminals. He said he had 'a deep regard for Sierra Leoneans, and really wanted to help'. Speculating on how the RUF might get diamonds out of Sierra Leone or Liberia, he said it would be simple: just find a buyer – like himself. Anyone could do it. The industry is so porous, and there are so many buyers, that diamonds can be moved around the world with almost complete impunity – to London, Antwerp, Israel, New York. 'It has always been like that.' He talked of his own trips – buying rough in Africa and mixing parcels in toilets on aircraft bound for Europe.

I walked through the dark, rain-swept streets of Kensington none the wiser as to whether Karras and Carlos were the same. Karras had not provided any confidence one way or the other, but I felt the trail was cooling. Six weeks later, when the *Esquire* story appeared, the trail changed again. In 'The Opportunist', author John Richardson flayed Karras alive, but not for dealing in weapons.

'There is a certain kind of man who, in unspeakable human suffering and chaos, sees an opportunity to make himself rich. Take, for instance, the diamond war of Sierra Leone. Nick Karras couldn't get there fast enough.' For some odd reason, Karras had allowed Richardson to travel with him on a rented Lear jet from South Africa to Sierra Leone and to watch as he threw money around among airport customs officials, met with government ministers, mercenaries and whores, and worked his dubious diamond deals. Karras 'sits back with his big belly bulging into his silk polo shirt, with the fat silver Dunhill pen and the Bulgari watch and the Tiffany bracelet that comes with its own gold screwdriver, and it's no surprise that he had his first heart attack at thirty-two – while working three phones from a barstool. "I want to be king," he says, cupping his balls.'

King, maybe, but of what? In his stream of consciousness Karras rambles for Richardson as he did for me, from boasts about his donations of computers and medical equipment, to the war and a view of Sierra Leoneans that he certainly could not have wanted to appear in *Esquire*: 'Think of them as hairless monkeys, it makes them easier to kill.' Blood on the diamonds? 'Yeah, but it washes right off,' he laughs, repeating the line. *Esquire* had not been on the stands more than two days when the head of the World Diamond Council wrote to the Editor, David Granger, to complain that the Richardson article was 'in no way a fair representation of the diamond industry at large'. Nick Karras, he said, 'is not typical of the diamond industry.'[2]

He might not have been typical of the industry as a whole, but he was typical of a kind of dealer that was all too common in the diamond universe we were discovering. Did Karras's dark side, however, extend further than diamonds – to guns? In a Hollywood world it might, but in the world we were investigating there was no obvious motive. Karras could get all the diamonds he wanted, and make whatever money might be left over after paying for his rented Lear jet and his Tiffany bracelets without going into the weapons trade. And it was unlikely that such a chatterbox would last more than fifteen minutes in a weapons world dominated by Russian mafiosi well versed in avoiding the prying eyes of police, UN inspectors and writers from *Esquire*.

Carlos, in fact, turned out to be the nickname of someone completely different: he was a Lebanese citizen named Mohammed Jamil Derbah who had, with a large clan of relatives in the Canary Islands, developed a lucrative criminal and gun running operation, courtesy, in part, of Russian mafia operating from southern Tenerife.[3] Russians shipped weapons to the Canaries, and Derbah sent them on to Africa. By the late 1990s, he had become a purveyor of arms to Charles Taylor, and was selling diamonds out of Spain. According to Spanish police, Derbah's weapons shipments included automatic rifles, assault rifles, sub-machine guns, pistols, revolvers and ammunition. Derbah also ran a lucrative time-share fraud, along with extortion, credit card forgery, and money laundering said to be worth over $10 million a year at its peak. Derbah was finally snared in the rush to capture al Qaeda suspects in the immediate post-9/11 worldwide police crackdown. His arrest came in the wake of a two-year investigation into his criminal activities and an alleged connection with Hezbollah and the pro-Syrian Shi'ite AMAL faction in Lebanon – a connection later denied by Hezbollah. Derbah was subsequently named in a UN Security Council report at the end of 2002 for alleged links to al Qaeda.[4]

The story returns to 'Carlos' Derbah shortly. But first, a detour into the huge Lebanese Diaspora that has settled all along the coast of West Africa, from the Canaries to South Africa. The first Lebanese arrived in West Africa at the end of the 19th century. For hundreds of years Lebanese silk had been prized in Europe, but the industry grew especially rapidly during the 1840s. It was a boom-and-bust business, however, and there were collapses in 1877 and again in 1888 as a result of silkworm disease, growing mechanization and quality control problems. Recession in the silk industry, growing population pressures in Lebanon, and the collapse of the Ottoman Empire created waves of Lebanese emigration to North and South America, and eventually to West Africa.

The first Lebanese Maronite Christians arrived in Freetown in 1893. They were soon followed and overtaken in number by Shi'ites from South Lebanon, escaping their own population pressures and agricultural downturns. Gradually, Lebanese families moved further south, to Côte d'Ivoire, Ghana, Nigeria and the Congo. Today there are an estimated 100,000 Lebanese in Côte d'Ivoire, and some 20,000 in Sierra Leone. There, the Lebanese quickly displaced the Creoles as commercial middlemen, making their way up-country and soon dominating the trade in agricultural produce and dry goods, along with much of the retail trade in Freetown. With the building of feeder roads, the Lebanese came to dominate the transportation industry as well, and when diamonds were discovered in Kono District in 1930, the first colonial officials posted to the area found that a Lebanese shopkeeper had already been there for two years.

When the Sierra Leone Selection Trust (SLST) established its monopoly on diamond mining throughout the country in 1935, it should have put an end to Lebanese interest in minerals. But it did not. Because the alluvial diamonds were so easy to mine and so hard to police over such a wide area, the Lebanese became the most obvious alternative to a British company that offered few jobs and low pay. The Lebanese were also an obvious vehicle for moving illicit diamonds out of the country. They had ready cash, a wide network of shops that could double as buying offices, and on top of a secret language (Arabic), they had a wide network of friends and relatives throughout the country and across the region.

By the early 1950s, the smuggling of diamonds from Sierra Leone had reached epic, multimillion dollar proportions, with near anarchy in the diamond fields and a haemorrhage of potential tax revenue that the colony could ill afford. The story of Sir Percy Sillitoe and the creation of the International Diamond Security Organization is told in Chapter 1. Although the cloak-and-dagger operation along the border between Liberia and Sierra Leone had dramatic appeal, the real solution to smuggling then, as now, was economic. In 1955 the SLST lease was reduced to 450 square miles in return for, 1.6 million in compensation. And the following year an Alluvial Mining Scheme was introduced, which legalized the mining of diamonds by ordinary Sierra Leoneans outside the SLST lease areas. Mining licences were issued only to Sierra Leoneans, but dealer's licenses were open to all, and soon much of the legal diamond trade beyond the SLST lease was dominated by the Lebanese. Even inside the lease, illicit digging continued, and these diamonds too needed an outlet. Lebanese dealers were the most obvious avenue.

Siaka Stevens became head of government in 1968, and soon set about dismantling all formal diamond arrangements. In 1971 he created the National Diamond Mining Company, buying 51 per cent of SLST's shares and effectively nationalizing the diamond industry. His closest ally in what he did next was an Afro-Lebanese named Jamil Sahid Mohamed. By 1988 Jamil was the country's diamond czar, although officially, the industry had simply vanished. From exports of two million carats a year when Stevens took power, official exports had dropped to only 48,000 carats by 1988. As much as $400 million worth of Sierra Leone's best diamonds were now submarined out of the country each year, lining the pockets of Jamil and his network of thieves, as well as the President and *his* network of thieves.

The Lebanese civil war that raged between 1975 and 1992 had a profound effect on the Lebanese Diaspora and on the diamond industry in West Africa. The changes were manifested at the top of the political chain, as well as at the bottom. Jamil, a Shi'ite, had been a childhood friend of Nabih Berri, another Sierra Leone-born Lebanese who had moved to Lebanon where he became leader of the armed AMAL faction.* Jamil had large investments in Lebanon, and Berri helped him obtain a Lebanese passport. Jamil reciprocated by assisting AMAL in its fundraising efforts. By 1980, AMAL had become the most powerful of the Shi'ite militia, and following the Israeli invasion of Lebanon in 1982, it was used by Syria to push the US-led multinational force out of Lebanon, weakening the Lebanese state and forcing it to cancel an agreement with Israel. Berri and his AMAL colleagues leaned on their compatriots in Africa for financial support. According to one writer, Lebanese expatiates in Côte d'Ivoire were required to help in sharing the burden. 'As in Beirut itself, the youngest members of the community are recruited to collect these dues while immigrants are continuously having the good fortune of their immunity from the war impressed on them, and their moral obligation to make at least a financial contribution to national liberation or to the new Lebanon.'[5] The same was true in Sierra Leone; a Shi'ite diamond dealer in Kenema explains how it worked:

> Maybe every two or three months or so, [a Kenema Lebanese community leader] would call small groups of us around to his house. Firstly, he would give us a report on how things were going for AMAL back in Lebanon; you know, what Berri was doing and whether ground was being lost or gained... Then we would all sit down and talk about contributions – everyone pretty well knows how everyone is doing – so [the community leader] knew how much everyone could afford. It was just a small percentage of monthly earnings – if people were in the shit they didn't have to pay – it was no problem. You know, nobody ever complained, in fact everyone I knew was happy to help – it was for our people back in Lebanon and we all wanted them looked after. I just used to send parcels [of diamonds]; what happened to them I don't know – either they were sold for cash in Antwerp or Lebanon or Israel or whatever, it wasn't my problem – I knew that the matter was in good hands.'[6]

---

* AMAL is an acronym for *Afwaj al Muqawama al Lubnaniya*, ('Lebanese Resistance Detachments').

The tactic was not unique to Ivory Coast or Sierra Leone: AMAL was raising funds in the same way in Liberia, Angola, Namibia, South Africa, Guinea, Zimbabwe, the Congo and elsewhere. The pressure sometimes developed into a protection racket, with gangs attacking the shops and businesses of the unconvinced. In West Africa, all of the Lebanese factions plied their trade – the Christian Phalange, the Druze militia and AMAL.

In 1986, Jamil was forced to flee the country, charged with plotting a coup against the new president, Joseph Momoh. This heralded the arrival of the small-time Israeli crooks and the Russian mafia described in Chapter 7. But through it all, the Lebanese diamond dealers in Sierra Leone barely skipped a beat. The little Lebanese shops selling cloth and hardware and tinned goods in Koidu and Bo and along Hanga Road in Kenema continued to buy diamonds, shipping them out through friends and family who paid whatever 'taxes' or protection was necessary in Freetown, or through friends and family across the borders in Guinea and Liberia.

Things were about to turn considerably more dangerous, however. Hezbollah – Hizb Allah, the Party of God – was created in Lebanon by disenfranchised and disillusioned Shi'ites in 1982 when Israel invaded Beirut and Southern Lebanon in an effort to destroy the PLO. Here too, Jamil had assisted. With Berri's help, he had made contacts with Iran, a major backer of Hezbollah, and he helped in having an Iranian diplomatic mission established in Freetown in 1983. When the first Iranian ambassador arrived, he was greeted at the airport not by government officials, but by Jamil.[7] In return for loans, Iranian oil and other considerations, the all-but-bankrupt government allowed the new embassy to become the centre of Iranian operations in West Africa. During the mid 1980s, backed by Iran and Syria, Hezbollah grew. It conducted a series of major operations against American and Israeli targets – bombing a US Marine barracks and the US embassy in Beirut, and finally forcing a Western withdrawal from Lebanon. It was involved in kidnapping westerners through the rest of the civil war, and was largely responsible for forcing the Israeli withdrawal in 2000 from its last positions in Lebanon. It has subsequently become a political party with representation in the Lebanese parliament, and it enjoys great support throughout the Middle East for its purist Muslim views. Although it denounced the 9/11 terrorist attacks on the United States, the American government maintains that Hezbollah is a terrorist organization, with links to al Qaeda.

More purist and more secretive than AMAL, Hezbollah too raised funds throughout the Lebanese Diaspora, making deals wherever it could. A Belgian military intelligence report identified several Lebanese diamond traders said to have links to Hezbollah.[8] One was Imad Bakri, sometimes known as Imad Kabir and Emad/Emat Bakir, a man also identified by the United Nations as being UNITA's primary broker for importing arms and military equipment through the Congo during the last half of the 1990s.[9] And there were other connections. Ibrahim Bah, the 'real general' from Burkina Faso was one. Bah, who worked closely with the RUF in Sierra Leone, was always the odd man out in that crowd. Ten or fifteen years older than most of Foday Sankoh's young 'commanders', he also came to the RUF from a greater distance. A Senegalese, he had trained at Muammar Gaddafi's secret *al-Mathabh al-Thauriya al-Alamiya* – World Revolutionary Headquarters – in Benghazi, where he met Foday Sankoh, Charles Taylor and other would-be heads of state. But he had also trained and fought with Hezbollah in Lebanon's Beeka Valley, and in the late 1980s he fought with Mujahidin against the Russians in Afghanistan. He fought with Charles Taylor during the 1990s, helping him to power in 1997.

In addition to being a 'real general', Bah often served as the diamond bag man for the RUF. The UN Expert Panel on Sierra Leone said that he was also known as Ibrahima/Abrahim Baldé and Baldé Ibrahima and that he was 'instrumental in the movement of RUF diamonds from Sierra Leone into Liberia, and from there to Burkina Faso.'[10] A story in the *Washington Post* shortly after 9/11, tied Bah directly to al Qaeda. Written by long-time war correspondent Doug Farah, the article said that the al Qaeda network 'reaped millions of dollars in the past three years from the sale of illicit diamonds mined by [RUF] rebels in Sierra Leone', and that Ibrahim Bah acted as 'a conduit between senior RUF commanders and the buyers from both al Qaeda and Hezbollah.'[11] It said that three al Qaeda officials, all on the FBI 'most wanted list' as suspects in the 1998 al Qaeda bombing of the US embassies in Kenya and Tanzania, had paid visits, arranged by Bah, to RUF-held areas of Sierra Leone that year and later. All of this had been facilitated, the article said, by Liberian President Charles Taylor.

The denials were fast in coming. In Sierra Leone, acting RUF leader Issa Sesay denied any connection with al Qaeda in an interview with Radio France International. 'No. No,' he said. 'We would never do business with this type of people, and I have no knowledge with that, and I have no business with them. We have nothing to do with them, you know, as far as I'm concerned with the present peace process in Sierra Leone, and even as far as talking of 1998 or 1999, we have no idea. We have no idea with being in contact with these people you're talking of. We never came across with the [?Algerians], we have no business with them, and we never worked with them. We never happened to, and we've never been in contact with these people. We never knew them and we don't know them. We have no dealing with them. We have no business with them at all, as far as I'm concerned.'[12] So angry was Charles Taylor that the *Washington Post* decided to move Farah and his family back to the United States from Abidjan, for fear of reprisals.

The diamond industry held its breath, dreading more bad news. But none appeared. Gradually, as time passed, it seemed that the story might be discounted. But former US Ambassador to Sierra Leone Joe Melrose had told a US Senate Committee the previous February about evidence that al Qaeda and Hezbollah were buying diamonds from the RUF. And Peter Hain, Britain's Minister for European Affairs made an indirect connection between al Qaeda and the RUF. He told reporters that Viktor Bout 'undoubtedly did supply al Qaeda and the Taliban with arms.'[13] An infamous gun runner and sanctions buster, Viktor Bout has been named in UN Expert Panel reports on Sierra Leone, Liberia and Angola as a weapons supplier to the RUF and UNITA rebels, as well as to Liberia's warlord president, Charles Taylor.

A year after the first report, the *Washington Post* published an even longer and more detailed Farah article.[14] According to Farah, the al Qaeda diamond operation in West Africa began in September 1998, six weeks after the bombing of the US embassies in Tanzania and Kenya, and shortly after the US had moved to freeze $240 million in Taliban and al Qaeda assets. Al Qaeda needed a way of both hiding and moving money outside normal banking structures. It had already invested in diamonds, tanzanite, rubies and other gemstones in Tanzania, and so the move into West Africa made sense. That month, a senior al Qaeda financial officer, Abdullah Ahmed Abdullah, arrived in Monrovia and was introduced by Ibrahim Bah to senior Liberian and RUF officials. Abdullah, a swarthy 35-year old Egyptian with a scar on his lower lip, was of great interest to the FBI because he was a member of al Qaeda's powerful finance committee and was suspected of having masterminded the US embassy bombings.

Another of the visitors was Fazul Abdullah Mohammed, a young computer expert born in the Comoro Islands and a veteran of the wars in Somalia. Indicted for the embassy bombings but never arrested, Mohammed is also suspected of involvement in the bombing of a Mombasa tourist hotel in 2002. He had reached such heights on the international terrorism wanted list that a mere sighting of him in Kenya was enough for the British government to halt all commercial airline flights to Nairobi in May 2003. Five years earlier, the first exchange of diamonds and cash had taken place between Abdullah Ahmed Abdullah and the RUF's Sam Bockarie.[15] The following year, Fazul Ahmed Abdullah and another al Qaeda operative spent time in both Liberia and RUF-controlled areas of Sierra Leone, travelling at will in and out of Burkina Faso and Liberia on false Yemeni passports.

In July 2000, Bah approached a company named ASA Diam about handling gems. ASA Diam was an appropriate choice. Two of its associates, Samih Ossaily and Aziz Nassour had long careers in the diamond underworld. Ossaily and Nassour were cousins, both born in Koidu, the centre of Sierra Leone's diamond area. Nassour eventually found his way into the diamond business in the DRC and Liberia, and spent time in Egypt, Lebanon and Spain where he did business with Mohammed Derbah – the infamous 'Carlos'. A UN report in October 2002 linked him directly to a clan of Lebanese criminals operating in the Congo:

The Panel has documents showing that three 'clans' of Lebanese origin, who operate licensed diamond businesses in Antwerp, purchased diamonds from the Democratic Republic of the Congo worth $150 million in 2001, either directly through Kinshasa or through *comptoirs* in the [neighbouring] Republic of the Congo. The three 'clans' – Ahmad, Nassour and Khanafer – are distinct criminal organizations that operate internationally. Their activities, known to intelligence services and police organizations, include counterfeiting, money-laundering and diamond smuggling. Several credible sources have reported that the clans also have ties with AMAL and Hezbollah. Some businesses associated with the clans are Sierra Gem Diamonds, ASA Diam, Triple A Diamonds and Echogem.[16]

According to the *Washington Post*, Nassour's cousin Ossaily and another Lebanese diamond dealer, Ali Darwish, met the al Qaeda operatives in Monrovia in December 2000, and along with several RUF commanders travelled to Sierra Leone to inspect the goods. Back in Monrovia just after New Year's Day 2001, a courier handed $300,000 over to Ibrahim Bah for the shipment. Meanwhile, at the ASA Diam offices in Antwerp, someone was running up phone bills to Afghanistan, Pakistan, Iran and Iraq. And ASA

Diam phone records showed that in the first five months of 2001, there were 31 hours of calls to Liberia. In January alone, Ibrahim Bah was called nine times and Issa Sesay 17 times.[17] According to a European intelligence report, Nassour flew from Beirut to Dubai in July 2001 where he picked up $1 million in cash. From there he went to Burkina Faso where the report says that two al Qaeda operatives were staying in the compound of President Compaoré in the Zone du Bois district. Nassour then flew on to Monrovia where he is reported to have given the $1 million to Charles Taylor to hide the two al Qaeda operatives at a military camp near Taylor's private farm.

During the same month, Issa Sesay, the RUF's acting leader – soon to issue the grovelling denials quoted above – allegedly wrote a letter to Charles Taylor saying, 'We have agreed to sell all of our diamonds to Mr Aziz Nassour through your offices'. He reminded Taylor that Nassour had been introduced to the RUF by 'General Abrahim Balde [Bah] upon your recommendation'.

As late as the summer of 2002, after his cousin Samih Ossaily had been picked up in Belgium and charged with money laundering, arms dealing and trading in embargoed diamonds from Sierra Leone, Nassour was still in business. According to the British NGO, Global Witness, he delivered two shipments of weapons to Liberia and, in light of the *Washington Post* allegations, Taylor offered him sanctuary in return for investments he might make in the logging industry. Presidents Taylor and Compaoré denied all allegations. From his home in Burkina Faso, Ibrahim Bah could hardly deny that he worked with the RUF, but he said he had never heard of Osama bin Laden until 9/11. From prison, Ossaily admitted some of his bad behaviour, and Nassour acknowledged his peregrinations around West Africa and the Middle East, but denied everything connected to illegal weapons sales, bribery and an al Qaeda connection.

The stories of all this criminal behaviour were uncovered for a variety of reasons, not least, good sleuthing by Doug Farah at the *Washington Post* and by Global Witness in London. Intelligence services are notoriously chary with information, always fearful of compromising sources and holding onto secrets long past their 'best by' date. But they too contributed dribs and drabs that could be triangulated. Suspects indicted in the US Embassy bombings also provided a great deal of information at their trial in 2001. Both Ossaily and Nassour spoke at length to investigators and journalists, perhaps in hopes of lighter prison sentences, and their stories have been triangulated with those of their partner, Ali Darwish, who bubbled with information like a soapy drain.

The UN Expert Panels picked up useful information as well, although there was little coordination among them, a major failing in such an important undertaking. Like slugs crossing a path, most of the suspects left trails: telephone records, hotel registration forms, plane tickets, visa applications, computer records and notes found when they were arrested. In a memo to himself about an arms deal worth $1,067,142, Ibrahim Bah priced AK 47s at $150 each, rocket-propelled grenades and their 'lunchers' at $500 each and 400 boxes of 'ammo' at $30,000.

The diamond industry hoped against hope that these stories would go away, that they could be denounced as unsubstantiated, or that they could be dismissed as a minor irritation, a tiny problem which could be expunged with ease from an otherwise respectable trade. It would not, however, be quite that easy. Fundraisers and money launderers from al Qaeda, Hezbollah, AMAL and other organizations had simply opened the same unlocked doors as had the RUF, UNITA and Charles Taylor. They found a substance of great value that could be bought with ease, transported in small parcels, and sold through already existing back channels into an unregulated industry that asked absolutely no questions.

One of Farah's best sources was a man whose identity he was still protecting when he published a book in 2004 on the terrorist diamond connection, *Blood from Stones: The Secret Financial Network of Terror.*[18] Farah identified him only as 'CR' and he protected him because as it turned out, the man was Charles Taylor's own brother-in-law, Cindor Reeves. Others talked as well. Al White, Chief Investigator for the Sierra Leone war crimes court, said that the 9/11 Commission, which looked briefly into the al Qaeda diamond connection, 'missed the boat', failing to interview credible witnesses offered by the Court.[19] And Mike Shanklin, who headed the CIA's operations in Liberia during the 1990s, said, 'Al Qaeda, Bah, Taylor, they were there. There is no question in my mind that these people were there. They were there during the period in question. And clearly they were involved in some sort of diamond business. That's a fact.'[20]

◆

In retrospect, some of the adventures of a 'UN expert' seem comical, if not inane, although at the time it was all deadly earnest, and sometimes just deadly. On one occasion, our Expert Panel travelled up-country to Kenema, a diamond trading town in Sierra Leone not far from the front. We flew on a draughty UN helicopter, an ancient Russian MI-8 with Ukrainian pilots flying under the low-hanging clouds and not very far above the treetops. At the ruined Kenema airstrip we were greeted by dozens of bristling UN peacekeeping troops from Ghana, and we raced into town – the five of us in two jeeps, accompanied by half a dozen armoured fighting vehicles, sirens blaring, vehicle-mounted .50 calibre machine guns at the ready. At each stop we were kept in our jeeps until the perimeter was secured by gun-toting troops in blue helmets whose intention was what? To disperse crowds? Our arrival and their behaviour achieved the opposite. Within minutes of our appearance at each meeting – UNHQ, the District Commissioner's Office, Sierra Leone army HQ – we were besieged by noisy, jostling crowds. It was as though Princess Diana had arrived in some kind of thrill-starved town in Missouri.

I wanted to have a serious discussion with some of the town's Lebanese diamonds dealers, so I asked the team to fly on to the next stop and return for me before dark. As the helicopter chopped off into the distance, I realized that I was now alone with one of these dealers, a man with bad English and a face like a catfish. The enthusiastic Ghanaian troops had simply vanished. That is what I had wanted, but in the event, it seemed a little foolhardy, especially when the dealer took me to a secluded house where Lebanese diamond traders had been asked to gather. What 35 Lebanese diamond dealers were doing in a town that close to the front, at a time when Sierra Leone was exporting only $80,000 worth of diamonds a month, was something they could not explain. And my idea of a quiet, off-the-record discussion with five or six of them drowned in a noisy shouting match, as each tried to outdo the other in demands that Kofi Annan come immediately to Sierra Leone, arrest Charles Taylor and stop the war.

I was glad when the helicopter returned, not least because it had no radar, and once the sun had set all navigation was by compass and whatever the Ukrainians could see in the gathering gloom. If the day had not been so odd, if the down-market diamond dealers and cut-rate Lebanese mafiosi I met had not seemed faintly ridiculous, I'd have been hard-pressed to take what we were doing seriously. What is it Hannah Arendt said about the banality of evil? These diamond dealers, just like others I would meet in Israel and Belgium and New York, denied everything and were oblivious to the consequences of what they were doing. And like the others, they were up to their knees in blood diamonds. The difference was, these guys knew it.

CHAPTER 10

BOILING FROGS:
COMPANIES IN HOT WATER

Long-term planning in the diamond industry: What to order for lunch.

– Diamond Industry Joke

In October 2002, a UN Expert Panel investigating the illegal exploitation of resources in the Congo issued a devastating report on the activities of companies engaged in the diamond trade and other resource extraction.[1] The report documented systemic and widespread corruption in the diamond industry of the DRC, and the flagrant collusion of allied governments, notably Zimbabwe. It detailed the pillage of Congolese diamonds and other natural resources by Rwanda and Uganda. The report described bribery, asset stripping, tax fraud, sanctions busting, embezzlement, extortion, the use of stock options as kickbacks and the diversion of state funds by groups that 'closely resemble criminal organizations'. The report said that in areas controlled by the Congolese government, at least US$5 billion worth of state mining assets had been transferred to foreign companies, with no benefit to the state since 1999. It estimated that the *Armée Patriotique Rwandaise* had been 'earning' US$320 million a year from commercial operations in eastern Congo. These practices, the report said, had led to, and fuelled war, human rights abuse and the extinction of an almost inconceivable number of human lives. Citing studies by humanitarian organizations, the report said that as many as 2.5 million more people had died since the beginning of the war than would been the case had the war not occurred.

The report concluded with three lists. The first contained the names of 29 companies, most registered in Africa. Six were involved in diamond trading and three of these were based in Antwerp. So egregious and so blatant were the alleged transgressions of these companies that the report asked the Security Council to place financial restrictions on them, freezing their assets and suspending their banking facilities. A second list contained the names of 54 individuals the Panel wanted barred from all international travel and from access to money. Some were businessmen in Africa, some were arms dealers, some were serving officers in the armed forces of Uganda and Zimbabwe. The Congo's Minister of Planning and Reconstruction was on the list, as was the Chief of Military Intelligence in Uganda and the Speaker of Zimbabwe's parliament.

Earlier chapters of this book have dealt with some of these individuals and their involvement in trafficking illicit diamonds. One of them, the infamous gunrunner Viktor Bout, had been named in other UN reports as the most prominent supplier of illicit weapons to African rebel movements. The reports listed several of his aliases – Bont, Butte, Boutov, Sergitov and Vitali – along with five different passport numbers. Bout, however, continued to travel freely, if carefully. Although supposedly wanted by several governments, he continued to work in the air cargo business long after this report was released, and planes of Air Bas, a company with Bout connections, were even used by the US military for moving cargo in the early years of the Iraq war. The UN Panel's third list was of companies it considered to be in violation of OECD Guidelines for Multinational Enterprises. On this list were 85 firms, many of them very large and well known: Ashanti Goldfields, Barclays Bank, Bayer A.G., Standard Chartered Bank, Anglo American, and its kissing cousin De Beers. The reaction was as quick as it was furious, and some of it was justified.

Those on the first and second lists squealed like tires at Sebring. Oryx Natural Resources stated that the allegations against it were 'completely baseless', and dared the Panel to repeat the allegations in public, outside the protection of the United Nations. Niko Shefer, a former commodities broker who had been jailed in South Africa for fraud, and who had once represented Charles Taylor as Liberia's honorary consul, said he had not been out of southern Africa since 2000. Asked about the panel's claim that one of his companies had a 50 per cent stake in Thorntree Industries, a joint venture diamond-trading company with the Zimbabwe Defence Forces, Shefer said he never had any equity in the company. Zimbabwean Defence Force Commander General Vitalis Zvinavashe – recommended for the travel ban – said that the claims against Zimbabwe and against him were 'meaningless'. Rwandan presidential aide Theogene Rudasingwa said that reports about his country were untrue. [The Panel] 'has no factual evidence to prove we are plundering Congolese resources,' he told Reuters, despite the extensive details about Rwanda laid out in the report.[2] Ugandan Lt-Gen Salim Saleh, half brother of Ugandan President Museveni, denied charges against him. 'I have accounts in London and Geneva,' Saleh said. 'I can assure the world that they don't hold more than $10,000.' Regarding claims that he looted diamonds from the DRC, he said, 'I have never done anything like that. But why,' he added, perhaps tellingly, 'should Antwerp be the diamond market of the world when they don't even have a mine? As Africans we should be selling our own diamonds and other resources.' He neglected to mention that Uganda and Rwanda, like Antwerp, 'don't even have a mine'.[3]

A Belgian Senate Parliamentary Commission of Inquiry investigating the exploitation of natural resources in the DRC concluded in 2003 that no illegal acts were committed by the people and companies it investigated. The commission had been established after an earlier UN report had criticized Belgian companies, and the commission examined the new charges as well. Despite the outrage of opposition senators at the apparent whitewash, a spokesman for the commission said that 'the boundary between moral and immoral, legal and illegal is not obvious.'[4] Or at least the boundary was not obvious to some Belgian senators.

The third list in the UN report was more problematic because the transgressions of most of the companies named were not detailed in the report, and so most had no idea what they were being accused of. This was not the case with a Canadian firm, First Quantum Minerals Ltd., which was accused of attempting to buy access to Kolwezi copper and cobalt tailings by making cash payments and holding shares in trust for government officials. Four officials were named and the Panel said that it had 'extensive documentation' on the case.[5] This did not stop First Quantum from saying that 'all allegations included or implied within the report are categorically refuted.' For many of the companies, however, the most galling thing, apart from the embarrassment, was the fact that they had never even heard of the OECD Guidelines on Multinational Corporations.

The OECD, the Organisation for Economic Co-operation and Development, is hardly a household name but in some ways it carries more clout than the United Nations. Its 31 member states include all of the Western industrialized countries of Europe and North America, as well as Japan, Korea, Mexico, Turkey and a growing number of former East Bloc nations. OECD agreements aim at coordinating domestic and international policies – labour and the environment, codes for the free flow of capital and services, and agreements that aim to clarify the impact of national policies on the international community. In the 1970s, amidst international clamour about the growth in size and power of transnational corporations, the OECD developed its 'Guidelines for Multinational Enterprises'. Refined over the years, the guidelines encourage 'high standards' and 'best practices' in corporate behaviour, practices that 'contribute to economic, social and environmental progress with a view to achieving sustainable development.' Of particular relevance to the diamond trade is its section on disclosure, which calls on companies to provide 'timely, regular, reliable and relevant information' on their ownership, their financial position and performance, and 'foreseeable risk factors'. Companies are enjoined from establishing output restrictions and quotas, and from price fixing – mother's milk to some parts of the diamond industry. And finally, companies are told that they should not rig bids, nor should they 'directly or indirectly, offer, promise, give or demand a bribe or other undue advantage to obtain or retain business or other improper advantage.'

Some of these latter injunctions sum up in a more polite way the findings of the UN Congo Panel, practices honoured more in their absence than in their application. The OECD Guidelines are, in fact, much like the Boy Scouts' solemn oath: Be clean in thought, word and deed. But the Boy Scout code does not begin with an escape clause. The very first 'principle' in the OECD Guidelines states that they are only recommendations, that they are 'voluntary and not legally enforceable'.

A tougher OECD agreement can be found in its 'Convention on Combating Bribery of Foreign Public Officials in International Business Transactions', negotiated in 1997 and put into effect in February 1999. This convention, which had been ratified by 35 industrialized countries by the end of 2002, made the bribery of foreign public officials punishable by 'effective, proportionate and dissuasive criminal penalties.' The convention and the national laws, however, had rarely been invoked, and in five years of UN Security Council investigation into weapons smuggling, diamond theft and sanctions busting, they had simply not arisen.

The UN Panel argued that 'home governments have the obligation to ensure that enterprises in their jurisdiction do not abuse principles of conduct that they have adopted as a matter of law.'⁶ But in reality there are few examples of a government attempting to regulate the behaviour of one of its companies in another country. National sovereignty is only one of a dozen problems in reaching beyond one's own border, not least because all countries have their own laws, and are responsible for implementing them accordingly. Proof is obviously essential to making a good case, and then there is the problem of politics. Few governments are likely to go eagerly into the prosecution of a corruption case involving high level officials in another country – the *very* highest in the case of the Congo, Uganda, Zimbabwe and Angola. So apart from some 'naming and shaming', momentary embarrassment, and indignation at the UN report's lack of specificity, the 85 companies charged with breaking OECD Guidelines actually had very little to fear. The behaviour that had so exercised the panel could continue with impunity.

The incident, however, raises important ethical issues for the legitimate diamond industry, issues intrinsic to a growing debate on corporate social responsibility. This term, 'corporate social responsibility' has in fact become a catch phrase for a very large body of issues. In essence, it is about the overall behaviour of companies, and the responsibility they have to the societies in which they operate. A 'socially responsible' company goes beyond the interests of its shareholders, taking into account human rights, environmental concerns and the interests of employees, customers and the communities in which it works.

But corporate social responsibility and the diamond industry are two concepts that for a century were related to one another only tangentially. This is, in part, because 'the diamond industry' itself is little more than a concept. At one end of the scale is the quiet ambience of the Cartier showroom where the diamond is a glittering symbol of love, purity, wealth and eternity – here diamonds are *forever*. At the other end there is a raucous free-for-all where nothing is forever: here diamonds come and go with lightning speed. In Africa where almost 60 per cent of the world's diamonds, by value, are mined, the industry is characterized on the one hand by a few gigantic, well-fenced holes in the ground, and on the other by hundreds of thousands of diggers, known variously as *garimpeiros* in Angola and Brazil, *creuseurs* in the Congo and Central African Republic, *diggers* in Sierra Leone and Liberia.

The most productive and profitable diamond mines in the world are those in Botswana, where De Beers, in 50-50 partnership with the government, digs straight down into volcanic kimberlite pipes and pulls up huge amounts of sparkling stones – 34.9 million carats in 2007, representing sales of $2.9 billion. This is a capital-intensive, high technology operation which employs about 6000 people, about three per cent of the formal labour force.[7]

Where Africa's kimberlite pipes have been eroded by millions of rainy seasons, the result is alluvial diamonds. Scattered over hundreds of square miles – along river beds, in valleys where rivers once flowed, on beaches and on the seabed where rivers eventually deposited them, alluvial diamonds are close to the surface. They are often available to individual diggers with little more than shovels, sieves and a source of water for straining gravel. This is where hundreds of thousands of *garimpeiros* and *creuseurs* dig, often illegally, always under unhealthy, unsafe and frequently unprofitable circumstances. Here the industry is essentially unregulated, unwatched and nameless. Here the concept of corporate social responsibility exists only in its absence. Corporations as conceived in industrialized countries – even governments – barely exist in the diamond fields. The middle men to whom the diggers sell pass the diamonds on to other middle men and then still others. If and when the diamonds are noticed by government, they may be taxed, but few of the benefits filter back to those who dig, or to those on whose land the diamonds were found. Here, corporate social responsibility is nonexistent.

Botswana is often cited as the best example of what diamonds can do for development. By and large, Botswana has invested its diamond resources wisely. One result is development statistics that are the envy of many other African countries: 80 per cent adult literacy and an impressive 94 per cent among youth; clean drinking water for 95 per cent of the population; high rates of child immunization, good primary health care and other positive indicators. The economic growth rate for much of the past decade has been an enviable five per cent, and GDP per capita in 2005 was a stunning $12,387,[8] compared with only $216 in Sierra Leone. But diamonds, it seems, cannot do everything, even if they yield more than $3 billion a year in a country with fewer people than Houston. More than 55 per cent of the people of Botswana still live on less than $2 a day and half of the country's income is shared by the wealthiest ten per cent of the population.

Where South Africa and Namibia are concerned, De Beers and its partner conglomerate, Anglo American, have to accept some of the historical responsibility for badly skewed social and economic development. The company was party to the contract labour system, and it thrived in an environment which held back social development. But the Oppenheimer family, which has controlled De Beers since the 1920s, were consistent critics of apartheid, and Harry Oppenheimer sat as an opposition Member of the South African Parliament for many years. De Beers, if nothing else, has over the years been very successful in its pragmatism. The company defends its labour record in South Africa and points to the many schools and colleges established through its charitable De Beers Fund, for many years the largest source of private sector philanthropy in South Africa. When Harry Oppenheimer, father of current De Beers Chairman Nicky Oppenheimer, died in 2000, Nelson Mandela spoke highly of him. And President Thabo Mbeki recalled that Harry Oppenheimer 'supported and funded the organizations that sought to end white supremacy... Abroad, all too often, he was ignorantly damned for his association with South Africa's apartheid policies.'[9] In the historical context of the day, De Beers was well ahead of the South African business sector on corporate social responsibility.

De Beers, of course, attracts attention. Because it is big, and because it dominates much of the diamond industry, it is a lightning rod for activists. Diamonds, however, are mined by many companies; they are bought and sold by many companies. And many of these companies are not public. Few, in fact, of the hundreds of companies that buy and sell rough diamonds are publicly traded (including De Beers after 2001). Until the blood diamond campaign began to shed light on the industry, little, and often nothing, was known about their labour and environmental practices, or about whether they gave anything at all back to society. And many companies, like some named in the UN report on the Congo, have been formed *only* to take advantage of war and corruption. They have been fronts for warlords, neighbouring governments and criminal networks. For them, the concept of corporate social responsibility does not arise.

An effort to polish the diamond industry's public image was made at a major diamond conference held in Antwerp in 2002. A gala fund-raising dinner for a thousand guests inaugurated a 'Diamond Relief Fund' which raised about $250,000 for community projects in African diamond producing nations. Keynote speaker Al Gore told the audience that the diamond trade was 'a beacon of cooperation, from which other industries could take a lead'. Nobody thought to ask why the money raised that night was going to Botswana, the one conflict-free African country whose government earned more from diamonds than any other. And nobody thought it polite to mention that Al Gore's fee for the evening was more than $100,000.

Between the mines and diamond pits of Africa and the showrooms of Cartier, Tiffany and Harry Winston, lie the other diamond worlds described in this book. Diamonds have always lent themselves to theft and smuggling, and they have served a wide variety of interests as a ready alternative to both soft and hard currency. They are small; they have a high value-to-weight ratio; they hold their price. And historically they have been completely unregulated. Most governments gave up long ago trying to tax diamond exports and imports in any meaningful way because diamonds have been virtually impossible to trace and to police. And the diamond trade is secretive; perhaps more secretive than any other. Multi-million dollar deals are made on a handshake, in closely guarded rooms and in crowded diamond bourses, where men gather with scales, tweezers and loupes. Until 2003, tens of millions of dollars worth of diamonds were sent across borders and across continents on approval, with little or no paper work. Some of this was traditional – a way of doing business in a trade heavily populated by small (and a few very large) family-run businesses, and by people who have known each other for generations. Some of it has to do with a trading and cutting industry heavily populated by Jewish families who, for generations, were persecuted and driven from one place to another, and for whom the diamond itself – rather than the industry – was often a primary form of security. Some of it had simply to do with protection and the transportation of high value goods from one place to another.

But there have been other reasons for secrets. In order to retain control over the market, De Beers had to deal in the 1950s and onward with a wide array of strange and incompatible bedfellows. Apartheid South Africa, the home of De Beers, was an inappropriate partner for newly independent diamond producing nations elsewhere in Africa – Congo, Sierra Leone, Guinea, Tanzania. And a South African cartel was an even more inappropriate partner for the Soviet Union after its discovery of diamonds in the 1950s. In addition, having dealt with Portuguese colonists until the mid 1970s and the apartheid regime of Southwest Africa until the late 1980s, De Beers had some fancy and confidential footwork to do in making friends with the new management in Angola. It did all of this very successfully, in part because it avoided the spotlight of public attention.

As some African diamond producing countries slipped into corruption and chaos during the 1960s and 1970s, diamond buyers remained on the scene, but they began to conduct their business in new ways. Formal diamond production in Mobutu's Congo fell from 18 million carats in 1961 to 6.5 million carats by the late 1990s. The drop reflected not so much a fall in actual production, as a drop in what was being recorded in the national accounts. The difference, and a lot of informal production as well, was being siphoned off by Mobutu and his cronies. And as the government's hold on institutions slipped, other players became involved. The same was true in Sierra Leone where the two million carats produced officially in 1970 had fallen to only 48,000 carats by 1988, courtesy of one of the most corrupt regimes on the continent's west coast. There was no drop, however, in the overall supply of diamonds reaching the world's trading centres, of which Antwerp was the most important. All that was required was a degree of secrecy, and few questions would be asked when the diamonds were declared at Belgian customs. And so, between the 1950s and the mid 1980s, the diamond scene in Africa changed dramatically. A significant proportion of the production of several countries was being hidden under thick layers of secrecy, cloaking a vast network of corruption, theft and smuggling. Diamonds were also being used for money laundering – as a medium of exchange in cashless societies, or in economies where currency no longer had value. In a hothouse like this, the dangerous bacillus of conflict diamonds would thrive.

The question then arises: what is a reputable company to do in a situation of encroaching corruption, conflict and state collapse? How will a code of conduct help when a company with major investments is asked by the president of the country if there might be a job for his nephew? If the company might allow him to use the company jet? If there might be an additional 'signature bonus' to sweeten contract negotiations? What if it is not about bribery or bribery by another name, but about a decaying democracy, a military takeover, human rights abuse or ethnic cleansing? What role in this, if any, is there for a legitimate foreign company with legitimate diamond interests? And who is to say if, when and even whether a state is collapsing? The questions bring to mind the boiled frog syndrome: it is said that if you drop a frog in boiling water, it will jump out immediately. But if you put a frog in cold water and gradually turn up the heat, it will boil to death.

Organizations campaigning on corporate social responsibility tend to take an *ex post facto* approach to the most egregious cases of abuse. In other words, they have clear views on what companies should and should not do once a situation has spun out of control. The strong views expressed about foreign investment in apartheid South Africa developed long after the institutionalization of apartheid. They may have provided potential new investors in the 1980s with clear alternatives, but they could not have been very helpful to those already there. New foreign investment in present-day Burma may be ill-advised, given the brutal and undemocratic nature of the regime, but at what stage should a company with established investments have taken a position, spoken up, or pulled out? What might the consequences be for shareholders in a company that 'speaks out'? How is a corporate investor to calculate the risks and the cost of action versus inaction in a volatile political situation – which tomorrow could turn better, or worse? The OECD Guidelines are completely silent on these issues, which are made more complex by the situational ethics of various Western governments.

Recognizing that its Guidelines did little to address these problems, the OECD took another crack at the issue in 2002, preparing a paper on 'Multinational Enterprises in Situations of Violent Conflict and Widespread Human Rights Abuses'.[10] The study describes some of the conditions under which foreign firms operate in countries like Angola and the Congo, where fiscal frameworks and accountability are weak, and where confidentiality is built into most government relations with the private sector. Add to that the suppression of political and civil liberties, mix in some industrial-strength corruption, and it is not long before fashionable recipes for corporate social responsibility show their inadequacies. The IMF reported, for example, that in 2000, less than two per cent of government expenditure in the Congo was 'executed through normal procedures'. Most expenditure was from diverted revenue without any form of control, through direct orders from the central bank without prior knowledge of the treasury, and through what the IMF euphemistically called 'fast track procedures'. 'Overall, the proliferation of parallel channels deprived the Ministry of Finance of its capacity to record and control expenditure,' assuming that it actually wanted such control.[11]

Nicky Oppenheimer explains what the phenomenon means in practical terms: 'Natural resources can be a source of great good... or dreadful ill. The key element is not the resource itself, but how it is exploited. An orderly mining regime, operating within a transparent and predictable legislative and fiscal framework, can be a major source of prosperity for governments and people. Without it, mineral wealth... will be a magnet for the greedy and corrupt to line their own pockets at the expense of the people.'[12] But on the question about what is to be done – where these predictable legislative and fiscal frameworks will actually come from – the answers are by no means clear.[13]

The easiest, although not necessarily the most businesslike corporate move, might be to pack up and leave, to get out of the pot before it boils. De Beers did close its buying offices in the Congo in 1999, but that, of course, did not stop Congolese diamonds from reaching world markets; it simply deprived De Beers of the business. Smaller companies flowed in to fill the void, caring nothing about OECD guidelines, UN Expert Panels or anything else aside from the bottom line. In a 20 page discussion of the problem, the OECD study, in fact, has only four pages on 'multinational enterprises in search of solutions'. These 'solutions' include the promotion of greater transparency in financial transactions ('where allowed by law...'), the creation of development trust funds for 'future generations'; socially responsible investment funds, and anti-corruption initiatives for industry associations. In other words, precious little. In fact another OECD survey examined 246 codes of conduct among businesses and business associations. Most addressed labour standards and environmental stewardship; some addressed bribery; all were voluntary. And none seemed to have had any effect on corporate behaviour in countries like the Congo.

The diamond industry too created a wide variety of codes as the conflict diamond issue found its way into media headlines. In July 2000, De Beers adopted 'Best Practice Principles' which committed the company not to buy or trade in rough diamonds 'from areas where this would encourage or support conflict and human suffering'. It further stated that it would require its sightholders to comply with the same standard. Diamond bourses around the world announced policies to eject from their membership any diamantaire found trading in conflict diamonds. The Israel Diamond Exchange was one of the first. The Antwerp Diamond Bourse called on its 22 counterparts around the world to emulate its 'zero-tolerance policy for conflict diamonds', saying that any individual or company with links to the arms trade would be barred permanently from the diamond industry. Over the next two years, UN Expert Panels on Sierra Leone, Angola, Liberia and the Congo released many reports containing the names of dozens of individuals and companies involved in trading conflict diamonds and weapons. Not one, however, was barred from the diamond business or from a diamond bourse anywhere. The standard explanation was that unless companies had broken a national law, it would be improper and legally actionable for a bourse to deprive them of their means of livelihood. In other words, the codes and the zero tolerance policies meant absolutely nothing where transgressors were concerned.

Chapter 5 discussed UNITA diamonds and the war in Angola. In all the concern to keep conflict diamonds from rebel movements, however, sight is sometimes lost of the other side of the coin. While UNITA was a brutal, illegitimate rebel movement that paid for its war with diamonds, the legitimate Angolan government was never much better. Corruption, mismanagement and brutality have been its stock in trade. Massive oil revenues were used in part to fight the war against UNITA, but much of the money simply went missing, and little was done for the people living in areas under government control. Where diamonds are concerned, the Angolan government has given the international diamond industry a merry roller coaster ride of confusion, capriciousness and arbitrary behaviour, canceling deals and responding to new offers every second year. Having encouraged De Beers during the 1990s in new mining ventures and new selling arrangements, and having accepted De Beers loans and the building of a new diamond sorting facility in Luanda, the government arbitrarily cancelled its selling arrangements with the diamond giant and other buyers in 2000. Then it made a deal that would benefit a new corporation of its own, Ascorp, and two new players, the Russian-Israeli mogul, Lev Leviev and Sylvain Goldberg of Antwerp (who would later be charged in Belgium in connection with a multi-billion dollar diamond tax fraud). Tales about the personal involvement of top Angolan government officials and their family members abound, not least because none of the parties had the slightest interest in the OECD guidelines or any other codes of conduct dealing with transparency, price-fixing and bribery. De Beers, owed something close to $100 million by the Angolan government, went to the Court of International Arbitration and the UN's Commission on International Trade Law (and eventually lost). But the issue was never really justice; it was always the diamonds.

Following a visit by its officials to Angola in 2002, the IMF issued a damning report. It was couched in anodyne banking jargon, but it is not difficult to see what the IMF was driving at when it talked about the lack of transparency in government operations. The report said that the government needed to 'identify and eliminate or include in the treasury account all extra-budgetary and quasi-fiscal expenditures, including the total amount of signature oil bonuses.' It felt obliged to mention that government revenues should actually be channelled through the central bank, but it demanded as well an audit of the central bank and the scandal-plagued national oil company, Sonangol, which is reputed to mislay as much as a billion dollars worth of revenue every year.

Like Nicky Oppenheimer, the IMF talked about 'issues of governance', saying that poverty indicators had shown no improvement in recent years and that the humanitarian situation had reached dire proportions. By 2006, there had been improvements. Most Angolan refugees had returned home, and the IMF said there had been progress on transparency. But not much. Transparency International continues to place Angola among the most corrupt countries on the planet. Most of the population still lives on less than $2 a day, and where Angola ranked 146th on the United Nations Human Development Index in 2001, it had dropped to 157th place, very close to the bottom, by 2008.

For the diamond industry, discouraging words and dark clouds like these always seem to come with silver linings and new opportunity. Somehow, De Beers and the government of Angola were able to patch up all their terrible differences and, as though nothing had happened at all, in 2005 they announced a new love-in. Managing Director Gary Ralfe said that De Beers now 'embraced a solid commitment to establish a successful partnership'.[14] Although De beers would limit its role to exploration for the time being, it was far from alone. All the big players were crowding into Angola: Petra Diamonds, SouthernEra, Latin America's largest engineering and construction company, Odebrecht, along with the Russian giant, Alrosa. Maurice Tempelsman's LKI was back, and Leviev was everywhere.

One proposal for getting around the corruption problem has been put forward by George Soros's Open Society Institute and a group of NGOs, including, Global Witness. In a campaign entitled 'Publish What You Pay', these organizations and a coalition of members in 70 countries argue that all publicly traded resource companies should be required by regulators to disclose information about taxes, royalties, fees and other transactions with governments in all of the countries where they operate. If this revenue were to be effectively and transparently managed, it could serve as a basis for growth and poverty reduction. Campaign organizers point out, however, that the state institutions which manage these resources are too often, in practice, unaccountable to the parliaments and ordinary citizens of their countries. Revenues from resource extraction are disclosed neither by the governments nor the companies involved – often because legal injunctions have been deliberately created to hide information. This lack of accountability facilitates corruption, and in extreme cases, conflict.

The British government took up the issue as well in the 'Extractive Industries Transparency Initiative' (EITI). Bringing together government officials and the leaders of some of the world's largest companies, including Anglo American, BHP Billiton, Rio Tinto, Shell, Chevron and BP, in 2003 the British proposed a 'compact' on transparency that would make it more difficult for companies to conceal, and governments to extract, illegitimate payments. This would, of course, be in the interests of good corporate citizenship as long as the playing field was level and the same behaviour was required of all. But 'required' is a dirty word in most corporate circles. The debate at one of the earliest meetings on the British transparency initiative turned before long to the venerable old chestnut that has bedevilled OECD Guidelines and most corporate codes of conduct: should such a compact be voluntary or mandatory? The EITI has now been endorsed by more companies and governments, but the going is slow. At the start of 2010, 28 countries were EITI 'candidates', but only two, Azerbaijan and Liberia, were deemed to be 'EITI-compliant'.

It is hard for those who do not attend meetings of bodies like this to understand the debate. All countries have laws against theft. These are not 'voluntary'. Most countries have laws against bribery and corruption. These are not 'voluntary' either, unless those administering the laws are corrupt themselves. If they are not corrupt, what is to be lost by making a compact on corporate transparency mandatory? This, of course, is just a rhetorical question. The truth is that many officials *are* corrupt, and they have no difficulty in finding like-minded private sector counterparts. And that is what drives a large part of the debate about social corporate responsibility.

In the film, *Pirates of the Caribbean*, Jack Sparrow attempts to forestall his execution at the hands of Captain Barbossa by invoking the pirate code. Barbossa replies that the code is really nothing more than a set of 'guidelines'. Even children in the audience get it.

Where diamonds are concerned, instead of citing toothless OECD guidelines, the UN's DRC Expert Panel might have been better advised – where it had real evidence – to consult some basic definitions of war crimes. The Constitution of the Nuremberg Military Tribunal, for example, included as a war crime the 'plunder of public or private property' and said that 'leaders, organizers, instigators and accomplices participating in the formulation or execution of a common plan or conspiracy to commit [war] crimes are responsible for all acts performed by any persons in execution of such plan.'[15] The Prosecutor for Sierra Leone's Special Court obviously looked at Nuremberg precedents. In announcing the Court's first indictments in March 2003, David Crane quoted Robert Jackson, Chief US Prosecutor at Nuremberg: 'We are able to do away with tyranny and violence and aggression by those in power against the rights of their own people only when we make all men answerable to the law.'

By the beginning of the new century, the issue for responsible diamond companies was not the temperature in the Congolese pot or the Angolan pot, but in the diamond industry as a whole. By ignoring, condoning and even participating in the corruption of countries like the Congo, Sierra Leone and Angola, the better parts of industry had allowed a long-standing infection to go septic. By ignoring tax evasion and the use of diamonds for money laundering, the industry only encouraged it. By hiding details of their contracts with, and payments to corrupt governments, they abetted graft and embezzlement. By pretending for years that diamonds had nothing to do with the worsening conflicts in Africa, they provided tacit and tangible support for terrorism, human rights abuse, state collapse and death.

CHAPTER 11

ICE STORM:
THE NGO CAMPAIGN

There's a battle outside and it's raging. It'll soon shake your windows and rattle your walls. For the times they are a'changing.

– Bob Dylan

By the end of 1992, it was clear that Angolan rebel leader Jonas Savimbi would not end his drive for power until he was in charge of the country, or dead. Exhausted by 16 years of war, however, he and the government were willing to attempt to break the stalemate by testing popular opinion. Peace accords signed in 1991 led to elections in September the following year. The elections were reasonably fair and there was a very high voter turnout. Angolans too wanted an end to the conflict, and hoped that the ballot might prove more effective than the bullet. Savimbi would not have risked the gambit had he not been reasonably confident of winning, and he made a respectable showing. His UNITA won 40.7 per cent of the presidential vote, against 49.6 per cent for the ruling MPLA. But as leader of the opposition, Savimbi preferred the bush to the legislature, and he soon returned to war. Within a year, as many as a thousand people were dying every day as a result of the renewed conflict. The government financed itself from the sale of oil, and Savimbi sold more diamonds.

Intense international pressure brought the two parties back to the negotiating table at the end of 1993, and as the result of an accord signed in Lusaka, a 'government of national unity' was formed, with members from both groups taking key positions. A UN Peacekeeping force was deployed to monitor the agreement, but as in so many other peacekeeping operations, the conditions needed for a genuine peace were absent. UNITA never participated actively in the new government, and never gave up control of its most important geographic strongholds.

No book about diamonds would be complete without reference to the enigmatic Maurice Tempelsman – the Belgian-born American Chairman of Lazare Kaplan International, a company with an annual turnover just shy of half a billion dollars, specializing in ideally proportioned diamonds and a great deal more. Unlike De Beers, little is written about Tempelsman. In a 550 page book on the diamond industry, Chaim Even-Zohar makes only nine passing references to the man and his company, even though Tempelsman has been linked by conspiracy theorists to almost every negative event in Africa since the murder of Patrice Lumumba and the overthrow of Kwame Nkrumah. At the opposite end of his legend are distinctions that are easier to verify. A major donor to the Democratic Party, Tempelsman has been close to several American Presidents, travelling with Bill Clinton to Moscow in 1995 on Air Force One and more than once sailing off Martha's Vineyard with the First Family of the day. An art collector, he has served on the boards – among others – of the Academy of American Poets, the African American Institute, the Center for International Policy and the International Advisory Council of the Harvard AIDS Institute. He was directly involved in the creation of the New Partnership for Africa's Development (NEPAD). For more than a decade he was Jackie Kennedy's constant companion, and was with her when she died. In 2003, in the presence of the Presidents of Botswana and Senegal, the 73-year old Tempelsman was awarded the Corporate Council on Africa's Lifetime Achievement Award for his 'longstanding commitment to Africa's economic development'.

This was perhaps fitting in several ways, not least because Tempelsman has shown a willingness to work with almost anyone in Africa, not just for their economic development, but for his own as well. He became very close to Mobutu Sese Seko and is said to have smoothed out bad patches for De Beers in the Congo. Despite his friendship with Mobutu, Tempelsman was present when the young Joseph Kabila arrived in Washington in January 2001, two weeks after the assassination of his father. Tempelsman told the new president that he had a unique challenge and an opportunity to bring peace and prosperity to the Congo. In this, Tempelsman said, the US business community stood ready to assist in every way it could.[1]

It was in Angola, however, in 1996, that the extent of his influence would be tested. At a time when UNITA and the government were ostensibly 'at peace', it was more than a little obvious to most observers that Savimbi would not soon be parted from his quest for power or from diamonds. Tempelsman devised a diamond sharing proposal that would see UNITA retain the rights to some of its diamond operations as a means of paying for a political party that many hoped might become part of a democratic process. The key to the deal was money, needed for investment in costly deep-mining equipment. For this, Tempelsman needed the US Export-Import Bank, an independent federal agency. The deal would be similar to a $62 million Ex-Im credit facility he was working on for Alrosa, the Russian diamond giant. But the Ex-Im Bank had placed Angola off-limits in the 1970s because of its lack of 'free and fair elections'. In order to get around the bureaucracy and the rules, Tempelsman went to National Security Adviser, Anthony Lake, Assistant Secretary of State George Moose and others to help grease the skids. Calls were made and letters were written. According to one government official, the proposal was handled with 'unusual intensity' and State Department aides 'were told to support Tempelsman'.[2] Tempelsman was ably assisted by his lawyer, Ted Sorensen – once a speech writer and Special Counsel to President Kennedy – and no doubt by officials' awareness of his proximity to the current President and his generous donations to the Democratic Party.

Sorensen explained the whole thing this way: 'Maurice Tempelsman has been willing to do whatever he could to secure the completion of the peace process.' The fact that Tempelsman would become the chief buyer of diamonds in the arrangement he hoped to broker – a deal that would have been worth billions of dollars – was not highlighted. In the end, the deal fell apart because of Angolan government suspicion and valid worries in the State Department about commercial entanglements in a dirty business and a dirty country.[3] As government forces began to encroach on UNITA territory, fighting erupted once again. But Savimbi's military position started to weaken in 1997 with the fall of his long-time Congolese supporter, Mobutu Sese Seko. More isolated, Savimbi became more desperate. And more desperate, he became more ferocious. By 1998 the Angolan war was in full spate.

Angola had certainly not gone unnoticed at the United Nations. The various cease-fires, peace accords and elections were the result of strenuous efforts by the Security Council to extinguish the violent legacies of colonialism and the Cold War. With the fall of the Berlin Wall, a new era of world peace was foreseen, not least in Angola, where the proxy war between the United States and the Soviet Union quickly lost its geopolitical meaning. The Cuban troops could go home, South Africa could withdraw, elections could be held, and everyone could move forward into the bright sunlit uplands of peace and prosperity. Protracted wars that have caused the deaths of hundreds of thousands of people, however, do not often end quite like that.

The first 'UN Angola Verification Mission' (UNAVEM) was established in the dying days of the Cold War to oversee and verify the withdrawal of Cuban troops. By 1991 the job was done – at a cost of $16 million. A new mission, UNAVEM II, was then established to verify the cease-fire and the elections of 1992. UNAVEM II comprised 350 military observers and for a time as many as 400 electoral observers, costing $175 million in total. UNAVEM II clung to life as the country returned to war. A new peacekeeping operation was sanctioned in 1995. Between February 1995 and June 1997, UNAVEM III maintained a little more than 6000 troops, observers and police in Angola, costing over $750 million by the end of 1996. Recognizing by the summer of 1997, however, that there was no peace to keep, the Security Council decided to pull the troops out.

Abject failure is rarely acknowledged in the diplomatic world, and so the Security Council worded its humiliation this way: 'Recognizing the successful contribution of the United Nations Angola Verification Mission (UNAVEM III) to the restoration of peace and the process of national reconciliation in country, the Security Council on Monday decided to establish, as of 1 July, the United Nations Observer Mission in Angola (MONUA).'[4] This new follow-on mission replaced UNAVEM III. MONUA's stated aim was 'to assist the Angolan parties in consolidating peace and national reconciliation, enhancing confidence-building and creating an environment conducive to long-term stability, democratic development and rehabilitation of the country.'[5] George Orwell couldn't have said it better in Newspeak, in which 'the expression of unorthodox opinions, above a very low level, was well nigh impossible.'[6] Thus, in Orwell's Nineteen Eighty-Four, 'War is Peace; Freedom is Slavery; Ignorance is Strength'.

In the Angolan case, war was peace (or peace was war), and MONUA's main purpose was not so much to 'consolidate' a non-existent peace as to get the UN out of the Angolan quagmire. MONUA spent most of its 18 months downsizing from the 3500 personnel it began with to fewer than 400 when it pulled out completely in February 1999. By the time it was over, MONUA had cost $300 million and had achieved very little beyond the pullout. The four UN peacekeeping efforts had cost well over a billion dollars and had consumed the lives of 54 UN personnel, including the Secretary General's Special Representative, Alioune Beye, who died along with five other UN staff and two pilots in a plane crash in June 1998.

The Security Council had tried to tackle the issue in other ways as well. It had imposed sanctions against UNITA in 1993 after Savimbi refused to accept the results of the 1992 election, banning arms, military equipment and fuel. When the Security Council makes a decision, it is incumbent upon governments everywhere in the world to comply. As a result, no arms or fuel should have reached Savimbi. But they did. Countries across Africa and around the world simply ignored the sanctions, in part because Savimbi had the cash to pay for what he wanted, in part because most sanctions-busting governments and entrepreneurs knew that there would be few, if any consequences. Recognizing the financial aspect of the problem, the Security Council toughened the sanctions in 1997, freezing UNITA bank accounts, closing all UNITA offices abroad, and placing a travel ban on senior UNITA officials. And finally, getting closer to the heart of the matter, the Security Council finally recognized in June 1998 that diamonds were a key to Savimbi's survival. As a result, it banned the purchase of any diamonds originating in Angola unless they were certified as legitimate by the government in Luanda. Like so many other Security Council sanctions, however, this too was largely ignored. With one exception.

Working out of a cramped office in a former primary school in a shabby part of London's Archway district, a small British NGO was paying attention. Global Witness had been created five years earlier by three campaigners who had broken away from the Environmental Investigation Agency. Global Witness too would investigate environmental crime, but the purpose would be different. Where the aims of the EIA were essentially environmental – tigers, elephants, bears and orang-utans – the primary concern at Global Witness was people. Their first investigative campaign focussed on illicit logging in Cambodia, not because they were concerned about deforestation, but because they saw that the proceeds were being used by the still active Khmer Rouge to prosecute its rear-guard war against the government.

Global Witness then turned its attention to the role of diamonds in fuelling the war in Angola. Their December 1998 report, *A Rough Trade*, demonstrated that the United Nations embargo on UNITA diamonds was being openly flouted. They said that a 'lack of understanding and government scrutiny of the functioning of the diamond trade has resulted in the absence of any serious examination of corporate culpability, allowing many diamond companies to continue to operate without fear that their actions may be called into question by consumers.'[7] The Global Witness report claimed that UNITA had taken in at least $3.72 billion in diamond revenues between 1992 and 1998, and that 300,000 Angolans had died violently between 1992 and 1995. They pointed their collective finger at two culprits: De Beers and the Antwerp diamond trade. Global Witness quoted De Beers' own annual reports on the subject of buying up Angolan supplies that undoubtedly originated with UNITA. It accused Belgian authorities of incompetence if not collusion in failing to halt illicit diamonds emanating from Angola.

Only fifteen pages in length, the Global Witness report landed in diamond circles like a fragmentation bomb. The organization was accused of being a tool of De Beers, the CIA, the oil industry and the mining giant, BHP Billiton. The report was something of a bombshell at the UN as well, because it demonstrated the toothlessness of the UN Security Council sanctions and embargoes – debated long into the night in New York perhaps, but ignored with impunity by UNITA, by denizens in the underground worlds of diamonds and weapons, and most notably, by many of Angola's neighbouring governments.

In 1999, things began to change in the Security Council. Canada, elected to one of the rotating two-year seats, had been asked to Chair the Iraq Sanctions Committee. Robert Fowler, Canada's UN ambassador, opted instead for Angola and he persuaded the Council of a new approach. Instead of passing more resolutions, it would become more aggressive in monitoring sanctions busting, taking into consideration the demands and allegations made by Global Witness. In May 1999 the Security Council agreed to create a 'panel of experts' whose job would be to trace violations in arms trafficking, oil supplies and the diamond trade, as well as the movement of UNITA funds. The panel, which included individuals from ten different countries, gathered in New York at the end of August to begin a job that would eventually take them to 30 countries in search of the truth about Angola's conflict diamonds.

Meanwhile, unaware of Global Witness, a Canadian NGO called Partnership Africa Canada (PAC), had also started to work on the issue of diamonds. In 1998, a group of Sierra Leoneans and concerned Canadians began meeting in the PAC office on the top floor of a Victorian mansion in Ottawa. Old photographs in the former drawing room show 323 Chapel Street as it was in its heyday, probably one of the largest and most luxurious homes in the city. Today, largely intact but showing the wear and tear of a century, the house is a warren of NGO offices and meeting rooms. Convening in what would once have been servants' quarters, the PAC group sought to raise funds for peace-building work in Sierra Leone, and hoped to draw Canadian government attention to what was essentially a forgotten emergency. Sierra Leone had never been a Cold War pawn, had never been of great strategic or geopolitical interest to wealthy aid-giving countries, and as it descended into the horrors of war, it attracted none of the United Nations Security Council attention and largesse that had been lavished with so little effect on Angola. At a PAC meeting in 1998, one of the participants threw up his hands in frustration at the seeming hopelessness of the situation. 'This war is about diamonds,' he said, 'and until something is done about the diamonds, we are wasting our time.'

The story of how a trio of PAC researchers came together, obtained funding and wrote a report on diamonds and the war in Sierra Leone is told in the Prologue of this book. It took almost a year – all of 1999 – to write *The Heart of the Matter: Sierra Leone, Diamonds and Human Security*.[8] The title recalled Graham Greene's gloomy 1948 novel, *The Heart of the Matter*, set in the British colony of Sierra Leone with diamonds as the *leitmotif* in a tale of corruption and melancholy. PAC's report told the story of Sierra Leone's Revolutionary United Front (RUF), a rebel movement devoid of ideology, without ethnic backing or claims to territory. Charles Taylor, the Liberian warlord, had financed the early stages of his brutal fight for power by selling timber. As Global Witness had shown in Cambodia, the market for tropical hardwood is lucrative. Once Taylor secured a sea port, he had both the supply and the means to export. But diamonds would prove to be even more lucrative. Taylor backed Sierra Leone's fledgling Revolutionary United Front, giving it a Liberian base, weapons, and an outlet for whatever it could steal in Sierra Leone. The RUF's grisly trademark – chopping the hands and feet off civilians, often small children – was a terror technique aimed successfully at clearing the country's alluvial diamond fields.

The Heart of the Matter traced Sierra Leone's diamond history from its decline into corruption in the 1970s through to 1999 when formal diamond mining had come to an almost complete halt. By then, there were almost no government supervised diamond exports, while across the border in Liberia, diamond exports were thriving. In the 1990s, billions of dollars worth of diamonds said to be from Liberia were imported into Belgium. Liberia, as shown in Chapter 6, however, is a country with a tiny diamond production of its own. Partnership Africa Canada's report exposed diamond fraud of vast proportions. It accused the diamond industry at large of complicity. And it accused the Belgian authorities in particular of closing their eyes to massive corruption in order to protect the Antwerp diamond trade.

Like the Global Witness report a year earlier, the PAC report made headlines – in Britain, Belgium, Canada, Sierra Leone, South Africa and elsewhere. Feature articles appeared in *The Financial Times, The Guardian, The Los Angeles Times, De Morgen, The Globe and Mail, de Volkskrant, La Presse, the International Herald Tribune* and a dozen others. The story was carried on CNN, the BBC, CBC, Reuters and the Associated Press. Mostly the reaction was one of horror at the connection between diamonds – supposed symbols of love – and the brutality that had become so rampant in Sierra Leone. Some of the Belgian media, however, saw a conspiracy. The first Canadian diamond mine was about to begin production. The Chairman of the Angola Sanctions Committee and the power behind the UN expert panel was Canada's Ambassador to the United Nations, Robert Fowler. And now here was a report from a Canadian NGO that devoted a dozen of its 85 pages to an attack on the Belgian diamond industry.

Large parts of the PAC Report described the structure and nature of the generic diamond trade, pointing out the pivotal role of Antwerp, not just in the legitimate trade, but in the illegitimate trade as well. PAC showed that the stated imports of rough diamonds into Belgium bore absolutely no resemblance to the production capacities of countries where they were said to originate. Billions of dollars worth of rough diamond imports came from Liberia, Côte d'Ivoire, Guinea – far in excess of what could ever have been produced there. [9]   Not only were Belgian authorities oblivious to the massive discrepancies contained in their own statistics, there was a major conflict of interest in the supervision of imports. The Diamond Office of the HRD (*Hoge Raad voor Diamant* – the Flemish acronym for 'Diamond High Council' – acted on behalf of the government as the clearance and customs bureau for diamond imports and exports. As a nongovernmental lobby group working on behalf of the Belgian diamond industry, the HRD was hardly a disinterested party.

The PAC report created waves in the diamond world, but it also created waves in Sierra Leone, where every single living adult knew of diamonds, but where there had never in history been anything resembling a public debate on the issue. Few Sierra Leoneans doubted that diamonds were at the heart of their misery. They had watched as the diamond fields were overrun by the RUF, fuelling the rebel war machine and pushing the remnants of governmental authority back towards the Freetown peninsula. They had watched mercenaries fight off the RUF in exchange for diamond concessions. They had watched as the government, its back to the sea, was led to the negotiating table by the United States to make one of the most cynical and unjust agreements in the history of Africa – no small achievement.

Like Global Witness, PAC was accused of many things, including being a stooge of De Beers. This was in part, perhaps, because the report took a relatively balanced approach to the diamond giant, an approach thought by some to be uncharacteristic of an NGO. 'De Beers is part of the problem,' the report stated. 'It is no doubt purchasing diamonds from a wide variety of dubious sources, either wittingly or unwittingly. The breadth of its control, however, is also its major strength, and is part of the solution to the problem. If De Beers were to take a greater interest in countries like Sierra Leone, and if it were to stop purchasing large amounts of diamonds from countries with a negligible production base, much could be done to end the current high levels of theft and smuggling.' PAC's approach to De Beers had been moderate in tone, and De Beers reciprocated. The company said that there were a number of factual inaccuracies in the report, but 'for the most part these are not relevant to the main thrust of the report.' De Beers said that it 'welcomes the initiative undertaken by Partnership Africa Canada in highlighting the tragic situation in Sierra Leone,' but it also stressed the importance of the legitimate diamond trade to many countries.

Mild as it was on the surface, there was a sub-text to the De Beers press release, which seemed to anticipate an approaching storm. The release said that the company was 'extremely concerned that actions taken or initiated by pressure groups could unintentionally disrupt and damage the legitimate international diamond market, without effectively addressing the intended objective of bringing peace to parts of Africa.' 'This misguided campaign,' it added, 'could be little short of disastrous' and it warned against 'the blunt instrument of the threat of a consumer boycott'.[10] De Beers also quoted former South African President Nelson Mandela, who with the end of apartheid seemed to have changed his mind on the political usefulness of boycotts. 'The diamond industry is vital to the South African and the Southern African economy,' Mandela said. 'We would be concerned that an international campaign on these issues does not damage this vital industry. Rather than boycotts being instituted, it is preferable that through our own initiatives the industry takes a progressive stance on human rights issues.'[11] In fact, the only talk of a boycott up to that point had come from De Beers and Mandela. The PAC report talked instead of a 'campaign', the objective of which would be 'to create greater interest among the public, public institutions and within the diamond industry in doing exactly what Mr Mandela suggests... The point of a campaign would be to help the industry take responsibility for its actions – not damaging it, but improving it.'[12]

In truth, De Beers and the wider diamond industry were more than a little alarmed by the growing chorus on conflict diamonds. A month before the PAC report appeared, Tony Hall, a Democratic Congressman from Ohio, had risen in the US House of Representatives to propose a bill that he called 'Consumer Access to a Responsible Accounting for Trade' – the CARAT Act. The bill would, if passed, require diamond importers to demonstrate clearly that their goods did not emanate from a war zone. Hall had been a Peace Corps volunteer in the 1960s, and was elected to the House of Representatives in 1979. As a congressman he travelled widely and had become a champion of human rights and a campaigner against world hunger. When he spoke in the House of Representatives on 1 November 1999, Hall referred to Sierra Leone's Revolutionary United Front:

'The revenues from the diamond mines they seized ensured they never wanted for the best in weapons or gear, and they enabled these butchers to cut off the hands and arms of civilians in punishment for casting ballots. In all, $200 million a year in diamond exports funded the bloodshed that killed 50,000 people in Sierra Leone this decade. Angola's seemingly endless war is another example. Rebels again are waging the war that has cost a million people their lives, has driven more than a million from their homes in the past year, and now threatens two million with famine. Their weapons, including land mines that make Angola the deadliest place in the world, are purchased with diamond revenues totalling nearly $4 billion this decade. Through their greed and craven brutality, rebels and dealers in dirty diamonds risk tarnishing the appeal of diamonds to consumers, and their promise to impoverished African nations. I believe the CARAT Act will help protect these democracies from the shame that these outlaws are bringing to the diamond trade.'[13]

Hall was even more incensed a month later, after he returned from a visit to Sierra Leone with Republican Congressman Frank Wolf, another human rights campaigner with a strong interest in Africa. He and Wolf became bipartisan comrades on the diamond issue, and when the CARAT Bill was revised in 2000, Wolf became a co-sponsor. He too spoke out after the visit to amputee camps in Sierra Leone. 'The civil war is largely being funded by the sale of unregulated diamonds,' he said. 'Not only are the profits from these illicit diamonds used to fund a war of terror against the people of Sierra Leone, but the people are being deprived of the benefits that these natural resources could offer their society. Passage of Congressman Hall's Bill would be a huge stride in ending this practice.'[14]

Then, in March 2000, the UN Expert Panel on Angola released its report. The 'Fowler Report' as it became known, was something of a landmark in UN history. Gone was the diplomatic *Newspeak*. Not only was the report blunt, for the first time in history it named sitting heads of state for complicity in sanctions busting. In 1993, the report said, Col. Alcides Lucas Kangunga (known as 'Kallias') had been sent by Jonas Savimbi to make a deal with the President of Togo, Gnassingbé Eyadéma. Kallias arranged for weapons to reach UNITA via Togo, using Togolese end-user certificates. Eyadéma could take 20 per cent off the top of each shipment, in either cash or kind. 'As a token of appreciation,' the report said of one visit, 'Kallias gave to Eyadéma a "passport sized" packet of diamonds on Savimbi's behalf.'[15] The Togo connection became more important after the 1997 fall of Mobutu Sese Seko, with whom Savimbi had a similar deal: 'Mobutu provided Savimbi with Zairian end-user certificates, and in exchange, Savimbi gave Mobutu diamonds and cash.'[16] Then Vice President (now President) of Rwanda, Paul Kagame, also helped Savimbi. Another supporter was President Blaise Compaoré of Burkina Faso, who also assisted Liberia's Charles Taylor in sanctions busting and provided direct assistance to Sierra Leone's murderous RUF. The Panel reported that Savimbi would call President Compaoré to alert him that a delegation with diamonds was coming to Ouagadougou. On their arrival, they 'would be met by someone from the President's office and provided with protection and an escort. This was necessary not only to ensure that there were no difficulties with customs or other Burkinabe authorities, but also to ensure the safety of the diamonds or cash during the delegation's stay in the country.'[17] The report also spoke of UNITA diamonds being smuggled through Zambia, Namibia and South Africa. And it reserved special scorn for Belgium where, it said, 'authorities have failed to establish an effective import identification regime with respect to diamonds. Nor has any effective effort been made to monitor the activities of suspect brokers, dealers and traders – virtually all of whom appear to be able to travel freely and operate without hindrance.'[18]

While De Beers had been warning politely against boycotts, others in the diamond industry were starting to take notice. Martin Rapaport is a prominent diamond industry iconoclast who divides his time between New York and Ramat Gan, the diamond district of Tel Aviv. Known variously as 'Rap' and 'Mike' as well as Martin, his sometimes avuncular nature belies a fiery temper, fuelled by long days and longer nights managing a huge family and a network of companies and publications. Among the latter is an influential monthly *Rapaport Diamond Report*. In it, in November 1999 he wrote a rambling article about diamonds and war in Africa. He used the term 'conflict diamonds' for the first time. He called Global Witness 'a feisty little troublemaker human rights organization'. 'As the name implies,' he continued, 'Global Witness runs around the world witnessing and documenting very bad things. Not content to merely witness the bad stuff, it then packages and markets guilt trips to powerful governments and organizations that are in a position to do something to stop the bad stuff.'

Although open to thinking about the issue, Rapaport was suspicious about all this reportedly 'bad stuff'. 'Is the diamond industry being used as a scapegoat, as an easy target for manipulation by the political establishment because we sell a high profile product that they think can easily be damaged by negative publicity?' he asked. 'Should we allow ourselves to be blackmailed to support the FAA (Angolan Armed Forces) against UNITA? Are the motivations of the politicians humanitarian? Are they economic? Do they have anything to do with Angola's huge oil reserves? Is the diamond industry being used by the political establishment as a shill, a fake target, a way to show the world that the politicians are supposedly doing something to end the war but in reality they are supporting the war through oil purchases and arms sales?'

Frankly, the whole situation stinks,' he concluded. 'I don't know the answers to these questions. I don't know if there are any answers, if there is any way to stop the wars. What I do know is, given the historic role of foreign governments in Africa, it is a good idea for the diamond industry to tread with great caution and to suspect the intentions of all parties involved in this issue. We must be very careful about how we allow ourselves to be manipulated.'[19]

Four months later, Rapaport went to Sierra Leone to see for himself, and when he returned, his tune had changed. 'I don't know how to tell this story,' He wrote in an article he called 'Guilt Trip'.[20] 'There are no words to describe what I have seen in Sierra Leone. My mind tells me to block out the really bad stuff, to deny the impossible reality. But the images of the amputee camp haunt me and the voices of the victims cry out. "Tell them what has happened to us," say the survivors. "Show them what the diamonds have done to us."'

> Friends, members of the diamond trade. Please, stop and think for a minute. Read my words. Perhaps what is happening in Sierra Leone is our problem. Perhaps it is our business... The real problem facing Sierra Leone is... how to stop the illegal diamond industry from stealing the country's resources. But it goes beyond that. The bastards are not just stealing Sierra Leone's diamonds, they are trading them for guns. Guns which are used to kill people to keep the war going, which assures that the government will not be able to control the illegal trade, assuring that the bad guys can continue to steal the diamonds... While the industry in general cannot solve Sierra Leone's problems, it can, and must, take realistic measures to assure that illegal diamonds are excluded from the marketplace.

Rapaport, regarded within the diamond industry as something of a 'feisty little troublemaker' himself, proposed a number of solutions. One was economic – paying fair prices to those who actually dig diamonds in countries like Sierra Leone, and making sure that everyone within digging distance of a mine would know what diamonds are worth. A transparent pricing policy and the return of immediate benefits to mining communities would go a long way to reducing the attraction of selling to smugglers. He also talked about the need for an industry-wide system of voluntary disclosure regarding the sourcing of diamonds. 'The diamond industry needs to tighten its standards. The days when one could simply take the position – "I don't know where my diamonds are coming from" – are drawing to a close. The time has come for us to band together and make sure that we can be trusted to ensure the legitimate origin of our diamonds and the legitimacy of our diamond industry. The bottom line is that our industry must stop dealing with questionable diamonds. If you don't know where or who the diamond comes from – don't buy it.'

Global Witness had recommended that the UN Security Council make it mandatory for all diamonds in trade to carry a certificate of origin, subject to independent scrutiny by internationally recognized diamond experts. Partnership Africa Canada recommended the establishment of a permanent, independent international diamond standards commission. Rapaport recommended better industry self-regulation and Tony Hall proposed national legislation to control the diamond trade. Each of them made other recommendations, but these, in fact, were the general drift of what would begin to emerge in discussions during the months ahead. The Fowler Report recommended that a conference of experts be convened 'for the purpose of determining a system of controls that would allow for increased transparency and accountability in the control of diamonds from the source or origin to the bourses.'[21]

By early 2000, Global Witness, PAC, Fowler, Rapaport, Tony Hall and De Beers had all made each others' acquaintance. And other NGOs were beginning to take an interest: Physicians for Human Rights in the United States, Fatal Transactions in Europe, Human Rights Watch and ActionAid in Britain, Amnesty International and two of the biggest NGOs in the world, Oxfam and World Vision. At the same time, despite the reports, and despite growing industry acceptance of at least some responsibility, the wars in Sierra Leone, Angola and the Congo raged, and diamonds continued to flow from rebel armies into the cutting and polishing centres of the legitimate trade. The stage was set for a battle, and battle lines were being drawn.

CHAPTER 12

KIMBERLEY: A HOPE
IN HELL

*By now we are all familiar with the day when the world changed and
unspeakable acts of terror took the lives of more than 5,000 civilians. I am
referring, of course, to January 6, 1999, when rebel gunmen killed, maimed
and raped their way across Freetown, Sierra Leone's capital.*

– David Keen[1]

John Wodehouse, a stern diplomat and minister of the crown, was one of
those bearded men who for some reason shave their upper lip. He served
the British government in many capacities during the latter half of the 19th
century: as Lord Lieutenant of Ireland, Secretary of State for India, and Foreign
Minister. In 1866 when he was 40, Queen Victoria conferred an earldom on
him, and casting about for a title, he decided on the name of the house he
and his wife shared in Norfolk: Kimberley House, near the tiny village of the
same name. 'Kimberley' is derived from the Anglo Saxon word *ynburgh-leah*,
which means 'women were entitled to own land'. In 1870, Lord Kimberley
became Colonial Secretary. Meanwhile, in the South African province of
Griqualand West, all hell was breaking loose in a sprawling diamond boom-
town known as New Rush, springing up on a farm named Vooruitzicht.
'New Rush' seemed vulgar, 'Vooruitzicht' stumbled inelegantly off English
tongues, and John Blades Currey, the government secretary of the day, saw a
golden opportunity to attract favourable notice to himself at the highest levels
in London by proposing a new name. Today the capital of the Northern Cape
Province, Kimberley is a small South African city of 75,000 people. It has a
mine museum, an Ernest Oppenheimer Memorial Garden, an art gallery, a

fine historical tramway, the largest hand-dug hole on the planet (393 metres deep), and at 36 Stockdale Street the registered head office of the biggest diamond company in the world.

If there were such a thing, Kimberley would be the spiritual capital of the modern diamond industry. Kimberley is where the first significant diamond find since antiquity was made, and the place where the largest cheque in history up to that point was written – to consolidate the birth of the grandest diamond company of all time. It was perhaps appropriate, but not a little ironic, therefore, that South Africa's modern-day Minister of Minerals and Energy, Phumzile Mlambo-Ngcuka, would invite NGOs, diamond industry leaders and representatives of a dozen diamond producing and trading countries to gather in Kimberley in May 2000 to discuss the issue of conflict diamonds. Mlambo-Ngcuka had been an educator and an NGO activist herself during the last decade of apartheid, had run for parliament successfully in 1994 and was made Minister of Minerals and Energy by Thabo Mbeki on his first day as South Africa's President in 1999. Mlambo-Ngcuka knew perhaps better than others that the NGO campaign would not go away of its own accord. She also recognized, as many governments and much of the industry did not, that there was a genuine problem that had to be addressed. Conflict diamonds were not a figment of over-heated NGO imaginations. She had talked to the Global Witness campaigners and had met with Partnership Africa Canada at a mining conference in Toronto. More importantly, she had read their reports and was well aware of the Canada-led United Nations investigation into Angolan diamonds. She knew that the problem had two elements. The first was humanitarian in nature, with widespread security ramifications for large parts of Africa. The second was economic. If the diamond campaign were to spiral out of control, the cost to the economies of South Africa, Botswana and Namibia would be enormous.

The issue had caught fire in South Africa, with De Beers Chairman Nicky Oppenheimer and others condemning potential, but so far non-existent, NGO boycotts. The Kimberley meeting brought together for the first time officers of the diamond industry, senior government officials from almost a dozen countries, and representatives of the most active NGOs. De Beers sent a small army of men in suits, and Belgium sent its Foreign Minister. Martin Rapaport, the 'feisty little troublemaker', flew in. Several other countries with an interest in diamonds sent delegations: Botswana, Namibia, Angola, the Democratic Republic of the Congo, the United States, Britain and Canada. Notable for their absence, however, were some of the diamond heavies: Russia, India, Israel and Australia. Once past the pleasantries (and some unpleasantries), it was generally agreed that the issue could be wrapped up quickly. De Beers proposed a nine-point plan aimed at excluding conflict diamonds from the legitimate trade. Belgium, which had vociferously denied charges of mismanagement and conflicts of interest in its management of diamonds, announced new tighter government controls. But the meeting was, in fact, far from conclusive.

At the end, Phumzile Mlambo-Ngcuka proposed a wider meeting at ministerial level, to be held two months hence in order to settle the matter once and for all, and she announced that she would have the matter raised at the Okinawa G8 Summit in July. Through the next three years, Mlambo-Ngcuka's optimism never failed but her timetable certainly did, more than once. Other governments thought better of rushing such a highly political issue with so many technical complexities, and at a 'working group' meeting held in the capital of Angola the following month, it became clear that the ministerial meeting would have to be postponed. The Luanda meeting was chaotic. There was no sense of purpose, and many delegates arrived without instructions from their governments. JFK speechwriter Ted Sorensen flew in, claiming to represent industry, and caused a dustup by saying that the NGOs in the room had no place in the negotiations and should be thrown out. Charmian Gooch from Global Witness shot back, saying she was there on behalf of many NGOs, representing hundreds of thousands of people. She said she was immensely disappointed that a man of his stature should take on such a disgraceful, hatchet-job consultancy. After that there was never any argument about whether NGOs would be an integral part of the Kimberley Process. And in the end, despite the confusion and recriminations, the Luanda meeting actually managed to outline all of the elements that would be contained in the final agreement, ratified at the 13th meeting of what was becoming known as the 'Kimberley Process' 29 months later.

The Luanda participants agreed that there should be a global system to prohibit the importation of rough diamonds into any country unless accompanied by a 'forgery-proof certificate of legitimacy and/or origin'. Anyone found to be dealing in conflict diamonds should be expelled from the diamond trade, with provisions for punishment and forfeiture of the goods in question. The diamond industry should establish a 'chain of warranties'. And the United Nations, the G8, the World Trade Organization and relevant diamond industry bodies should all be engaged on the issue, 'in order to enable the scheme's earliest possible adoption and implementation'.[2] The Luanda meeting also proposed 'a centralized and standardized data base, incorporating information from producer countries... on diamond production, exports and imports, evaluating any substantial discrepancy in these figures and any reports of violations within the system, and exposing violators.' Without good statistics on trade and production, it would be difficult to find violators. The meeting called for 'transparency, disclosure and oversight of all diamond operations' although it stopped short of saying precisely who might make this happen or, in an industry based on secrecy and riven with corruption, what it might mean in practise.

But when the 'ministerial meeting' finally took place in Pretoria that September, few ministers showed up. Only the Southern African diamond producing countries and Sierra Leone sent anyone of rank, and the meeting – now attended by newcomers from Russia, Israel and elsewhere – broke up without agreeing to anything more than a date for another meeting.

♦

An issue raised by many observers of the Kimberley Process as it began to take shape was the possibility of physically identifying diamonds, or in some way marking them for tracking purposes. It is true that experienced diamantaires and geologists can sometimes look at a parcel of unmixed diamonds and say with some confidence where they originate. There are also cases where an expert may be reasonably sure of the geographic origins of a small parcel because of special and outstanding characteristics. Some Russian crystals, for example, have particular distinguishing features; some from Angola and the Congo have a 'frosted' appearance; Zimbabwean diamonds from Marange are distinctively brown.

But identifying such stones would be possible only in the case of unmixed parcels, and in most cases would not provide the level of evidence required in a court of law. Further, this sort of visual identification only works with rough diamonds. Once diamonds have been mixed or cut, it becomes impossible to distinguish – on the basis of 'characteristics' – where they have come from. An experienced eye might well be able to identify where a good diamond does *not* come from, because good diamonds are not found everywhere. But a single, fine, gem-quality diamond from Sierra Leone could look very much like one from

Namibia, Angola or South Africa. This problem is made more complicated where alluvial diamonds are concerned, because while they might originate from a single source, over the aeons they could have been scattered down riverbeds and across several countries.

A company named Gemprint developed a technology for 'fingerprinting' a polished diamond. The shape, size, weight and cut of one diamond will always be slightly different from all others – a bit like one snowflake always differing in its crystalline formation from another. Once measured and registered, the diamond can be identified later using a Gemprint machine. But the technology deals only with polished diamonds.

Other technologies can be applied to rough diamonds. A small mark or a chemical can be applied and read by special machines – just as a scanner reads bar codes. There is a problem, however. About 150 million carats in non-industrial diamonds pass through Antwerp alone in a single year – perhaps a billion individual stones. Marking each of these diamonds would represent hundreds if not thousands of person-years of work annually. This could be reduced if marks were applied only to stones of, say, one carat and more, but rebel armies do not distinguish diamonds in quite that way; nor do thieves, smugglers and sanctions-busters. A further problem is that any mark applied to a rough diamond can be removed, and *will* be removed anyway in the polishing process. Altering stones, even those of a carat or more, would not be difficult, and it would be worth the effort to thieves if it helped them evade the law.

The Royal Canadian Mounted Police (RCMP) has been pursuing the development of a different kind of diamond 'fingerprinting' at their Central Forensic Laboratory in Ottawa. Diamonds are typically thought of as pure carbon. However, even the best quality diamonds have trace amounts of over 50 different impurities. Research has shown that by comparing the relative amounts of these impurities, the origin of diamonds can be determined using something called laser ablation inductively-coupled plasma mass spectrometry.

The technology is workable. However, in order for this fingerprinting process to be practically applied, a reliable data base must be created. This means that diamond samples from all of the world's important diamond mines, and from different depths of these mines, would have to be 'fingerprinted'. Once that was accomplished, any rough diamonds on the market could be tested and matched against specific mine characteristics in the data base.

As with other techniques, however, the problems in applying it to even a fraction of the millions of carats of diamonds produced in a year is a proposition of staggering magnitude. And as with the other technologies, this one can only identify what a diamond *is* – assuming there is a good data base – not what it is not. An untagged, unmarked, un-fingerprinted diamond could only be called illicit if all legitimate diamonds in the world had been tagged, marked or fingerprinted using a common system. Delegates to the Kimberley Process actually spent hours at one meeting debating whether a certificate should be in landscape or portrait format, and whether it should use metric A4 paper or North American letter size. Getting from that level of debate to a serious discussion about the global adoption of laser ablation inductively-coupled plasma mass spectrometry was never even a remote possibility.

♦

In addition to the 11 meetings that were required after Luanda to reach a workable Kimberley agreement, there were almost as many informal meetings during the same time period, all of which helped to grease the wheels of the formal sessions. The first and perhaps most important was the World Diamond Congress, held in Antwerp in July 2000. Usually a kind of diamond trade show and schmooze-in, this one was given over almost completely to the issue of conflict diamonds. NGOs were invited, Robert Fowler was invited, and US Congressman Tony Hall was invited. Hall was given the podium at a special morning session that was held in a newly renovated Victorian opera house. As participants filed into the theatre, a chamber orchestra played. Tony Hall spoke for nearly an hour, flaying the industry for its callous apathy towards the diamond wars in Africa. The audience, including mining company executives and diamond traders who had barely heard of the issue, was stunned. When Hall finished there was a genteel reception in the foyer, where lashings of champagne steadied those who had been shaken by his noisome intrusion into their hitherto private world.

The inclination to dig in and fight back against the NGOs and Tony Hall was resisted by younger members of the diamond trade and by people like Martin Rapaport, who understood the issue and its wider implications. Young Turks in the International Diamond Manufacturers' Association (IDMA) and the World Federation of Diamond Bourses (WFDB) were able to stifle the industry's anger and bewilderment, and managed to get a resolution passed creating a new body, to be called the World Diamond Council (WDC). The WDC would include representation from the mining, trading and retail sectors of the diamond industry. Its mandate would be 'the development, implementation and oversight of a tracking system for the export and import of rough diamonds to prevent the exploitation of diamonds for illicit purposes such as war and inhumane acts.'

This was a huge step, an almost complete about-face from earlier industry positions. Late one night, an IDMA member was given the job of calling the man they hoped would lead the WDC, a New York diamantaire and a past president of the WFDB, Eli Izhakoff. Without thinking about the time difference in New York, they phoned Izhakoff at home and got him out of bed. 'They told me about the NGO problem,' Izhakoff recalled later, 'and the conflict diamond issue, and how they wanted me to be the president of this new thing. And I thought to myself, "*NGO, NGO*; Is it Nicky *G*. Oppenheimer?"'[3] Izhakoff may not have heard of NGOs before that night, but he was soon to hear a lot more.

There were other gatherings. In October there was a government Kimberley Process meeting in London. And in New York the United Nations General Assembly passed a resolution introduced by South Africa in support of the process, asking participating governments to 'give urgent and careful consideration to devising effective and pragmatic measures to address the problem of conflict diamonds.' Phumzile Mlambo-Ngcuka was successful in getting the G8 to endorse the process as well. In their final communiqué at Okinawa, the heads of government of the world's eight largest industrialized countries said, 'We express special concern that the proceeds from the illicit trade in diamonds have contributed to aggravating armed conflict and humanitarian crises, particularly in Africa. We therefore call for an international conference, whose results shall be submitted to the UN... to consider practical approaches to breaking the link between the illicit trade in diamonds and armed conflict, including consideration of an international agreement on certification for rough diamonds.' And in the ebb tide of the Clinton administration, the White House organized a conference to discuss conflict diamonds. National Security Advisor Sandy Berger told the gathering that 'the United States sees the trade in conflict diamonds as a genuine and important national security problem – one that we are determined to fight. It is also one that we have a moral obligation to fight, because we in the developed world are the leading consumers of diamonds.'[4] But with ten days to go before

George W. Bush took over the building, Sandy Berger was already clearing out his desk and did not plan to be around himself for any of the fighting.

During 2001, six Kimberley Process meetings were held – in Windhoek, the capital of Namibia, in Brussels, Moscow, London, Luanda and in Gaborone, the capital of Botswana. Before each one, it seemed – especially to the NGOs – that a breakthrough was imminent. But it didn't happen. Although the meetings struggled with concepts enunciated at the Luanda meeting the previous year, there were endless problems. Every time a consensus neared, at least one delegation – often the Russians and sometimes the Americans – objected. Some delegates came, it seemed, only to thank the host government for its hospitality. Usually the hospitality *was* good, often at the expense of the diamond industry. But too often that was all that was good. The Brussels meeting in April 2001 was perhaps the worst of the entire series. A badly chaired plenary and even worse chairing of 'working groups' led to virtually nothing of substance. The first achievement reported in the final communiqué was almost embarrassing: the much-discussed certificates of origin should be on A4-sized paper and in landscape format. But there had been no agreement that certificates – or anything else for that matter – would actually be issued, so these were non achievements. Even the draft communiqué prepared for the media became a problem. It said that 'substantial progress had been made' but this wording was debated for more than two hours, in part because many delegations had come with no mandate to make any progress on anything, and didn't want to be scolded back home for allowing 'substantial' progress. The final wording said only that 'There was emerging consensus on the common elements of the certificate of origin as a building block for a certification scheme for rough diamonds,' – shorthand for saying that apart from the size of the paper for a certificate that nobody endorsed, nothing at all had been achieved.

Part of the motivation to continue was the hope that something could eventually be achieved. Besides, by the middle of 2001, the Kimberley Process had developed a momentum of its own. It was prodded along by the government of South Africa with growing assistance from its neighbouring countries and Britain. It had been endorsed by the G8 and the UN General Assembly, and the problem that it sought to address, conflict diamonds, had not abated. The UN Security Council had appointed Expert Panels to follow the Fowler Report – one for Sierra Leone, a continuation of the Angola mechanism, one for Liberia and another for the Congo. In all, a dozen damning reports were issued between March 2000 and October 2002, cataloguing the horrors of the diamond wars and describing the industry rot that had made conflict diamonds possible. Still, the debate continued, narrowing on two issues. The first was statistics. The Russians said that diamonds were a 'strategic mineral' in their country and details could not be divulged. The Israelis and others fretted about the sanctity of commercial confidentiality. The second issue had to do with monitoring. In the various proposals now floating about, there was a strong propensity among many governments and the industry to make everything 'voluntary', and to ensure that the emerging scheme not be monitored by any institution outside their own national jurisdiction. The Russians kept playing the 'strategic mineral' card, the Israelis warned of the cost and the Chinese spoke of 'national sovereignty'.

The NGOs readied themselves for the eighth meeting of the Kimberley Process by organizing a petition signed by more than 200 organizations around the world. Bright red in colour, its headline demanded that 'Governments and Industry Stop Blood Diamonds Now!'

Self-regulation will not work... All countries involved in the production, movement and processing of rough diamonds *must* agree to minimum international standards, and these *must* be open to international scrutiny. Nothing less will suffice if consumers are to have the confidence they need and deserve when they purchase something as expensive and as important as a diamond, and all governments have to take responsibility in the fight against conflict diamonds.

That meeting was held at the Twickenham Rugby Ground convention centre in a London suburb, beginning at 9:00 a.m., 11 September 2001 – 4:00 a.m. New York time. After lunch the meeting resumed, but within a few minutes a buzz started going around the room. Cell phones were ringing and people were showing each other incoming text messages. The World Trade Center had been struck by hijacked aircraft. The meeting limped along until finally a member of the Russian delegation interrupted and announced what had happened. He suggested, out of respect for the American delegation, that the meeting be adjourned for the day. But there were no buses to take delegates back to their hotels, so everyone gathered in a lounge overlooking the silent rugby field and watched in stunned silence as the BBC showed over and over the same footage of the Twin Towers collapsing.

The United States government, the United Nations and the world took action within a few short weeks of that terrible event to clamp down on money laundering and terrorist financing, passing laws and regulations, forming action-oriented task forces, and finally putting together a military coalition to crush the Taliban regime in Afghanistan and its al Qaeda friends. But the Kimberley Process would stumble along for more than another year, requiring five more meetings, more prodding from another G8 Summit and more UN reports on the diamond wars in Africa until it would conclude an agreement. Writing in *The Guardian*, David Keen, a long-time Sierra Leone watcher, started an article in November 2001 with the quote that begins this chapter: 'By now we are all familiar with the day when the world changed and unspeakable acts of terror took the lives of more than 5,000 civilians. I am referring, of course, to January 6, 1999, when rebel gunmen killed, maimed and raped their way across Freetown, Sierra Leone's capital.' Keen had put his finger on something: the quality of terror. Terrorists in Sierra Leone or Angola are one thing, but when terrorists strike the West, the quality is somehow different. The loss of innocent lives to terrorism in New York demands more urgent attention than the loss of lives to terrorism in Africa. Suddenly, it was no longer 'correct' to refer to men who chopped the hands off babies in Sierra Leone as 'terrorists'; they were not even remotely in the same league as the al Qaeda hijackers.

The tenth Meeting of the Kimberley Process was held in Gaborone, the capital of Botswana. If Brussels had been the A4 meeting, this was the Taiwan meeting. The issues of statistics and monitoring remained unresolved, but now a new issue arose: membership. The United States argued that the proposed certification scheme should be open to all countries. Otherwise it would restrict trade and might soon incur a challenge at the World Trade Organization. The European Union, NGOs and others argued for entry-level standards. Countries must be able to demonstrate that they could meet the minimum standards being thrashed out by the Kimberley meetings. China, a newcomer to the meetings and hitherto silent, weighed in on the side of entry standards. This club could not be open to just *anybody*. There would have to be scrutiny of credentials and agreement by the full plenary if a new country cared to join. As China dug in, it became clear that there was a sub-text, but the United States would not let go. The meeting went on and on, but the word 'Taiwan' was never uttered. At 10 pm there was a break for tea and cookies, with China playing Mad Hatter to the American March Hare. Oddly, China and Taiwan had each completed negotiations for entry into the WTO only nine weeks earlier, and now China was trying to block Taiwanese participation in the Kimberley Process – before either had actually been officially seated at the world trade body. An hour after midnight the meeting adjourned with the Taiwan issue unsettled.

Throughout the Kimberley Process, the NGO coalition continued to apply as much public pressure as it could. Amnesty International mimicked a De Beers television advertisement, placing a dramatic action cartoon on its website showing rebels hacking the hand off a civilian in order to get at diamonds. American NGOs such as Physicians for Human Rights, World Vision and Oxfam America worked with congressmen Tony Hall and Frank Wolf on their continuing efforts to get a 'Clean Diamond Bill' through Congress. The US diamond jewellery industry, worried about the provisions of the bill but understanding the demand for better regulation, enraged American NGOs by working with Republican Senator Judd Gregg on softer legislation. In fact no effort was spared to weaken the Hall-Wolf-NGO effort. The World Diamond Council had engaged one of Washington's most politically well-connected law firms – Akin, Gump, Strauss, Hauer & Feld – to help draft the Gregg bill. The WDC also consulted specialists on how to deal with the NGO campaign: Powell Tate was headed by Jody Powell, a former spokesperson for Jimmy Carter, and Sheila Tate had served in the same capacity for Nancy Reagan. Shandwick Associates had advised Monsanto, Ciba-Geigy, Procter & Gamble, Royal Dutch Shell and others on how to deal with NGO campaigns. Jewelers of America hired Haake and Associates, and the Government of Botswana engaged Hill and Knowlton which had defended Nestlé (unsuccessfully) in a decade-long NGO campaign against the company's baby food marketing in developing countries. And the Government of Liberia hired Jefferson Waterman International, whose list of clients included the Burmese military junta.

Mostly these companies simply absorbed large amounts of diamond industry cash, doing little to advance the cause of their clients. Then, in May 2001, World Vision bought some time as the credits were rolling on the season's last episode of the popular television program, *The West Wing*. In the series, actor Martin Sheen played a likeable American President. The World Vision promo showed film of Sierra Leonean children without hands. The voice of Martin Sheen told viewers that diamonds were contributing to such atrocities, and they should ask their congressman to support the Hall/Wolf bill. Within days the Gregg bill had vanished, and the US industry made peace with NGOs and the Clean Diamond Bill.

NGOs worked the media. They worked closely with all the major international television networks; with national and international radio; with print journalists and the Internet. Major articles appeared in *Vanity Fair, National Geographic, USA Today, the New York Times, Der Spiegel* and *Jornal do Brazil*. Feature programs were shown on television in Britain, Canada, Japan and in the United States.

In addition to general material about conflict diamonds, NGOs also produced policy-related documents, op ed articles and background research. Early in the debate Global Witness published a detailed description of what a certification system might look like, and in 2003 it produced major papers on Liberian diamond and timber interests, and the al Qaeda diamond connection. Partnership Africa Canada published ten research papers on diamonds in Guinea, Canada, Southern Africa, India and elsewhere. It produced a follow-up report on Sierra Leone which examined the role of the Lebanese diaspora in the illicit diamond trade, and it reviewed other international agreements for their provisions on monitoring.

The NGO coalition was never a formal grouping; there were no regular meetings; no chair; no 'members'. There was no leadership as such, although because Global Witness and Partnership Africa Canada had dedicated resources and people to the issue, they tended to be more active and informed on day-to-day issues. Other key players were the British NGO, ActionAid, Oxfam International, the Amsterdam-based Fatal Transactions, World Vision and Amnesty International. Two African NGOs representing broad coalitions in their own countries joined: the Network Movement for Justice and Development in Sierra Leone, and CENADEP (*Centre National d'Appui au Développement et à la Participation Populaire*) in the Democratic Republic of the Congo. This coalition was supported and backed by a loose grouping of 200 other NGOs around the world, including an important set of American organizations. It was an eclectic mix: development and human rights NGOs; NGOs in the North and the South; very big NGOs and very small NGOs; faith-based organizations and secular, activist, campaigning NGOs. While there were occasional disagreements, there was never anything like a dispute. Each organization carried out its own activities, but there was regular sharing of information by e-mail, frequent telephone conference calls, and meetings before and after each Kimberley session. The coalition's energy came from its commitment to ending the diamond wars in Africa, but organizationally it derived strength from its informality and the broad range of interests, and from a willingness to share, to listen, and to cooperate when common stands were required.

The 11th Kimberley meeting was held in a snowy Ottawa, in March 2002. Here one of the outstanding issues was at last resolved. Governments agreed that they would provide quarterly diamond trade statistics and semi-annual production statistics, even though it would take another 18 months to get a data-gathering system up, if not exactly running. This would make it possible to verify whether exports from Angola to Belgium, for example, equalled Belgian imports from Angola. The massive discrepancies of the past would now no longer be possible. A delegation from Taiwan arrived but the Chairman of the Kimberley Process – the head of South Africa's Diamond Board – nimbly avoided them. When the delegation phoned his hotel, they found his line blocked. They were then told he had checked out, and when they went to the Westin Hotel and sat in the lobby planning to corner him in person, they had no way of identifying him, short of accosting each of the many Africans who had come for the meeting. This was diplomacy in the Kimberley Process.

On the cusp of an agreement, the NGOs now had to make a choice. In its basics, the overall proposal was elegantly simple. The seemingly endless debates and drafting had paid off. Governments of all participating countries would agree to certify that diamonds leaving their borders were clean. Importing countries would reject any diamonds not accompanied by an official certificate. The same standard would apply to Sierra Leone as to the United States, Russia and Switzerland. Any country, whether producing diamonds, trading rough diamonds, or cutting and polishing diamonds, would have to ensure that all rough diamonds leaving its borders were clean, and there would be a series of internal controls to prove it. Diamonds would be sealed in tamper-proof containers. The certificate issued by each participating government or its surrogate (on A4 paper – *landscape*) would be the transit document, and receiving countries would inform shipping countries that parcels had arrived intact. The certificates would be forgery-resistant, produced by security printers.

So, what would now prevent someone from walking past customs with illicit goods and going straight to Hovenierstraat in Antwerp or 47th Street in New York? Nothing. But the industry chain of warranties – part of the system – was designed to provide an audit trail. Dealers handling rough diamonds would be required to keep records showing incomings and outgoings, by weight and value. The approach might vary from country to country. But each participating government agreed to 'maintain dissuasive and proportional penalties for transgressions' – something that had never before happened in the diamond industry.

The system was not perfect. Diamonds are small and easy to conceal. But the illicit trade on which conflict diamonds had piggy-backed was founded on tax evasion and money laundering. Those trading in illicit diamonds in order to evade tax would now have to think twice, because some countries began to write the word 'forfeiture' into their regulations. Avoiding a thousand dollars in taxes might not be worth the risk of losing a million dollars in diamonds. Volume is the attraction for money launderers, and with better statistics and audit trails, large-scale money laundering would become more visible. Diamond theft, of course, will never be stopped completely, any more than car theft will be stopped completely. In the case of automobiles, the first deterrent – a hundred years ago – was door locks. Then came ignition locks, steering locks, serial numbers, alarms, fuel disablers and tracking devices. All serve to make car theft more difficult. That is what the Kimberley Process was all about: making it more difficult in a hitherto unregulated industry, to exchange stolen diamonds for weapons.

The dilemma for NGOs centred squarely on the problem of monitoring, which seemed like a no-brainer. They were wrong. Although the industry had been slow, the barriers to an effective certification system were now being erected by governments. As the Kimberley negotiations progressed, it became obvious that some, notably Russia, Israel and China, would not agree to regular independent monitoring. Cost, commercial sensitivity and national sovereignty became their mantra – chanted at every meeting while most other governments sat on their hands and said nothing. Commercial sensitivity, however, was not a real issue because the standards to be monitored were systemic rather than financial in nature. No commercial secrets – in fact no commercial information of any kind – would be sought in a review mission. And if the total bill for all review missions in a year cost one or two million dollars, it would not add more than fifteen cents to a five hundred dollar diamond ring – in an industry that spent $170 million more in advertising than it had only two years earlier.[5]

Compromises to national sovereignty can only be traded against a greater good if a government deems this to be in its own interest – as in the case of airline safety, nuclear safety, food and maritime safety and provisions related to money laundering. If monitoring is acceptable for these threats, why not for diamonds when the issue was the human security of millions of Africans? The real answers were obvious enough, but they were never discussed at the Kimberley Process meetings: some governments were protecting thieves. And many did not care about Africans. Those with vested interests in the status quo understood that a system that would effectively stop *conflict* diamonds would also expose the much larger trade in *illicit* diamonds. If you trawl for tuna, you will catch porpoise. If you look for piranha, you will also find catfish.

The final draft Kimberley agreement said only that monitoring could take place if there were 'credible indications of non-compliance' with its standards, and that this would require the agreement of all participating countries. On top of that, all participating countries would work out the terms of reference for each mission at the annual plenary meeting, and they would also appoint the team. This from a group – now expanded to more than 60 governments – that had taken six months to agree on A4 paper for certificates. The NGOs came under withering pressure at the eleventh Kimberley meeting in Ottawa to back off their demand for effective monitoring. They knew, in fact, that they had the power to break the agreement entirely, but if they did, there would be no return to the table and no agreement of any kind. Finally, they gave in, hoping that the question could be revisited in the future.

On a cold, rainy November day in 2002, in the small Swiss resort town of Interlaken, the world's diamond industry, representatives of the NGO coalition and the governments of 52 countries, plus another fifteen represented by the European Union, put their seal of approval on an agreement to end the trade in conflict diamonds. After 1 January 2003, no rough diamonds would be traded internationally anywhere in the world without an accompanying certificate of origin from the government of the exporting country. Without the NGOs, without Phumzile Mlambo-Ngcuka, without the United Nations expert panels, without the World Diamond Council, it would never have happened. High on the Jungfrau overlooking the town, it had snowed during the night, and for a few moments the clouds broke to reveal the mountain, looming over the town in its brilliant cloak of new white snow. Unresolved issues notwithstanding, it seemed like a metaphor for the event: a brief opening and a small step towards solving a problem that a group of NGOs had been battling for more than four years.

Four years. It seemed like an eternity in NGO time. For the diamond industry it also seemed like an eternity: four years of accusation, demonstrations, fear that a powerful consumer boycott might suddenly erupt into a diamond world that had been badly hit by the 1997 Asian economic meltdown and then again by a market downturn after Nine-Eleven. For the governments that gathered at Interlaken, however, four years was nothing. It was, in fact, a record in reaching a complicated international agreement on anything, especially an issue that transcended the political and trading interests of countries on every continent. The agreement cut across evolving political and economic sensitivities in the European Union, cut into perceived WTO obligations and drew strength from still smouldering Cold War embers. It had engaged the United Nations Security Council in a dozen detailed investigations and it lay at the centre of debates about African development, underdevelopment, sanctions busting, resource exploitation, mercenaries, theft, murder, state collapse and war.

CHAPTER 13

ENDGAMES

We shall find peace. We shall hear the angels, we shall see the sky sparkling with diamonds.

— Chekov, *Uncle Vanya*

In March 2003, the Special Court established by the United Nations and the Government of Sierra Leone indicted rebel leader Foday Sankoh and several others. By then, Sankoh had slipped into a fantasy world, unable to respond to simple questions even from his own lawyers. He had become dishevelled and with his hair uncut for months, he looked like a confused old Rastafarian. It was a rapid transition from the madness of the jungle, where he had commanded a force of drug-addled teenaged killers, to a madness induced by solitary confinement and little more than his own ideas for company.

A month later, the Chief Prosecutor demanded that Liberian President Charles Taylor hand over Sam 'Maskita' Bockarie and escaped coup leader, Johnny Paul Koroma. Both had been indicted along with Sankoh and others for war crimes. Taylor denied all knowledge of their whereabouts, but there had been sightings of the narcissistic Bockarie in Liberia, and it was widely reported that he was leading ex-RUF and Liberian combatants in a civil war that had erupted in Côte d'Ivoire. Never one to miss a chance, Taylor had turned his attention from Sierra Leone and Guinea to his eastern border and to Ivorian rebels attempting to overthrow the elected government of that country. New Ivorian rebel movements sprouted like mushrooms along the Liberian frontier, and hundreds of thousands of people fled the fighting in a country once regarded as an exemplar of African peace and development.

Bockarie was at the centre of it until one day in May 2003 when he was shot dead. The Liberian government, forever trying to convince the world of its benign intentions, announced that its 'gallant' soldiers had attempted to apprehend Bockarie while he crossing into Liberia near the Ivorian border town of Bon-Houn. In the official version, Bockarie was to be arrested for possible transfer to Sierra Leone to face justice.[1] When he resisted, he was killed in a shootout.

As his body lay in a mortuary in Monrovia, a diplomatic argument broke out over returning it to Freetown for DNA testing and forensic examination. Meanwhile, other versions of Bockarie's demise began to surface. Moses Blah, Taylor's Vice President, would later testify that Bockarie had been murdered by senior officers close to Taylor to prevent his extradition and possible testimony at the Special Court.[2] Soon, reports would arrive in Freetown that Johnny Paul Koroma too had been killed in Liberia. And not long afterwards, the Chief Investigator of Sierra Leone's Special Court said there was evidence that Taylor had ordered the death of Bockarie's mother, wife and two children. One by one the Special Court's suspects and potential witnesses were disappearing in a gangland-style bloodbath.

It was not be long before Taylor himself was forced to step down. To the disgust of the world's human rights organizations and the outrage of Sierra Leone's Special Court, Nigerian President Obasanjo offered Taylor asylum as battles pushed the number of desperate Liberians, living rough on the streets of Monrovia, into the hundreds of thousands. When Foday Sankoh died of a stroke in prison, Charles Taylor may have seen this as a harbinger of things to come, but until Obasanjo made the offer, there seemed no way out. So at long last, in a tawdry ceremony complete with a church choir singing hymns of praise while the Presidents of South Africa, Mozambique and Ghana looked on, Charles Taylor, clad in the sashes and ribbons of a Ruritanian princeling, handed power to his Vice President. 'History will be kind to me,' Taylor said. 'I have fulfilled my duties. I have accepted this role as the sacrificial lamb... I am the whipping boy.' That afternoon, Nigeria's Presidential jet whisked him off to exile in Nigeria. Two cargo planes loaded with an estimated three million dollars in cash, furniture, cars and other ill-gotten gains followed. 'By the grace of God,' Taylor said ominously, 'I *will* be back.'[3]

He did return, but neither he nor his listeners could foresee then how it might occur, or how brief his stay would be. For almost three years Taylor languished in a luxury villa in the Nigerian port city of Calabar, in a district fittingly known as 'Diamond Hill'. Nigerian President Olusegun Obasanjo steadfastly protected Taylor from the Special Court, saying he would only hand him over to a democratically elected Liberian government if such a government were to make the request. In January 2006, Liberia's first-ever truly free and fair elections took place, and in March, the country's new President, Ellen Johnson-Sirleaf, asked that Taylor be surrendered to the Special Court. Obasanjo, besieged by human rights organizations and trapped by his own excuse for inaction, said with not a little bad grace, that Liberia was 'free to take' Charles Taylor.

Liberia, with no military, no aircraft, and no money, did not have the wherewithal to 'take' Taylor, and in any case, the last thing Johnson-Sirleaf wanted was Charles Taylor back in Liberia. At issue was Taylor's indictment for crimes against humanity, not whether Liberia wanted him. As negotiations began, Special Court officers demanded that Nigeria step up the guard on Taylor's Calabar villa to prevent an escape. It was too late. Obasanjo said on a Saturday that Liberia could take Taylor. By Monday Taylor had vanished.

International outrage was sudden and fierce. En route to Washington to discuss other matters entirely, Obasanjo was told that his meeting with President Bush might be cancelled. Kofi Annan expressed his anger, and Human Rights Watch said that history would judge Nigeria harshly for what was certainly indirect if not direct collusion in Taylor's disappearance.[4] Then, on the Tuesday, at a remote Cameroonian border crossing in northern Nigeria, Charles Taylor was dragged out of a Range Rover stuffed with Euros and American dollars. He was driven immediately to Maiduguri and then flown to the Nigerian capital, Abuja. The next morning a Nigerian aircraft flew him to Monrovia. There, on the tarmac, in a driving rainstorm, he was handcuffed by UN peacekeeping troops and read his rights. Within an hour, a UN helicopter lifted him away from Liberia for the last time. In Freetown, the Special Court had constructed a helipad for precisely this kind of eventuality. Two hours later, dishevelled former warlord, Charles Ghankay Taylor, was led to his cell and to the beginning of a long-awaited rendezvous with justice.

◆

The cost of dealing with the diamond wars has been enormous. UNMIL, the UN peacekeeping force that was established in Liberia in 2003, grew to absorb a budget of $560 million in 2009-10. The peacekeeping force in Sierra Leone cost $2.8 billion by the time it ended operations in 2005. The annual cost of the peacekeeping force in Côte d'Ivoire was half a billion dollars a year in 2009-10, and in the Democratic Republic of the Congo, MONUC was running a $1.35 billion dollar 12-month budget over the same period. As of January 2010, 152 UN personnel had lost their lives in the DRC operation. At something between $2.3 and $4 billion a year, not counting the peacekeeping efforts in Angola, it has taken a great deal of money and troops to control the fires that were fuelled by diamonds. These wars might or might not have happened without diamonds, but they would never have been so brutal, would never have taken so many lives, would never have attended the destruction of so much infrastructure and humanity had there never been diamonds.

When the campaign against conflict diamonds began, there was a sudden rush of academic papers and conferences, suggesting that greed rather than grievance was at the root of more conflicts than had previously been imagined. Diamonds became a kind of stalking horse for studies on oil, timber, coltan and other commodities being used by rebel forces to pay for weapons. In 2000, New York's influential International Peace Academy produced a book entitled *Greed and Grievance: Economic Agendas in Civil Wars*,[5] and before long 'resource-based conflict' had become something of an academic fad. The World Bank developed a Conflict Prevention and Reconstruction Unit that produced a widely-cited paper on the subject in 2001. Entitled 'Greed and Grievance in Civil War',[6] it examined 78 major civil conflicts between 1960 and 1999. While it found that rebellions are often caused by severe grievances – high levels of inequality, lack of political rights, ethnic and religious divisions – it found that opportunity was also a factor. Opportunity comes in a variety of forms, but the strongest has to do with the means of financing a rebellion, and the World Bank study found that economic opportunity was the predominant systematic explanation for rebellion.

This balloon was not in the air a month before it attracted heavy sniper fire. At one end of the firing range, the diamond industry resolutely insisted that diamonds do not kill people, guns kill people. More academics entered the fray, arguing that the real problem was 'lumpen youth', a 'predatory accumulation of the political class that enfeebled institutions', a 'crisis of modernity', the breakdown of 'traditional patrimonial relationships', social injustice, corruption, and so on. Resources are, in themselves, 'value neutral', it was said.

True, perhaps. Although much valued, diamonds are, in themselves, virtually worthless, although you might have a hard time convincing Elizabeth Taylor of it. And it is true that young people are in many cases attracted to a rebellion because they have grievances, many of them poignant and very genuine. But that does not excuse or explain butchery. Those who flocked to the Nazi Party had grievances, as did the Hutu who killed their neighbours in Rwanda. Grievances were always ready on the lips of those who stole diamonds to pay for weapons. But in the case of the RUF, UNITA and a dozen factions fighting in the Congo, it was diamonds and the criminal violence used to obtain them that became the vehicle for grievance – however just or evil, however real or imagined. Without diamonds, Jonas Savimbi, Foday Sankoh, Charles Taylor and the rest might never have become such monsters. Instead of conflating a false dichotomy, the academics might have used their time more productively in thinking about ways to halt wars that were obviously funded by the unrestricted sale of commodities – like diamonds – than whether or not Foday Sankoh had a 'grievance'. He did have a grievance, not one that needed much academic study: someone other than him was president of Sierra Leone.

♦

Had this story ended in 2003 with the conclusion of a somewhat incomplete Kimberley Process Certification Scheme, it would have left the reader hanging, just as participants in the scheme wondered after Interlaken whether it could ever be made to work. The Interlaken agreement, which remains the central working document of the Kimberley Process Certification Scheme – often quoted by diplomats of participating countries as though it were gospel – reflected many of the concerns expressed during the negotiations, and at face value it appeared rather weak. The KPCS is not a legally binding formal international treaty, and no government signed any document. The KPCS preamble recalls the early General Assembly Resolution, carefully worded by anonymous officials, which said that the KPCS should be 'a simple and workable international certification scheme based on national certification schemes and on internationally agreed minimum standards.' It recognized 'the differences in production methods and trading practices' that might require 'different approaches'. It recognized the importance of state sovereignty and said that everything should be agreed by consensus.

Consensus, which in the real world means generalized agreement, in the Kimberley Process came to mean unanimity: if one government dissents from a position, that position cannot go forward. It was a one man-one veto arrangement that would hobble the KPCS on more than one occasion in the months that followed. The provision for monitoring was weak in the extreme, with no sanctions in the unlikely event that a review mission ever took place. And membership was to be open to any government 'willing and able to fulfil the requirements of [the] scheme', with no credentials review of any kind. There would be no secretariat, no staff and no budget. Plenary meetings would be held once a year in the country of the KP Chair, who would rotate annually.

None of these weaknesses were lost on those who wanted a tough, binding agreement with tough admission and verification standards. For them the question at Interlaken had been whether to accept a weak agreement and work later to strengthen it from the inside, or to leave the table entirely and for good. Given the obvious inability of the process to move beyond what was agreed at Interlaken, the latter would probably have destroyed the entire process, culminating in the consumer boycott that the industry feared, hurting hundreds of thousands of innocent diamond miners and polishers in many developing countries.

The agreement had several strengths, however, that were not obvious at first. One was that although participation was completely voluntary, members undertook not to trade with those outside the system. Countries that 'voluntarily' stayed out of the KPCS, therefore, could not trade diamonds with countries that were in. This created a situation where virtually any country with a rough diamond business – production, trade or consumption; gems and industrial – *had* to be a member. It was voluntary, but in *real* terms it was compulsory.

The KPCS minimum standards were not *minimal* standards, and some were set quite high. It was necessary for almost every serious participant to pass new laws in order to enforce the KPCS at home. New Kimberley-specific laws were passed for the entire European Union, in Canada, Russia, the United States and virtually every one of the almost 80 countries that were eventually covered. So while the KPCS was not a legally binding international treaty, each participating country made its provisions legally binding within its own borders. Where an international treaty might have been difficult to enforce, laws in each participating country are much less so.

A Monitoring Working Group was struck to manage a system of 'peer reviews', with teams usually consisting of representatives from three other countries and one each from industry and civil society. Although the review provision was voluntary, when some countries began to request review visits, it became harder for others not to volunteer. By the end of 2005, 25 'voluntary' reviews had been carried out, and there were few countries left in the KPCS that had not requested one.

During 2003 and 2004 as the Kimberley Process began to gather strength, the signs were promising. The fact of the KP negotiations alone had helped choke diamond supplies to rebel movements in Angola and Sierra Leone, and contributed to the end of hostilities. And the KPCS was credited by several countries as having a direct impact on the growth in legitimate diamond exports, and thus of tax revenue. In 2005, Sierra Leone exported $142 million worth of diamonds, a huge increase on $26 million in 2001 and as good an indication as any that many more miners, buyers and exporters had decided that crime no longer paid. In 2003, the DRC had its best diamond export year in history. As important as stemming the flow of conflict diamonds might be, the KPCS also helped to formalize and clean up an industry that – at its edges – had operated for a century with little transparency and few paper trails, making it a fertile playground for all manner of illicit activity and for some of the world's most ruthless killers.

The Kimberley Process data base, weak at first, was gradually transformed into the best and most reliable set of statistics on the world's rough diamond production and trade. The peer review system showed that the Kimberley Process could bare its teeth when it became the basis for expelling Congo-Brazzaville from the system in 2004. The Republic of Congo (Brazzaville), a long-time conduit for smuggled diamonds from neighbouring Democratic Republic of the Congo (Kinshasa), had no explanation for the large volumes it continued to export, and the solution was obvious.

But the peer reviews, solid at first, soon became a hit and miss business. The cost of each participant on a team had to be met by his or her employer, which constrained many governments and limited participation. Some reviews were thorough, others were not. The worst example was a bloated 2008 review of Guinea. There the problem did not lie in finding enough members. Instead of the usual three government representatives and one each from industry and civil society, the team had nine members. But they spent less than two hours on the ground outside the capital city, and they did not complete their report for 11 months. This was not just dilatory, it was irresponsible in dealing with a country that had registered a staggering two-year 600 per cent increase in diamond production, and whose eastern border was immediately adjacent to the rebel diamond mining areas of Côte d'Ivoire.

Even where reports were thorough, recommendations often attracted little attention and no follow-up. Reviews in 2004 and 2005 of Angola and the DRC found that those governments could not say where as many as half of the diamonds they exported were mined. The same was true to a lesser extent in Guinea, Sierra Leone and other countries. This was the whole point of the Kimberley Process: to certify with confidence where diamonds came from. Subsequent studies by NGOs between 2005 and 2009, and by the Kimberley Process itself in 2009 showed that nothing had changed.[7]

Perhaps the worst example of blatant non-compliance occurred in Venezuela, a smallish diamond producer, but a founding member of the Kimberley Process and an important link in the overall diamond pipeline. Early in 2005, Venezuela simply stopped issuing Kimberley Certificates. There was no explanation, and no amount of correspondence from the Kimberley Process succeeded in re-establishing contact. Finally, at the end of 2006, Partnership Africa Canada sent an investigator to Venezuela. His report showed that diamonds were still being mined and were being openly smuggled into Brazil and Guyana.[8] When the story reached the media, the Kimberley Process and the government of Venezuela both appeared to awaken, as if from a siesta. Venezuela sent a senior official to KP meetings where he denounced PAC. Finally, in October 2008, the KP sent a high-level team to Caracas for discussions. NGOs, an integral part of the Kimberley Process and members of all reviews up to that point, were forbidden, and the Potemkin team obligingly ate up Potemkin promises, never visiting diamond mining areas or easy-to-reach trans-border smuggling points. It simply regurgitated the blandishments it had been fed in Caracas. Venezuela, it was agreed, did have some problems regulating its diamonds, and the government offered to suspend all exports for two years while it revamped its controls. But Venezuela had already 'suspended' shipments years before, in the sense that it had issued no certificates and submitted no production or export data since 2005.

That was perhaps beside the point for those looking for any excuse to avoid confrontation or the application of a penalty. The Kimberley Process, its heart too soon made glad, swallowed the offer, hook, line and sinker. Six months later, in May 2009, the PAC investigator returned to Venezuela and the border areas around Santa Elena de Uairén to find that nothing had changed. The Venezuelan government had reissued mining permits; diamonds were being openly bought and sold; and the blatant illegal traffic across the border to Brazil and Guyana continued. The Kimberley Process sat on its hands, effectively ignoring diamond smuggling. Incredibly, the institution that had been designed to halt diamond smuggling was now condoning it.

In October 2008, the Zimbabwe Air Force shot and killed as many as 200 illicit diamond diggers in the Marange region near the Mozambique border. It had been obvious for some time that Zimbabwe's diamonds were leaking openly into a resurging international swamp of illicit goods. Seizures of Zimbabwean diamonds had been made in Dubai and Bombay, and just a few miles into Mozambique near the Zimbabwean border town of Mutare, diamond dealers from around the world had gathered with their scales, their loupes and their cash. The media was full of the stories, and human rights organizations produced detailed studies of the smuggling and the atrocities.[9] It took months of internal wrangling for the Kimberley Process to finally send a review team. Once there, it found ample evidence of Zimbabwean non-compliance, but when it came to any discussion of human rights abuse or a possible suspension of Zimbabwe, some governments went into a kind of see-no-evil overdrive. India, Russia, China and Namibia led in denouncing any kind of chastisement over human rights abuse. 'The Kimberley Process is not a human rights organization,' they said, a view supported by the industry representative on the review team. South Africa, a long-time apologist for the Mugabe regime, gathered Southern African allies in a defensive laager around Zimbabwe. The KP Chair, Namibia's Deputy Minister of Mines, issued a series of contradictory statements, absolving the Zimbabwe government of wrongdoing before the team had even started its work, and stating before the report was written that Zimbabwe would never be suspended.

If Venezuela showed that the Kimberley Process had no teeth, Zimbabwe showed that it had no brains, and that its moral authority had evaporated. Despite the horrendous findings of the review team, and despite the efforts of a number of member countries, the best the KP Plenary of November 2009 could do was to provide Zimbabwe with technical assistance and a 'workplan' to help solve its problems. There was no censure, and the Zimbabwean Minister of Mines had been permitted to attend the meeting, insulting and threatening NGOs that had uncovered human rights violations in the diamond fields.

A month later, Namibia drafted the annual motherhood Kimberley Process resolution for the United Nations General Assembly. The text 'noted with satisfaction' and 'appreciation' the system's positive impact on peace and just about everything else. There was no mention of Venezuela, Zimbabwe or human rights, because strong paragraphs on these subjects had been stripped out of the document courtesy of Venezuela, Zimbabwe and China respectively. The one man-one veto arrangement meant that only good news would be taken to the General Assembly.

Before the anodyne text was presented for a vote, however, Sweden, Canada, Switzerland and the United States spoke out on the Zimbabwe problem. Then Zimbabwe itself had the last word. The Zimbabwean representative said that his country was 'a victim', and he denounced the 'charade' by countries that were supposed to be guarantors of the Kimberley Process. The charade, of course, was perpetrated not by Sweden, Canada, Switzerland and the United States. It was perpetrated by the countries in Southern Africa that rallied, as they had in the past, in protection of a criminalized neighbouring government. In the end, the UN resolution was proposed by Botswana, Namibia and South Africa, the very countries that had initiated the Kimberley Process, three countries with the most to lose if it failed. As if to add insult to the farce, there was a fourth presenter: Zimbabwe.

In short, the Kimberley Process was becoming an ineffective circus. Most of its members went to considerable lengths to comply with its minimum standards, and some were disgusted with its inability to deal with outliers. But as a regulatory system, its policing was a joke. It patrolled country roads looking for jaywalkers while criminals infested its downtown streets with impunity.

A few voices called for an end to the KPCS. It wasn't working, they said, and after all, the problem of conflict diamonds had ended. They were wrong on the second assumption. A small amount of conflict diamonds continued to leak into the system from Côte d'Ivoire. Regardless of whether it might be absolved, Zimbabwe was covering its diamonds with blood – an example if one was needed of how quickly a polite fiction can descend into chaos and murder. More to the point, however, the combined cost of the 2009-10 UN peacekeeping efforts in Liberia, Côte d'Ivoire and the DRC was $2.3 *billion*, and in some areas the effort was barely keeping a lid on the problem. While all of this was going on, the Kimberley Process, touting itself as a model for commodity regulation, could not track half the stones in some of the countries worst affected by the diamond wars. Some governments and parts of the diamond industry were demonstrating that common sense, human rights and even the long-term interests of the industry at large could be trumped by narrow, short-term vested interests.

If it were to happen, the cost of a general KP collapse would be extraordinarily high. The criminalized diamond regime of the 1990s would undoubtedly re-emerge. Criminals have already shown that they are not far back in the wings. Conflict diamonds would probably not be far behind, and then it would be necessary to start all over again. The alternative is simple. The Kimberley Process, a remarkable agreement that already binds some 80 governments, has most of the tools it needs to become an effective regulatory system. But it needs a few more.[10]

It needs to end its nonsensical veto arrangement and replace it with a voting system. It needs an independent, accountable, arms-length review mechanism. It needs much greater transparency and a problem-solving secretariat with a permanent home base to replace the annual rotation of Chairs whose main objective, it seems, is to avoid being stuck with a difficult decision. And the diamond industry needs to do more than nod politely at these ideas. It must lead.

Young men still buy diamond engagement rings for young women. But young couples are better informed, better connected, and more conscious than ever of the need for social responsibility in the products they buy. The issue will not go away. If the world learned anything during the great economic meltdown of 2008, it is that when regulators fail to regulate, the object of their attention runs away from them. And not in a good way.

◆

In 2005, something else began to develop, something quite unusual under the circumstances. The year before, Partnership Africa Canada and Global Witness had joined forces on a research project to examine the plight of the artisanal African diamond digger. What they found was striking. First, the number of artisanal miners is enormous. As many as 1.3 million people dig for diamonds in the Congo, Angola, Sierra Leone and half a dozen other countries, using the most rudimentary equipment and earning – on average – a dollar a day. Despite the hope each digger has of getting rich quick with a big find, the pittance they actually earn puts them squarely into that category of people the UN calls 'the absolute poor'. Social violence of every sort is rampant in the mining towns and at the digging sites. The work is dangerous and unhealthy, and the miners are vectors for malaria, HIV/AIDS and a host of other diseases. Child labour is common, and most of the miners, living completely outside the formal economy, are vulnerable to just about every kind of predator. This is where conflict diamonds were born, and while better regulation of the international trade makes sense, it is naïve to think that the diamond industry will ever be free and clear of criticism and peril as long as twenty per cent of its product is mined under these circumstances.

When PAC and Global Witness presented their finding to a Kimberley Process meeting, it was De Beers that was first to suggest a way forward. Would the two NGOs be prepared to co-host, with De Beers, a meeting of industry, NGOs and governments, to talk about the issue? The danger in this was obvious: many environmental NGOs have lost their *bona fides* over the years by getting into bed with corporations eager for endorsement. But the Kimberley Process succeeded, up to a point, because NGOs, the industry and governments had been willing to cut each other some slack, to pull punches, to talk and to listen. The objective for NGOs in the Kimberley Process was not to hammer the diamond industry, which is so important to many developing countries. It was to end the diamond wars. Now an opportunity was emerging for something that might take the Kimberley idea much deeper into Africa's diamond problem, with the potential not just to get at the ultimate cancer, but perhaps to make diamonds a force for development.

And so began a tentative new effort they called the Diamond Development Initiative (DDI). A first meeting brought interested parties together in London to see if the concept made sense. The idea was not to start a lot of small diamond mining cooperatives around Africa, although this could be part of what might emerge. The idea was to push the market price for diamonds closer to diggers, finding ways to formalize their work and to give them a stake in a *job* rather than the hope of a diamond. In order for this to work, it would require better information, new laws, tax harmonization across borders to discourage smuggling, enforceable health and safety standards. It would require the involvement of more companies, more NGOs, and more aid agencies, most of them hitherto wary of this volatile industry.

A second meeting was held in Accra at the end of 2005, and the representatives of governments, aid agencies, business and civil society came from nine African countries, and from as far away as Australia, India, Europe and North America. The first tentative DDI project left the runway in January 2006 and an executive director with the right mix of experience, compassion and vigour, Dorothée Gizenga, was appointed in 2008. By 2010 DDI was receiving support from the Tiffany Foundation, a range of diamond companies and the governments of Sweden, Britain and Belgium. More importantly, there was enthusiastic uptake from African governments and communities where diamonds are a troubled everyday fact of life. It is not yet clear whether DDI will have the impact it seeks. Detractors saw a De Beers plot; an NGO sell-out; a futile gesture; an impossibility. African supporters saw something else: an opportunity to change the very meaning of diamonds; an enterprise worthy of support; a possibility. If the decade-long investment in campaigning and in creating the Kimberley Process is to pay long-term, sustainable dividends, DDI looks like the right way to go, and perhaps the only way to go in ending a century of chaos in the diamond fields of Africa. If it succeeds, it could be one of the biggest development projects in Africa, and it could help to ensure that there will never be anything like blood diamonds again.

♦

There are many apocryphal tales in the diamond industry, but two stand out. One is the story of the *Star of Sierra Leone*, the largest alluvial diamond ever found, and the third largest gem diamond of all time. The size of a hen's egg, it weighed – at 968.9 carats – nearly half a pound. Appropriately, it turned up on Valentine's Day in 1972, on the picking table of Sierra Leone's National Diamond Mining Company. Before long it found its way to De Beers in London. There it was offered for sale, and in October that year, Harry Winston announced in New York that he had bought it for a price 'in the vicinity of several million dollars'.[11] Winston intended to have the diamond cut in a way that would yield one exceptional stone. But like the diamond industry and the government of the country it came from, the *Star of Sierra Leone* was flawed, and there were problems with Harry Winston's great 143.2 carat emerald cut when it finally emerged. In the end, the big diamond was divided into seventeen more gems, the largest of them only five per cent of the original stone's weight. The *Star of Sierra Leone* had simply disappeared.

The second story is told by Christian Dietrich in a diamond exposé written for Partnership Africa Canada, *Hard Currency*.[12] Dietrich quotes De Beers on its *Millennium Star*:

Imagine a diamond so flawless and so great in size that the world's diamond experts cannot put a price on it. The De Beers *Millennium Star*... It took over three years for their diamond cutters to shape the stone with lasers. What emerged was the world's only internally and externally flawless, 203-carat, pear-shaped diamond... De Beers created the [Millennium] collection as a way to symbolize the world's hopes and dreams for the future.[13]

Dietrich says that De Beers bought the stone from which the *Millennium Star* was cut in the early 1990s, near Mbuji-Mayi in the Congo, at a rumoured purchase price of £400,000. Other stories put the actual transaction at more than $7 million in cash, lugged to the Congo via Brazzaville in a trunk. Whatever the cost, the *Millennium Star* served as the centrepiece in De Beers' 'Diamonds for the Millennium' sales campaign. A BBC headline, 'Great Heists of Our Time',[14] later focussed public attention on the attempted theft of the collection from the Millennium Dome in London in November 2000. 'Nobody considered the irony,' Dietrich says, 'that such a priceless gem had been purchased in the 1990s in a country now gripped by a civil conflict, with its genesis in decades of mismanagement, corruption and exploitation by government authorities, as well as foreign commercial and strategic interests. Nor did anyone notice that the Democratic Republic of the Congo ranked as one of the world's top ten diamond producers, but remained one of its least developed countries.'

The ironies tripped over one another. In February 2002, the members of the gang that had bulldozed its way into the Millennium Dome 16 months earlier were sent to prison with terms ranging up to 18 years. The judge who sentenced them condemned their 'wicked' and 'professional' raid. The media reported that had it succeeded, the theft would have been the biggest robbery of all time. Not quite, and not least because the diamonds on display were actually all artificial. The real gems had always been locked safely away from prying eyes and grasping hands. More to the point, a quiet and equally wicked theft of diamonds, larger and just as professional, had been taking place every year across Africa. It was rarely reported as such, but hundreds of thousands of people died in the process. As a result, millions were deprived of government services that might have been available had the diamonds been sold through legal channels and been taxed in the process. No judge spoke; few perpetrators went to jail; no *diamantaire* was chastised; no fiancée was deprived of an engagement ring.

Can this trade in stolen and blood diamonds be stopped? The Kimberley Process Certification Scheme has helped to put a hold on the worst of it, but in the few cases where it has been tested – Côte d'Ivoire, Venezuela, Zimbabwe – it has stumbled. If a diamond fuelled conflagration were to erupt in the Eastern

DRC or anywhere else, there is little evidence that the Kimberley Process would be able to cope. It looks too much like the nearsighted Mr. Magoo, walking around in a fog, barely missing collisions with swinging girders and falling anvils through pure blind luck.[15]

The Kimberley Process is failing, and it will fail outright if it does not come to grips with its dysfunctional decision-making and its unwillingness to deal quickly and decisively with non compliance. African governments need to tighten their controls, and trading countries need to make sure there are no loopholes in theirs. The industry itself needs to be much more forthright in demanding protection and enforcement from the governments that have passed Kimberley Process laws aimed at doing precisely that. The campaigning NGOs are unlikely to go away, and sooner or later, consumers will get the message. If things don't improve, the reputation of diamonds will fall, along with their attractiveness for engagement rings and other expressions of love.

Despite the horror of the diamond wars, despite the continuing challenge, on balance this story should perhaps conclude on an optimistic note. In a world of failures, this is a story about NGO campaigning, corporate social responsibility and diplomacy that still has a chance of working, not just to end and prevent conflict, but to turn diamonds with secrets and blood in their pedigree into an engine of development and hope in places where these virtues are in tragically short supply.

EPILOGUE

The morning was cold, and at eight o'clock when the van with darkened windows came for me, the sun had not yet fully risen. It was early January 2008, but hardy crocuses were poking orange and purple heads up through frosty lawns along the short drive to the International Criminal Court in The Hague.

I was to be the first witness at the war crimes trial of Charles Taylor, former school teacher, former warlord, former president of Liberia. It had been a long time in coming. Taylor had helped turn his country into a charnel house on his way to achieving the presidency in 1997, but the victory was pyrrhic and it was not enough to slake his bloodlust. He enflamed the war he had helped to start in Sierra Leone and he engineered attacks on Guinea. He helped destabilize Côte d'Ivoire, causing death and destruction in every one of the countries along Liberia's 1500 kilometre border. His worst crimes were in his own country where some 200,000 people were killed in the rampage that concluded with his assumption of power. At least 50,000 more were killed in the subsequent effort to unseat him.

But it was his hand in Sierra Leone's bloody conflict that dragged Taylor at last to The Hague. Given a safe harbour in Nigeria after his resignation, for a time he lived comfortably in a Calabar villa, partying and wielding his cell phone as a long distance weapon against his enemies. Then, in March 2006, the Government of Liberia requested that he be handed over. A brief escape, an ignominious capture, three flights in two days, and Taylor was listening to the charges against him in Freetown, the capital of a country he had helped to wreck.

The Special Court for Sierra Leone was a hybrid, a joint effort of the United Nations and the Government of Sierra Leone. Its mandate was to try 'those who bear the greatest responsibility for serious violations of international humanitarian law and Sierra Leonean law, committed in the territory of Sierra Leone since 30 November 1996.' It was the first international criminal tribunal funded entirely by voluntary contributions, and it received support from over 40 different governments. In the end, it tried eight individuals in Sierra Leone, achieving a 100 per cent conviction rate. Among the eight were RUF rebel leaders, army officers who had joined with the rebels, and leaders of the *kamajor* – the popular government-aligned militia. As such, the Court tried a balanced set of cases and was not simply an exercise in victor's justice. In Taylor's case, the charges included acts of terrorism, unlawful killing, sexual violence, physical violence, the use of child soldiers, abduction, forced labour and looting.

The trial venue was moved from Freetown to The Hague because the Court, the governments of Sierra Leone and Liberia and others feared that a protracted trial in Freetown might attract Taylor's friends and other opportunists, and they feared that the likelihood of further mayhem was high. The International Criminal Court in The Hague agreed that its facilities could be used, but the government of the Netherlands balked, saying that a place had to be found for Taylor's imprisonment, should he be found guilty. The Netherlands did not want him and neither did half a dozen other countries, including Sweden, Denmark and Austria. It was Britain's offer to host a guilty Taylor in one of Her Majesty's Prisons that finally allowed for his transfer to The Hague.

It would take 18 months for the trial to begin. Taylor's lawyer fired opening salvos, complaining that the conditions of Taylor's incarceration were 'draconian', even worse than they had been in Freetown. Taylor was not allowed to make as many phone calls as had been the case in Freetown, and he was forced to eat 'Eurocentric food' at the United Nations detention Unit at Scheveningen.

When the trial opened, Taylor had been at Scheveningen for a year, but he did not appear in court, and his lawyer showed up only to announce that Taylor had dismissed him. It would take six more months to get Taylor into the courtroom, this time with a team of lawyers costing the Special Court an estimated $130,000 a month, more than a million and a half dollars a year. In fact the overall cost of the Special Court was enormous, and many criticized the wisdom of such an expensive set of trials for so few defendants. That Taylor should be receiving such costly legal counsel – at the expense of the court – when his victims received so little, seemed to fly in the face of common sense and decency.

But there was something else involved. A great many people in West Africa were pleased that the Court had got at least one of the big men into the dock. Foday Sankoh had died before he could be brought to trial. Hinga Norman, another defendant, had also died in jail. Sam Bockarie had been murdered in Liberia, and the coup-making diamond thief, Johnny Paul Koroma, had simply vanished, presumed killed in Liberia. So the Taylor trial was iconic. It was important for Sierra Leoneans and Liberians to be able to see the once-powerful man face his accusers in open court. And it was important to be able to see Taylor on live-stream broadcasts, glowering behind his dark glasses, even if he was denying everything. The trial was important in other ways. Slobodan Milosevic had the distinction of being the first former head of state to wind up in a war crimes court. But Taylor was the first former African head of state to be brought before such a body, and the trial accomplished two significant things. First, it set an important precedent. And second, it sent a powerful message throughout the continent to other leaders that criminal behaviour was beginning to receive a new kind of attention. In some ways, Taylor was a proxy for all the other men who had used diamonds to fuel their murderous ambitions: Mobutu Sese Seko, Jonas Savimbi, Gnassingbé Eyédema, Blaise Compaoré and their many acolytes.

Taylor complained repeatedly that the Court was a Western construct and that his accusers were racist. A more valid complaint might have been that the many others who made it possible for diamonds to be used so badly were not in court with him: a diamond industry that had looked the other way for a decade while its product fuelled so much death and destruction; the gun runners Viktor Bout, Leonid Minin and dozens more like them; the governments – Russia, Ukraine, Bulgaria and others – that willingly sold weapons obviously bound for African wars; and the other governments – Libya, Sudan, Burkina Faso, Togo – that provided transit facilities and false end-user certificates. Taylor was, in a sense, the fall guy for all of them, and he felt it. He would complain repeatedly during his trial that the whole thing was simply 'not fair'.

Between July and November 2009, in weeks of detailed questioning by his own legal team, Taylor described the prior testimony of witness after witness as lies, blatant lies, vicious lies, total lies, far right lies and diabolical lies. When questioned about my testimony, he said 'Smillie is lying through his teeth'.[1]

He spoke frequently and often about being demonized. 'It's such a travesty of justice, you know, that people in the public eye get these statements against them. It's a big thing now, when you want to demonize African leaders you are either eating human flesh, like this other person sat here and said, or you are stealing money. And they don't have to prove it.'[2]

He was asked about testimony that had been given about human heads and entrails being 'festooned' at his army's roadblocks. He tried to explain that these were skulls, not human heads, and that the display of skulls was rather normal in the general scheme of things, a kind of Oddfellows Lodge symbol. 'Let me tell you,' he told the court, 'I am a past noble father of the Grand United Order of Oddfellows. It's in Britain. It's in the United States. It is Western. If any Oddfellow member is hearing this, we know what symbols are. Those were only skulls that I saw and would not have tolerated anyone killing or putting some human head up. It would have never happened and did not happen.'

One of the judges asked why it was necessary to display human skulls at all. Taylor explained: 'When you use symbols, symbols are designed to give a lesson that, "Look, here is the situation. If you don't do this, then this happens, okay? This is the result of not following orders, okay?" That is why these skulls – not at every gate, but there were certain areas that skulls were there. I saw them, I investigated and I got to realize that they were enemy skulls and we did not think that that symbol meant anything wrong.'[3]

We did not think that that symbol meant anything wrong.

◆

Up-country in Sierra Leone, in Koidu Town where I taught school in the 1960s, damaged buildings are being reconstructed. Aid money has helped returning refugees to resettle. Markets are bustling. There was also, until not very long ago, something that none of us who lived there in the 1960s could possibly have imagined: Koidu Secondary School, once crowded with boys and girls eager for what looked like a bright future, was for a time the headquarters of UNAMSIL's Pakistan Battalion, there to prevent a recurrence of the terrible past. The last of the foreign troops left at the end of 2005, and Sierra Leone is once again on its own. Koidu Secondary School is once again a place where boys and girls attend class and think about what they will be when they grow up. Not more than a mile away, however, other children stand waist-deep in filth and mud at a place called Kaisombo. There, they dig for diamonds.

NOTES

CHAPTER 1. OF JUDGEMENT AND CUNNING WORK: DIRTY DIAMONDS

1. Percy Sillitoe, *Cloak Without Dagger* (London: Pan Books, 1956), 215.

2. Fred K. Kamil, *The Diamond Underworld* (London: Allan Lane, 1979), 31.

3. Ian Fleming, *Diamonds are Forever* (London, Jonathan Cape, 1956).

4. *Ibid.*, 28.

5. *Ibid.*, 148.

6. A.W. Cockerill, *Sir Percy Sillitoe* (London: W.H. Allen & Co., 1975) 193.

7. J.H. Du Plessis, *Diamonds Are Dangerous* (New York, John Day, 1961), 16.

8. Author's personal correspondence with Anne's daughter in 2002.

9. Global Witness, *A Rough Trade: The Role of Companies and Governments in the Angolan Conflict* (London: Global Witness, December 1998); Partnership Africa Canada, *The Heart of the Matter: Sierra Leone, Diamonds and Human Security* (Ottawa: Partnership Africa Canada, January 2000).

10. United Nations, *Report of the Panel of Experts Appointed Pursuant to UN Security Council Resolution 1306 (2000), Paragraph 19 in Relation to Sierra Leone* (New York: United Nations, December 2000), 28.

11. The total value of British diamond imports in 1997 would have been much higher than this. Other diamonds would have entered under different customs codes.

12. United Nations, *op. cit.*, 24.

13. Sharon Berger, Sharon, 'Congo signs $700m. agreement with IDI Diamonds' *Jerusalem Post*, 2 August 2000.

14. Christian Dietrich, 'Have African-based Diamond Monopolies Been Effective?' *Central Africa Minerals and Arms Research Bulletin*, Issue 2, (June 2001). Online: http://www.google.com/search?q=dietrich+www.diamondstudies.com&sourceid=ie7&rls=com.microsoft:en-US&ie=utf8&oe=utf8&rlz= (accessed 7 December 2009).

15. For a complete discussion of diamonds in Central Africa at this time, see Christian Dietrich, *Hard Currency: The Criminalized Diamond Economy of the Democratic Republic of the Congo and its Neighbours* (Ottawa: Partnership Africa Canada, 2002).

16. Figures from the Diamond High Council, Antwerp, and *Diamond Intelligence Briefs*, Tel Aviv.

17. United Nations Security Council, *Report of the Monitoring Mission on Sanctions against Angola, S/2001/966* (New York, United Nations, 12 October 2001), para 141.

18. 'Diamond Pipeline 2001', *Mazal U'Bracha*, No. 146 (June 2002).

19. Matthew Hart, *Diamond: A Journey to the Heart of an Obsession* (Toronto: Viking, 2001), 159–181.

20. Details of various Russian diamond frauds are contained in Hart, *op.cit.*

CHAPTER 2. THE RIVER OF BIG RETURNS: GEOLOGY AND HISTORY

1. M. Sevdermish and A. Mashiah, *The Dealer's Book of Gems and Diamonds*, (Israel: Mada Avanim Yerakot Ltd., 1995), Vol. II, 502.

2. Marian Fowler, *Hope: The Adventures of a Diamond* (New York: Random House, 2002), 8.

3. Adam Hochschild, *King Leopold's Ghost*, (Boston, Houghton Mifflin, 1998), 233.

4. Kimberley Process Statistics, https://mmsd.mms.nrcan.gc.ca/kimberleystats/default.asp (accessed 7 December 2009).

5. *Ibid.*

CHAPTER 3. DE BEERS: THE DELICATE EQUIPOISE

1. Stefan Kanfer, *The Last Empire: De Beers, Diamonds and the World* (New York: Farrar, Strauss Giroux, 1993), 95.

2. *Ibid.*, 116.

3. Edward Jay Epstein, *The Rise and Fall of Diamonds* (New York: Simon and Schuster, 1982), 84.

4. Hart, *op. cit.*, 141.

5. Anita Loos, *Gentlemen Prefer Blondes: The Illuminating Diary of a Professional Lady*, New York: Boni & Liveright, 1925), 100.

6. In fact De Beers did polish as much as half a million dollars worth of diamonds annually through the1980s and 1990s, but always kept very quiet about it because they did not want to seen to be competing with their own sightholders.

7. John. H. Shenefield and Irwin M. Stelzer, *The Antitrust Laws: A Primer* (Washington: American Enterprise Institute Press, 1993), 1; cited in Debora L. Spar, *Managing International Trade and Investment: Casebook* (London: Imperial College Press, undated), 213.

8. Kanfer, *op. cit.*, 317.

9. Speech at the Harvard Business School Global Alumni Conference, March 1999; reproduced in Spar, *op. cit.*, 220–223.

10. Epstein, op. cit. 115.

11. *Ibid.*, 116.

12. Nelson R. Mandela, 'Eulogy: Harry Oppenheimer', *Time Magazine*, 4 September 2000.

13. This story is told in Epstein *op. cit.*, 171–182.

14. This story is told in detail in Edward Wharton-Tigar, *Burning Bright: The Autobiography of Edward Wharton-Tigar*) London: Metal Bulletin Books, 1987), 183–200.

15. Kanfer, *op. cit.*, 344.

16. De Beers, *A Diamond is Forever*-1998 *Annual Report* (London: De Beers, 1999), 5.

17. Nicholas Stein, 'The De Beers Story: A New Cut on an Old Monopoly', *Fortune Magazine*, February 2001.

18. 'De Beers Cut Angers Antwerp Council', *Business Day*, Johannesburg, 13 June 2003.

19. In order to avoid the charge, the contract between De Beers and LVMH stipulated that none of the diamonds would be sourced from De Beers.

20. Stein, *op. cit.*

CHAPTER 4. STRANGE PLUMBING: THE DIAMOND PIPELINE

1. Tacy Limited and Chaim Even-Zohar: http://www.idexonline.com/pdf_files/IDEX_Online-2008_Diamond_Pipeline.pdf (accessed 7 December 2009).

2. Nicky Oppenheimer, interviewed in *Mazal U'Bracha Diamonds*, August 2000.

3. The story is told in Epstein, *op. cit.*, 238–240.

4. Peg Hill, 'Diamonds: For Love or Money?' *Globe and Mail* (15 February 2003).

5. Chaim Even-Zohar, 'Recycling Diamonds', *Diamond Intelligence Briefs*, Vol. 24, No. 575 (30 September 2009).

CHAPTER 5. ANGOLA: ANOTHER DISTRACTING SIDESHOW

1. Basil Davidson, *In the Eye of the Storm: Angola's People* (Garden City, N.Y.: Anchor Books, 1973), 70.

2. *Ibid.*, 130.

3. *Ibid.*, 241.

4. United Nations Foundation, 'Diamonds Worth $1 Million Smuggled Daily, U.N. Says', 16 October 2001, On Line: http://www.unwire.org/unwire/20011016/19671_story.asp (accessed 5 January 2010).

5. Christian Dietrich, 'Inventory of formal diamond mining in Angola' in Jakkie Cilliers & Christian Dietrich (eds.), *Angola's War Economy: The Role of Oil and Diamonds* (Pretoria: Institute for Security Studies, 2000), 146.

6. Others estimate a lower total. In a 1999 paper, Human Rights Watch estimated the total at $1.72 billion before the collapse of the Lusaka process in late 1998: Human Rights Watch, *Angola Unravels* (New York: Human Rights Watch, 13 September 1999). Philippe Le Billon estimates the net return to UNITA as something between 25% and 50% of this amount (Philippe Le Billon, 'A land cursed by its wealth? Angola's war economy 1975–99', World Institute of Development Economics Research, Helsinki, October 1999.

7. Oddly, as the De Beers Annual Reports indicate, there was nothing covert in any of this, and the Government of Angola was well informed of it. As early as 1992, Nicky Oppenheimer had written directly to Angolan President dos Santos: 'I am writing you once again to draw your attention to the continuing problem of theft from the

Angolan diamond mining areas... We have bought these diamonds as part of the CSO's continuing role of ensuring stability in the diamond market. It will be evident to you that the Republic of Angola has derived no benefit whatsoever from this sale and that is a matter which causes me great regret.' Letter, N.F. Oppenheimer to HE President Eduard dos Santos, 6 February 1992.

8. United Nations Security Council Document S/2000/203, (New York: United Nations, 10 March 2000), 23.

9. Quoted in Ian Smillie, Lansana Gberie and Ralph Hazleton, *The Heart of the Matter: Sierra Leone, Diamonds and Human Security* (Ottawa: Partnership Africa Canada, 2000), 31.

10. United Nations Security Council Document S/2002/486 (New York: United Nations, 26 April 2002).

11. United Nations Security Council Document S/2000/203 (New York: United Nations, 10 March 2000), paras 14–38.

12. United Nations Security Council Document S/2001/363 (New York: United Nations, 18 April 2001).

13. Peter Landesman, 'Arms and the Man', *New York Times Magazine*, 17 August 2003.

14. United Nations Security Council Document S/2001/966 (New York: United Nations, 12 October 2001), 39.

15. *Ibid.*, 42.

16. This story is detailed in United Nations Security Council Document S/2002/486 (New York: United Nations, 26 April 2002).

17. United Nations Security Council Document S/2001/966 (New York: United Nations, 12 October 2001).

18. Partnership Africa Canada, *Diamond Industry Annual Review, Angola,* 2007 (Ottawa: Partnership Africa Canada, 2007), 7–9.

19. 'Corruption Replaces War as Way of Life in Angola', *National Post,* 30 July 2002.

20. Jim Hoagland, 'Diamond-Backed Warriors', *Washington Post,* 28 February, 2002.

21. Nicholas D. Kristoff, 'The Angola Mirror', *New York Times,* 5 March 2002.

CHAPTER 6. LIBERIA AND THE LOVE OF LIBERTY

1. Graham Greene, *Journey Without Maps* (London: William Heinemann, 1936).

2. International Monetary Fund, 'Staff Report for the 2001 Article IV Consultation' (Washington: International Monetary Fund, February 2002.

3. H. L. Van der Laan, *The Sierra Leone Diamonds: An Economic Study Covering the Years 1952–1961* (London: Oxford University Press, 1965), 60.

4. Stephen Ellis, *The Mask of Anarchy* (London: C. Hurst & Co., 1999), 50.

5. Mark Huband, *The Liberian Civil War* (London: Frank Cass, 1998), 35.

6. William Reno, *Warlord Politics and African States* (Boulder CO: Lynne Rienner, 1998), 87.

7. Huband, *op. cit.,* 46. In August 2009, at his war crimes trial in The Hague, Taylor told his own version of the escape. He said that his prison cell was unlocked by a guard late

one night, and he was escorted to the minimum security area. He lowered himself from a window using a bed sheet and then climbed over the prison fence where a car awaited him. Taylor said the guard 'had to be operating with someone else.' He assumed that the mysterious car that took him to New York 'had to be a [US] government car' because the men driving him feared he might be 'picked up' if he changed vehicles to be with his wife, who had met the escape car with the cash needed to get out of the country.

8. Estimates of casualties in the Liberian civil war run as high as 200,000, but Stephen Ellis has compiled a detailed and convincing estimate for the lower numbers. Ellis, *op. cit.*, 312–315.

9. Reno, *op. cit.*, 99.

10. UN Security Council, S/2000/1195 (New York: United Nations, 20 December 2000), 24.

11. International Monetary Fund, 'Staff Report for the 2001 Article IV Consultation', (Washington: International Monetary Fund, February 2002).

12. Global Witness, *Taylor-made: The Pivotal Role of Liberia's Forests and Flag of Convenience in Regional Conflict* (London: Global Witness, 2001), 3.

13. UN Security Council, 'Report of the Secretary-General in pursuance of paragraph 13(a) of resolution 1343 (2001) concerning Liberia', S/2001/939 (New York: United Nations, 5 October 2001).

14. Global Witness, *op cit*, 17.

15. *Ibid.*

16 Charles Taylor Testimony, Special Court for Sierra Leone, 7 December 2009.

17. UN Security Council, S/2000/1195 (New York: United Nations, 20 December 2000), 17.

18. Logging details are documented in Global Witness, *The Usual Suspects: Liberia's Weapons and Mercenaries in Côte d'Ivoire and Sierra Leone* (London: Global Witness, 2003). Weapons imports are detailed in several UN Expert Panel reports, notably S/2003/498 of 23 April 2003.

19. Human Rights Watch, 'Back to the Brink: War Crimes by Liberian Government and Rebels' (New York: Human Rights Watch, Vol. 14, No. 4(A), May 2002).

20. Dennis, John, 'President Taylor Wins Peace Medal', 31 July 2002, Online: www. allaboutliberia.com (accessed 24 June 2003).

21. International Monetary Fund, 'Liberia: Selected Issues and Statistical Appendix' (Washington, IMF Country Report No. 05/167, May 2005).

22. Nicky Oppenheimer, 'Mostly a Matter of Marketing', Address to the American Gem Society, Vancouver, *Mazal U'Bracha*, No. 146, June, 2002

CHAPTER 7. SIERRA LEONE: DIAMONDS IN THE RUF

1. Lorna Duek, 'Hell Has Had Its Turn', *Globe and Mail*, 4 May 2000.

2. Graham Greene, *The Heart of the Matter* (Harmondsworth: Penguin, 1962), 143.

3. William Reno describes the 'shadow state' concept in *Corruption and State Politics in Sierra Leone* (Cambridge: Cambridge University Press, 1995).

4. David Caspar Fithen, *Diamonds and War in Sierra Leone: Cultural Strategies for Commercial Adaptation to Endemic Low-Intensity Conflict*, PhD Thesis, (London: University College, 1999).

5. 'Sierra Leone: The South Africa Connection', *Africa Confidential*, 17 September 1986. See also 'Sierra Leone – South Africa: the Strange Story of LIAT', *Africa Confidential*, 24 June 1987. The story is also summarized in: Francois Misser & Olivier Vallée, *Les Gemmocraties: L'economie politique du diamant Africain* (Paris: Desclée de Brouwer, 1997), 131–135. A brief outline of the Kalmanovitch case can also be found in William Reno, *op cit*, 155–157 and in Jeffrey Robinson, *The Merger* (London: Simon and Schuster, 1999)115–6. Additional information on 'hot money' and international crime can be found in R. T. Naylor, *Patriots and Profiteers: On Economic Warfare, Embargo Busting and State-Sponsored Crime* (Toronto: McClelland & Stewart, 1999).

6. Robinson, *op. cit.,* 115.

7. Robinson, *op. cit.,* 116.

8. Cited in Paul Richards, *Fighting for the Rainforest: War, Youth and Resources in Sierra Leone* Oxford: International African Institute & James Currey, 1996), 27ff.

9. Richards, *op. cit.,* 33.

10. Stephen Ellis, *The Mask of Anarchy* (London: C. Hurst & Co., 1999), 62.

11. Ibrahim Abdullah, 'Bush Path to Destruction: The Origin and Character of the Revolutionary United Front', Africa *Development*, Vol. XXII, Nos. 3/4, 1997, 68.

12. This story is detailed in UN Security Council Report *United Nations S/2000/1195* (New York: United Nations, 20 December 2000).

13. Janine Di Giovanni, 'Turning Killers Back into Children', *Ottawa Citizen*, 15 May 2000.

14. Steve Coll, 'The Other War', *Washington Post Magazine*, 9 January 2000.

15. Ryan Lizza, 'Where Angels Fear to Tread', *The New Republic*, 24 July 2000.

16. *Ibid.*

17. *Ibid.*

18. Coll, *op. cit.*

19. *Ibid.*

20. 'Extend a Trembling, Hesitant Hand', *New York Times*, 7 May 2000.

CHAPTER 8. PRESIDENT MOBUTU'S GHOST

1. Adam Hochschild, *King Leopold's Ghost* (Boston: Houghton Mifflin, 1998), 44.

2. Michela Wrong, *In the Footsteps of Mr Kurtz* (London: Fourth Estate, 2000), 45.

3. Hochschild, *op. cit.,* 259.

4. Edward Jay Epstein, *The Rise and Fall of Diamonds* (New York: Simon and Schuster, 1982), 87.

5. John Gunther, *Inside Africa* (New York: Harper & Brothers, 1953) 647 and 671.

6. The precise number of university graduates at independence is somewhat unclear. Basil Davidson, writing in 1964, put the number at 'fewer than a score' (Basil Davidson, *Which*

Way Africa? London: Penguin, 1964, 43). Wrong puts the number at 17 (Wrong, *Op. Cit,*. 50). A BBC history website states, 'There were no African army officers, only three African managers in the entire civil service, and only 30 university graduates.' BBC, Online: http://www.bbc.co.uk/worldservice/africa/features/storyofafrica/14chapter7.shtml (accessed 11 January 2010). Whatever the exact number, it was tiny.

7. The precise details of Lumumba's death remain unknown, but the CIA's involvement and a story of his likely execution by a Belgian officer are told in Wrong, *op. cit.*, 77–8.

8. Wrong, *op. cit.*, 118.

9. *Ibid.*, 197.

10. Christian Dietrich, *Hard Currency: The Criminalized Diamond Economy of the Democratic Republic of the Congo and its Neighbours* (Ottawa: Partnership Africa Canada, 2002), 13 and 17.

11. Quoted in Dietrich, *op. cit.*, 15.

12. United Nations Security Council, *Report of the UN Panel of Experts on the Illegal Exploitation of Natural Resources and other Forms of Wealth in the Democratic Republic of the Congo*, S/2001/357 (New York: United Nations, 12 April 2001), para. 32.

13. Dietrich, *op. cit.*, 41.

14. *Ibid.*, 42.

15. The is story is detailed in United Nations Security Council, *Addendum to the Report of the Panel of Experts on the Illegal Exploitation of Natural Resources and other Forms of Wealth in the Democratic Republic of the Congo*, S/2001/1072, (New York: United Nations, 13 November 2001), paras. 38–41 and 78–9.

16. Oryx Natural Resources, Online: http://www.oryxnaturalresources.com, (accessed 3 January 2003).

17. Les Roberts *et al*, *Mortality in Eastern Democratic Republic of Cong*, (New York: International Rescue Committee, March 2001).

18. Les Roberts *et al*, *Mortality in the DRC: Results from a Nationwide Survey* (New York: International Rescue Committee, April 2003); Benjamin Coughlan et al, *Mortality in the Democratic Republic of the Congo: An Ongoing Crisis* (New York: International Rescue Committee, 2008) Online: http://www.theirc.org/resources/2007/2006-7_congomortalitysurvey.pdf, (accessed 11 December 2009). The IRC numbers are challenged in the 2009 Human Security Report (Online: http://www.humansecurityreport.info/index.php?option=com_content&task=view&id=205&Itemid=91, (accessed 1 February 2010). Whatever the total, it is extremely high.

CHAPTER 9. ENTER AL QAEDA

1. David Caspar Fithen, *Diamonds and War in Sierra Leone: Cultural Strategies for Commercial Adaptation to Endemic Low-Intensity Conflict*, PhD Thesis, University College London, 1999.

2. Letter from Eli Izhakoff, Chairman & CEO of the World Diamond Council, to David Granger, Editor-in-Chief of *Esquire*, 14 December 2000; copy in author's possession.

3. Global Witness, *For a Few Dollars More* (London: Global Witness, April 2003), 47.

4. United Nations Security Council, *Third Report of the Monitoring Group Established Pursuant to Security Council Resolution 1363 (2001) and Extended by Resolution 1390 (2002)* (New York, United Nations, 17 December 2002).

5. Didier Bigo, 'Lebanese community in the Ivory Coast: A non-native network at the heart of power?', Albert Hourani and Shehadi (eds.), *The Lebanese in the World: A Century of Emigration* (London: I.B. Tauris & Co., 1992), 522.

6. Fithen, *op. cit.*

7. Stephen Ellis, 'Les prolongements du conflit israélo-arabe en Afrique noire: le cas du Sierra Leone,' *Politique Africaine*, No. 30, (Juin 1988), 69–75.

8. 'Angolan Diamond Smuggling: The Part Played by Belgium', ('*Algemene Dienst Inlichting En Veiligheid (Adviv),*) *Service Général du Renseignement et de la Securité (SGR)*, July 2000, cited in Global Witness, *op. cit.*, 20.

9. UN Security Council, *Report of the Panel of Experts on Violations of Security Council Sanctions Against UNITA*, S/2000/203 (New York: United Nations, 10 March 2000), para. 19.

10. UN Security Council Expert Panel Report on Sierra Leone, *United Nations* S/2000/1195 (New York: United Nations, 20 December, 2000), para. 73.

11. Douglas Farah, 'Al Qaeda Cash Tied to Diamond Trade, Sale of Gems from Sierra Leone Rebels Raised Millions, Sources Say', *Washington Post*, 2 November 2001.

12. Partnership Africa Canada, *Other Facets*, No. 3 (October 2001).

13. Bout had been supplying the anti-Taliban Northern Alliance from the mid 1990s, but later had direct dealings with the Taliban government for supplies and for servicing Ariana aircraft.

14. Douglas Farah, 'Report says Africans Harbored al Qaeda Terror Assets Hidden in Gem-buying Spree', *Washington Post*, 29 December 2002.

15. Global Witness, *op. cit.*, 41.

16. United Nations Security Council, *Final Report of the UN Panel of Experts on the Illegal Exploitation of Natural Resources and other Forms of Wealth in the Democratic Republic of the Congo*, S/2002/1146 (New York: United Nations, 16 October 2002), para. 34.

17. Global Witness, *op. cit.*, 49.

18. Douglas Farah, *Blood From Stones: The Secret Financial Network of Terror* (New York: Broadway Books, 2004).

19. MSNBC, 'Liberia's former president, a friend to terror?' *Dateline NBC*, aired 17 July 2005.

20. *Ibid.*

CHAPTER 10. BOILING FROGS: COMPANIES IN HOT WATER

1. United Nations Security Council, *Final Report of the UN Panel of Experts on the Illegal Exploitation of Natural Resources and other Forms of Wealth in the Democratic Republic of the Congo*, S/2002/1146 (New York: United Nations, 16 October 2002).

2. Reuters, 'Diamond Deaths in Congo' (22 October 2002), Online: http://www. zimbabwesituation.com/oct23_2002.html (accessed 14 December 2009).

3. Alfred Wasike, 'General Saleh Declares Foreign Accounts' (27 October 2002), Ugnet, Online: http://www.mail-archive.com/ugandanet@kym.net/msg00257.html (accessed 14 December 2009).

4. UNOCHA, 'DRC: "No evidence of illegal acts", says a Belgian pillage study' (New York, UN Office for the Coordination of Humanitarian Activities, Integrated Regional Information Network, 22 February 2003).

5. *Final Report of the UN Panel of Experts, op. cit.*, para 33.

6. *Ibid.*, para 178.

7. Production plummeted in 2009 because of the global recession: 17.7 million carats were mined, a 46 per cent drop over 2008.

8. Botswana statistics are from UNDP's *Human Development Report* 2008, Online: http:// hdrstats.undp.org/countries/data_sheets/cty_ds_BWA.html (accessed Dec. 14, 2009).

9. Ian Smillie, *Motherhood, Apple Pie and False Teeth: Corporate Social Responsibility in the Diamond Industry* (Ottawa: Partnership Africa Canada, 2003), 7.

10. OECD, 'Multinational Enterprises in Situations of Violent Conflict and Widespread Human Rights Abuses' (Paris: OECD Directorate for Financial, Fiscal and Enterprise Affairs, May 2002).

11. IMF, *Democratic Republic of Congo: Selected Issues and Statistical Appendix* (Washington: IMF, July 2001), 17.

12. Nicky Oppenheimer, Address at the Commonwealth Business Forum, November 1999, quoted in 'Multinational Enterprises in Situations of Violent Conflict and Widespread Human Rights Abuses' (Paris: OECD, May 2002), 14.

13. Interestingly, Nicky Oppenheimer has invested some of his personal fortune in the Brenthurst Foundation, a think tank dedicated, in part, to dialogue on some of these questions. See http://www.thebrenthurstfoundation.org/index.htm (accessed 19 February 2010).

14. De Beers, 'Angola' Online: www.debeersgroup.com/debeersweb/About+De+Beers/ De+Beers+World+Wide/Angola (accessed 12 July 2006).

15. Nuremberg Trial Proceedings: *Constitution of the International Military Tribunal*, Article 6, 8 August 1945, Online: http://www.gonzagajil.org/pdf/volume10/Nuremberg/ Nuremberg%20Charter.pdf (accessed Dec. 14 2009).

CHAPTER 11. ICE STORM: THE NGO CAMPAIGN

1. See, for example, Reed Kramer, 'Central Africa: A Moment for Peace?' *AllAfrica.com*, (5 February 2001), Online: http://allafrica.com/stories/200102050394.html (accessed 15 December 2009).

2. Susan Schmidt, 'Tempelsman Plan Got the Ear of U.S. Aides', *Washington Post*, 2 August 1997.

3. Some of Tempelsman's partnerships apparently caught up with him in 2009 when LKI was unable to complete some of its IRS filings and was forced to submit a plan to regain compliance with the New York Stock Exchange by May 2010. As the deadline approached, LKI announced a lawsuit against various Lloyds of London syndicates and European insurers for $640 million in damages arising from the disappearance of diamonds that were ensured by the defendants.

4. UN Security Council, *Resolution 1118 (1997)*, 30 June 1997.

5. *Ibid.*

6. George Orwell, *Nineteen Eighty-Four* (New York: Harcourt Brace and Company, 1949), 312.

7. Global Witness, *A Rough Trade: The Role of Companies and Governments in the Angolan Conflict* (London: Global Witness, 1998).

8. Ian Smillie, Lansana Gberie, and Ralph Hazleton, *The Heart of the Matter: Sierra Leone, Diamonds and Human Security* (Ottawa: Partnership Africa Canada, 2000).

9. A fine distinction was made in Belgium between the country where a diamond was mined, and the country of 'provenance' – the one from which it arrived. The distinction, used as an extremely thin veil to excuse the widespread corruption that allowed conflict diamonds to thrive, is discussed in more detail in Chapter 1.

10. De Beers, 'De Beers' Comments on "The Heart of the Matter"' (26 January 2000), Online: http://www.debeers.ca/, (accessed 29 January 2000).

11. Andrew Bone, 'Conflict Diamonds, The Kimberley process and the De Beers Group' in Alyson J.K. Bailes and Isabel Frommelt (eds.), *Business and Security: Public-Private Sector Relationships in a New Security*, (Oxford: Oxford University Press, 2004), 131.

12. Smillie *et al, op cit*, 73.

13 Capitol Hill Press releases, 'Hall Bill', 1 November 1999, Online: http://www.encyclopedia.com/doc/1P1-29424041.html (accessed 16 December 2009).

14. 'Observations by U.S. Rep. Frank R. Wolf of Virginia Visit to Western Africa: Sierra Leone After a Decade of Civil War November 30 - December 8, 1999', Online: www.house.gov/wolf/19991130SierraLeone.html, (accessed 16 December 2009).

15. United Nations Security Council, *Report of the Panel of Experts on Violations of Security Council Sanctions Against UNITA*, S/2000/203 (New York: United Nations, 10 March 2000), para. 33.

16. *Ibid.*, para. 20.

17. *Ibid.*, para. 83.

18. *Ibid.*, para. 90.

19. Rapaport, Martin, 'Blood Money', 5 November 1999, Online: http://www.diamonds.net/news/NewsItem.aspx?ArticleID=3347 (accessed 16 December 2009).

20. Martin Rapaport, 'Guilt Trip', 7 April 2000, Online: http://www.diamonds.net/news/NewsItem.aspx?ArticleID=3830 (accessed 16 December 2009).

21. United Nations Security Council. *Op. cit.*, para. 113.

CHAPTER 12. KIMBERLEY: A HOPE IN HELL

1. David Keen, 'Blair's Good Guys in Sierra Leone', *The Guardian*, 7 November 2001.
2. Kimberley Process, 'Recommendations of the Luanda Working Group Meeting', 13–14 June, 2000, author's possession.
3. Personal communication with the author.
4. National Security Advisor Samuel R. Berger, 'Remarks to White House Diamond Conference', 10 January, 2001, Online: http://www.sierra-leone.org/Archives/slnews0101. html, (accessed 17 December 2009).
5. The increased advertising was pushed by De Beers as part of its new strategy (See Chapter 3); 'The Genesis of a New Era' *Idex*, No. 158 (June 2003), 22.

CHAPTER 13. ENDGAMES

1. Taylor would later testify that he was unaware at the time that Bockarie had been indicted: Special Court for Sierra Leone, Charles Taylor Testimony (28 January 2010), Online: http://www.sc-sl.org/LinkClick.aspx?fileticket=STOt1nrouMM%3d&tabid=160 (accessed 15 February 2010).
2. Testimony of Moses Blah, Special Court for Sierra Leone, The Hague, 15 May 15 2008, Online: http://www.charlestaylortrial.org/2008/05/15/former-vp-moses-blah-discusses-beheading-of-ruf-commander-in-chief-and-other-events/ (accessed 17 December 2009).
3. BBC, 'Liberia Leader Defiant to the End', 11 August 2003, Online: http://news.bbc. co.uk/2/hi/africa/3140417.stm, (accessed 17 December 2009).
4. Human Rights Watch, 'Nigeria" Detain Taylor Immediately', 28 March 2006, Online: http://www.hrw.org/en/news/2006/03/28/nigeria-detain-taylor-immediately, (accessed 6 January 2010).
5. Mats Berdal and David Malone (eds.), *Greed and Grievance: Economic Agendas in Civil; Wars* (Boulder Colorado: Lynne Rienner 2000).
6. Paul Collier and Anke Hoeffler, 'Greed and Grievance in Civil Wars' (Washington: World Bank, October 2001).
7. See, for example, Annual Reviews of the diamond industries of Angola, DRC and Sierra Leone by Partnership Africa Canada between 2003 and 2007, and PAC's *Diamonds and Human Security Annual Reviews* for 2008 and 2009 at http://www.pacweb.org/index-e. php (accessed 6 January 2010).
8. Partnership Africa Canada, *The Lost World: Diamond Mining and Smuggling in Venezuela* (Ottawa: Partnership Africa Canada, 2006).
9. Partnership Africa Canada, *Zimbabwe, Diamonds and the Wrong Side of History* (Ottawa: Partnership Africa Canada, March 2009); Human Rights Watch, *Zimbabwe's Blood Diamonds* (New York: Human Rights Watch, June 2009).
10. Concerned that the Kimberley Process was proving unable to provide the assurances increasingly demanded by a discerning public, 14 organizations from across the gold and diamond supply chain created a body called the Responsible Jewellery Council in 2005.

The RJC has created a tough code of ethical standards that can be applied throughout the supply chain, from mine to retail. Unlike many codes, this one is compulsory for RJC members – now 140 strong – and requires independent third party verification. The code holds individual companies accountable, but as of 2010, coordination across the supply chain was still a work in progress. Van Cleef & Arpels, for example, does not use child labour, nor do RJC mining company members. But Van Cleef & Arpels is under no obligation to buy only from members of the RJC. When that mismatch is fixed, the gold and diamond industries, already well ahead of most extractives, will have something serious to boast about.

11. Ian Balfour, *Famous Diamonds* (London: William Collins Sons & Co., 1987), 206.

12. Christian Dietrich, *Hard Currency: The Criminalized Diamond Economy of the Democratic Republic of the Congo and its Neighbours* (Ottawa: Partnership Africa Canada, 2002).

13. De Beers, Online: www.adiamondisforever.com/jewelry/famous_star.html, 7 January 2001 (accessed 17 June 2001).

14. BBC, 'Great Dome Robbery Foiled' (7 November 2000), Online: http://news.bbc.co.uk/2/hi/uk_news/1010974.stm, (accessed 17 December 2009).

15. I would like to claim credit for this analogy, but it has to go to Shawn Blore, a great investigative journalist with a keen eye for metaphor.

EPILOGUE

1. Special Court for Sierra Leone, Charles Taylor Testimony (25 August 2009), Online: http://www.sc-sl.org/LinkClick.aspx?fileticket=prr6j5%2bbmsc%3d&tabid=160 (accessed 17 December 2009).

2. Special Court for Sierra Leone, Charles Taylor Testimony (3 August 2009), Online: http://www.sc-sl.org/LinkClick.aspx?fileticket=ouw2TzFKFHg%3d&tabid=160 (accessed 17 December 2009).

3. Special Court for Sierra Leone, Charles Taylor Testimony (16 July 2009), Online: http://www.sc-sl.org/LinkClick.aspx?fileticket=kMjmgkh4vT0%3d&tabid=160 (accessed 17 December 2009).

BIBLIOGRAPHY

Abdullah, Ibrahim. 'Bush Path to Destruction: The Origin and Character of the Revolutionary United Front.' *Africa Development*, Vol. XXII, nos. 3–4 (1997)

Balfour, Ian. *Famous Diamonds*. London: William Collins Sons & Co. 1987

Berdal, Mats and Malone, David M. (eds). *Greed and Grievance: Economic Agendas in Civil Wars*. Boulder, Colorado: Lynne Rienner 2000

Cilliers, Jakkie and Dietrich, Christian (eds.). *Angola's War Economy: The Role of Oil and Diamonds*. Pretoria: Institute for Security Studies 2000

Cockerill, A.W. *Sir Percy Sillitoe*. London: Allen Lane 1975

Davidson, Basil. *In The Eye of the Storm: Angola's People*. Garden City, N.Y.: Anchor Books 1973

Dietrich, Christian. *Hard Currency: The Criminalized Diamond Economy of the Democratic Republic of the Congo and its Neighbours*. Ottawa: Partnership Africa Canada 2002

Du Plessis, J.H. *Diamonds are Dangerous*. New York: John Day & Co. 1960

Ellis, Stephen. *The Mask of Anarchy*. London: C. Hurst & Co. 1999

Epstein, Edward Jay. *The Rise and Fall of Diamonds*. New York: Simon and Schuster 1982

Even-Zohar, Chaim. *From Mine to Mistress: Corporate Strategies and Government Policies in the International Diamond Industry*. Endbridge, Kent: Mining Journal Books, Ltd. 2002

Fithen, David Caspar. *Diamonds and War in Sierra Leone: Cultural Strategies for Commercial Adaptation to Endemic Low-Intensity Conflict*. (PhD Thesis), London: University College 1999

Fleming, Ian. *Diamonds are Forever*. London: Jonathan Cape 1956

Fleming, Ian. *The Diamond Smugglers*. London: Pan Books 1960

Fowler, Marian. *Hope: The Adventures of a Diamond*. New York: Random House 2002

Gberie, Lansana. *War and Peace in Sierra Leone: Diamonds, Corruption and the Lebanese Connection*. Ottawa: Partnership Africa Canada 2002

Gberie, Lansana. *A Dirty War in West Africa; The RUF and the Destruction of Sierra Leone*. Bloomington, Indiana: Indiana University Press 2005

Global Witness. *A Rough Trade*. London: Global Witness 1998

Global Witness. *Taylor-made: The Pivotal Role of Liberia's Forests and Flag of Convenience in Regional Conflict*. London: Global Witness 2001

Global Witness. *The Usual Suspects: Liberia's Weapons and Mercenaries in Côte d'Ivoire and Sierra Leone*. London: Global Witness 2003

Global Witness. *For a Few Dollars More: How al Qaeda Moved into the Diamond Trade*. London: Global Witness 2003

Hart, Matthew. *Diamond: A Journey to the Heart of an Obsession*. New York: Viking 2001

Gunther, John. *Inside Africa*. New York: Harper & Brothers 1953

Hazleton, Ralph. *Diamonds: Forever or for Good? The Economic Impact of Diamonds in Southern Africa*. Ottawa: Partnership Africa Canada 2001

Hochschild, Adam. *King Leopold's Ghost*. Boston: Houghton Mifflin 1998

Huband, Mark. *The Liberian Civil War*. London: Frank Cass 1998

Huband, Mark. *The Skull beneath the Skin: Africa after the Cold War*. Boulder: Westview Press 2001

Kanfer, Stefan. *The Last Empire: De Beers, Diamonds and the World*. New York: Farrar, Strauss Giroux 1993

Kamil, Fred. *The Diamond Underworld*. London: Allen Lane 1979

Naylor, R.T. *Patriots and Profiteers: On Economic Warfare, Embargo Busting and State-Sponsored Crime*. Toronto: McClelland & Stewart 1999

Reno, William. *Corruption and State Politics in Sierra Leone*. Cambridge: Cambridge University Press 1995

Reno, William. *Warlord Politics and African States*. Boulder: Lynne Rienner 1998

Richards, Paul. *Fighting for the Rainforest: War, Youth and Resources in Sierra Leone*. Oxford: International African Institute & James Currey 1996

Robinson, Jeffrey. *The Merger*. London: Simon and Schuster UK 1999

Sevdermish, M., and Mashiah, A. *The Dealer's Book of Gems and Diamonds* (Vol. II). Tel Aviv: Mada Avanim Yerakot Ltd. 1995

Sillitoe, Sir Percy. *Cloak Without Dagger*. London: Pan Books 1956

Smillie, I., Gberie, L., and Hazleton, R. *The Heart of the Matter: Sierra Leone, Diamonds and Human Security*. Ottawa: Partnership Africa Canada 2000

Van der Laan, H.L. *The Sierra Leone Diamonds: An Economic Study Covering the Years 1952–1961.* London: Oxford University Press 1965

Wharton-Tigar, Edward. *Burning Bright: The Autobiography of Edward Wharton-Tigar.* London: Metal Bulletin Books 1987

Wilson, Robert. *The Big Killing.* London: Harper Collins 2002

Wrong, Michela. *In the Footsteps of Mr Kurtz.* London: Fourth Estate 2000

UNITED NATIONS DOCUMENTS

Report of the Panel of Experts on Violations of Security Council Sanctions Against UNITA, S/2000/203. 10 March 2000

Report of the Panel of Experts Appointed Pursuant to Security Council Resolution 1306 (2000), Paragraph 19, in Relation to Sierra Leone, S/2000/1195. 20 December 2000

Report of the UN Panel of Experts on the Illegal Exploitation of Natural Resources and other Forms of Wealth in the Democratic Republic of the Congo, S/2001/357. 12 April 2001

Addendum to the Report of the Panel of Experts on the Illegal Exploitation of Natural Resources and other Forms of Wealth in the Democratic Republic of the Congo, S/2001/1072. 13 November 2001

Final Report of the UN Panel of Experts on the Illegal Exploitation of Natural Resources and other Forms of Wealth in the Democratic Republic of the Congo, S/2002/1146. 16 October 2002

INDEX

Breinigsville, PA USA
12 December 2010
251184BV00001B/6/P

9 780857 289636